INCURABLE
PHYSICIAN

INCURABLE PHYSICIAN

An Autobiography

Walter C. Alvarez, M.D.

PRENTICE-HALL, INC.
Englewood Cliffs, N. J.

Prentice-Hall International, Inc.
(*London, Tokyo, Sydney, Paris*)

Prentice-Hall of Canada, Ltd.

Prentice-Hall de Mexico, S.A.

"Condemn me not good Reader, or censure me too hardly, if some part of this treatise to thy thinking . . . be too light . . . I have inserted foolish trifles . . . and jests . . . I crave pardon for what is amiss; . . . wink at small faults . . . but if thou likest . . . wish me good success."

Robert Burton (1576-1639)

Contents

Introduction

WHY ANOTHER autobiography?

For several reasons.

I have an interesting story to tell—of medicine and its remarkable development during the last 70 years. I have watched it grow from the days when my father made his calls on horseback with his drugs and instruments in saddlebags behind him. I have seen the coming into wide medical use of X-rays, radium, and radioactive isotopes. I have seen the coming of the electrocardiograph, the electroencephalograph, and dozens of other delicate bits of apparatus now widely used in medical practice. I have seen the coming of many wonderful drugs, such as aspirin, the sleep-makers, procaine for local anesthesia, sodium pentothal and other splendid drugs for general anesthesia, the sulfas, penicillin, and the many other antibiotics, and, recently, the tranquilizers and the several drugs which now often help the mentally disturbed.

I have watched the development of bacteriology and virology. In 1905, when I was an intern, many people were dying of typhoid fever, and many children were cut down by the

awful diphtheria. A few years later, both of these diseases had
been practically wiped out. When I was a lad, tuberculosis was
a common disease—and often a fatal one. A brilliant chum of
mine died of it the year he left college. Today, the incidence
of the disease is only one-thirtieth of what it was, and there
are a number of drugs that tend to cure it.

For 13 years I worked alongside the great Mayo brothers.
The Mayos showed the world that the most effective way to
practice medicine is in a great Clinic in which are gathered
together many able specialists.

Later, I watched surgeons as they learned to operate in the
chest, and in the skull; and eventually I saw them putting a
new valve into a defective heart, or replacing a diseased artery,
perhaps with a tube made of Dacron. I watched the development of the great science of blood chemistry, now so useful in
diagnosis, and I saw the coming of modern anesthesia, which
today is so easy to take, and so safe. Since 1955 I have been
watching, fascinated, as the science of human genetics has
developed rapidly.

In 1905, when I was a surgical assistant, perhaps one out of
every four patients who had an abdominal operation promptly
died. Today, in a fine modern clinic, perhaps 99 out of 100 recover. In 1912, when I was seeing children with diabetes, it
distressed me terribly to have to watch all of them die within
a few months. Now, if they are properly taken care of, I see
them staying strong and well. These miracles of healing, and
hundreds more, I watched as they came to us in medicine.

I have been very fortunate in knowing so many of the great
men of medicine, many of them intimately. In San Francisco
after the turn of the century I knew Dr. Fehleisen, a handsome, distinguished, soldierly, and aristocratic-looking man
who, in his youth in Germany, was one of the group of men
who discovered the major germs that produce disease. In 1884,
the year I was born, he had demonstrated that erysipelas—that
red inflammation of the skin once so dreaded—is due to a special germ called a streptococcus.

Another link I have had with the great past in medicine was my friendship with dear old "Popsy" Welch, who, in his youth, went to Germany, and brought back to us in America much knowledge of the new sciences of pathology (the study of diseased tissues) and bacteriology (the study of germs).

Especially during my 25 years at the Mayo Clinic, I came to know not only scores of able leaders of medicine in the United States and Canada, but also most of the distinguished teachers and research workers of Europe and Latin America. All these friendships enriched my life.

Here is another reason for my writing this memoir: The head of a university once said to the great Scottish geologist Hugh Miller, "If you had received all of your magnificent education in the lecture rooms and laboratories of a college, it might not be worth talking about, but since you taught yourself all you know, you just must write and tell us how you did it. It can encourage many a young man to carry on until he gets the education he wants."

Before he died, my good friend Dr. Alan Gregg, the distinguished vice-president of the Rockefeller Foundation—who did so much for the advancement of medical teaching all over the world—urged me to write this book. He said that his talks with hundreds of fine young students of medicine and science in America, Europe, and Asia had shown him that many of them are hungry for information about how a man of science matures and eventually succeeds—intellectually, socially, emotionally, and spiritually. How does he climb up the ladder on his way to success? When and how does he first learn the need for absolute honesty in scientific observation and thinking? When does he get the idea that he can learn most from his patients? When does he develop the courage to criticize unwise medical practices, and when does he get the strength to stand up firmly in the face of opposition and perhaps bitter and unfair criticism? When does he learn to keep hard at his work even when he notes that some of his envious contemporaries are determined that, so long as he lives, they will see to it that his discoveries in their fields will be ignored and never mentioned?

I speak here with reluctance of the occasional unpleasant phases of a scientist's life—the jealousies and oppositions that are sure to assail him if he succeeds in doing anything worth while. But I feel I must describe those happenings which so often bring disillusionment and discouragement to the idealistic young scientist. As Dr. Gregg said, "In your book you must admit that you ran into opposition and sometimes into smallness of behavior on the part of men who should have been above doing anything small or mean. You must tell how, in spite of opposition, you kept driving ahead until you reached your goal. These things you must tell. Then the men all over the world who read of your experience will say to themselves, 'I no longer need feel so alone; evidently what I have been going through is a common experience; it is to be expected, and it is due to the fact that scientists are often more like ordinary men than like ideal scientists.' "

I hope that what I write here will strengthen the determination of many a fine young physician or surgeon to stick to his idealism and his desire never to practice medicine purely as a business or—at the worst—a racket.

I have been much helped in this writing by the fact that all through my life I have kept a diary. Often before retiring at night I recorded the essentials of a conversation I had had that day with some great man. Before writing this book I refreshed my memory by reading through all 62 volumes of my diary.

I have tried to be as honest as I have always been in writing up the results of a laboratory experiment. In choosing illustrative stories of patients, I have used only those told me 30 or 40 years ago by persons who were then in their middle life. I have done this so that no one living today, who may happen to read this book, is likely to guess who a particular patient was.

A discomfort that must be suffered by the writer of an autobiography is the constant use of "I," a repetition which sounds so immodest. Probably the best thing to do is just not fret about it. We human beings tend to think we are pretty good, and when on official occasions we conceal this self-estimate we do it because politeness and convention demand it. I might as well behave like the small child who admits he is pretty clever, and lets it go at that.

What Rufus M. Jones once said, I will say: "The repeated use of *I*, *me* and *my* sounds conceited and pitiably egotistic—and I have not used these pronouns because I love them. I am not in the least 'stuck' on the person I have been writing about. I know him too well!"

I never have felt that I could take much credit for whatever I have done in life because, as I shall show later, I was pretty much *driven* to whatever I did. I was driven by an energetic temperament, a great curiosity, and a great love of getting things done. And for all of these characteristics I can take no credit because they were bequeathed me by my two able and hard-working parents.

Through all this book I have tried to keep in mind a passage in Proverbs (27:1): "Let another man praise thee, and not thine own mouth—a stranger, and not thine own lips"; but still another thought comes to me from my friend Professor William B. Bean: "Blessed is he that tooteth his own horn, for he who has a horn and tooteth it not, the same shall not be tooted." In other words, if a man has a good story to tell to the world, he ought to tell it.

I cannot adequately thank my devoted wife for all the help she has given me in the writing of this book in the last eleven years—encouragement, much wise criticism, and endless hours of expert typing.

I

My Early Years as an Intern

On the morning of April 18, 1906, I was wakened at 5:13 A.M. by a tremendous roar. It sounded as if an enormous giant had taken hold of the big old wooden two-story City and County Hospital of San Francisco and was shaking it violently. In a few seconds, as I cleared the sleep out of my brain, I realized that what was happening was one of the world's great earthquakes. I jumped up and ran to the door of the big room in which four of us interns lived, dodging not only our chandelier as it came down but also part of the brick chimney that fell into the room through the fireplace. I ran downstairs, side-stepping a skylight that was breaking up and coming down. When I got to the big archway over the front door of the hospital, I had sense enough to stay there rather than risk running out, and having a big cornice come down on top of me.

Some minutes later, as the earthquake quieted, I saw out on the lawn three or four dozen nurses who had gathered there, together with a much-embarrassed senior medical student. The evening before, when he had stayed overnight to take the place of an intern who had suddenly been called home, I had offered him a pair of my pajamas, but he had said no, he'd sleep in his undershirt. So there was poor Whiting among the nurses, in an undershirt that was distressingly short. When he tried to get back into our dormitory he couldn't because the wife of the assistant superintendent, having become hysterical, was in the hall without her nightie!

I immediately realized that with the cracking of the brick-work around the dozens of little old-fashioned fire-places in the building, fire could easily creep into the wood-work, and a big general fire would mean the death of a few hundred bedridden patients. So I raced around through every ward of the hospital, telling the nurses to put out the fires as quickly as they could.

After the first big long shock, there came a number of shorter ones, but soon we quit paying much attention to them. Immediately our water, electricity, and gas were cut off. The huge water-main that then led into the city was broken clear across where it went through a "fault," along which the tremendous motion of the earth was taking place. What little water we had in the hospital was full of soot. Later, I got a little clean water from a nearby well.

Interesting was the narrow escape our chief cook had had. When, at 5 A.M., his alarm went off, he so hated to get up he took a 10-minute snooze. Three minutes after he got up—with the first big shock—some 1,000 pounds of brick-work flipped off the top of the high chimney, and falling first through the roof of the building and then through the ceiling of the cook's room, carried his bed down into the basement! The Chef assured me that always thereafter, whenever his alarm would go off, he would jump right out of bed!

Within half an hour after the first shock, ambulances began to bring in dozens of people with cracked skulls and broken bones, and I was hard at work in the operating room putting on plaster casts and trying to give comfort to the many people who were in great pain. Every few minutes an earthquake shock would come, so violently that I would look up expecting to see the big skylight falling in on us.

The cruelest thing our none-too-bright superintendent immediately did was to throw out of the hospital everyone who could be gotten out of bed. His idea was that soon hundreds of injured persons would be brought in, and we would need beds for them. But emergency committees of physicians had quickly built tent hospitals here and there in the parks of the city, and for some time these makeshift places took care of all of the sick and injured. For a few weeks the central committee remained unaware of the fact that there existed a large city hospital which was half empty!

One of the most unusual spectacles of the days during which most of the city burned to the ground was the procession of thousands of people who streamed out Potrero Avenue past the hospital. For two or three days they filled the street from one side to the other. Practically all were walking, and many were carrying bundles which contained the few possessions they had saved. Some were pushing pianos on casters! On top of the piano might be a couple of suitcases, a parrot in its cage, and a number of bundles. Alongside might be a woman pushing a baby carriage filled with some household belongings, or a woman would be pushing her beloved sewing machine. Next to her might be a man pulling a wagon, or a man pushing a wheelbarrow full of his extra clothes. Many people had their few possessions in a child's toy cart.

I remember well a horse-drawn wagon with three men on the seat. Lying on some straw in the bed of the wagon was their sister of 19 or 20 who, every so often, would go into one of the spectacular spasms of major hysteria. Suddenly, she would arch her back so that her weight rested solely on her head and her heels.

The first night after the earthquake my unlighted ward was an eerie place. Many patients were "seeing snakes"—either because of the sudden stoppage of their usual ration of alcohol, or because, with some of their bones smashed, fatty globules of marrow had been carried up into their brain by the blood stream and had plugged up a lot of little arteries.

Later my Chief told me about one man's curious experience in one of the famous old French restaurants in San Francisco. Here, there were upper rooms into which a man could take a woman for dinner and then stay for the night. In order not to be seen coming in, a couple could arrive in a cab with the curtains down and be taken up to the second floor in an elevator —cab, horse, and all.

On the morning of the earthquake, this man, who had spent the night in one of these restaurant rooms with "a friend," woke to find himself looking at flames in a building across the street. Not knowing that there had been a tremendous earthquake, and not knowing that with the first shock the whole front of the restaurant building had fallen off onto the sidewalk, the man's first thought was that he had waked in hell— to which he had been sent to atone for his sexual sins!

A few days after the earthquake I went down to the main post office where I sent brief notes on pieces of scratch paper to my girl and my family to say that I was safe and in good health. No envelopes or stamps were needed during those first few days after the quake and fire.

I had started my internship on July 1, 1905, and the nearly two years that followed were perhaps the most important and formative of my life.

A big city hospital is a remarkable place, filled as it is with human wreckage of all kinds. Most of the patients in my ward were men who were slowly dying of some chronic disease or combination of diseases. Many of them had acquired their illness through years of dissipation. Many had been out in bars drinking too much, staying up all night, then sleeping in some strange woman's bed.

Hundreds of these men were dying of some degenerative disease of the heart, the kidneys, the brain, the nerves, or the blood vessels. Many were suffering from the end-results of high-blood pressure, arthritis, asthma, cirrhosis of the liver, tuberculosis, or syphilis. Many were dying of a too-long neglected cancer.

I worked very hard, and for long hours each day. It was bad enough when I had only the 32 patients in my own ward to take care of, but one month I had charge of the receiving station as well. Another month I had a man-sized job in the contagious pavilion, where every day children came in, strangling to death with the awful diphtheria that nearly killed me when I was two years old.

At other times I was in the obstetrical ward, where I might have to work all night. Actually, our work as interns was so hard and unhygienic that two of my classmates soon came down with tuberculosis, and one promptly died of it. In those days the life of a conscientious intern was a killing job. And for those 16 or 20 hours of work all we received was a bed, some disgusting food—often full of cockroaches—our laundry, and some experience!

Because of the graft of that day, our food was so bad that we interns welcomed the invitations we sometimes got to come to a little party in a diet-kitchen—a party thrown about 10 P.M. by two or three of the more attractive nurses. This sort of thing was, of course, strictly forbidden, but it was a common practice.

No intern was ever supposed to date a nurse, but much of that sort of thing went on *sub rosa* and, as a result, many a doctor married a young woman who had worked in his ward. And this was a good idea because a good nurse makes an excellent wife, especially for a physician.

In my intern year came the report from Europe that Fritz Richard Schaudinn had at last discovered the cause of syphilis, and it was not a bacillus—it was a tiny little spiral organism called a spirochete. I immediately set to work to see if he was right, and I found that he was. I wrote up my work, and sent the paper—my first medical one—to the *Journal* of the

American Medical Association, where kindly old Dr. Simmons promptly published it.

Soon after I became an intern, there was an election in which the better element in San Francisco tried to throw out the gangsters and put in a reform mayor. At the hospital, we interns all voted the reform ticket. That evening Superintendent McQuaide called us into his office. He was a powerfully-built man who looked like a big toad standing on its hind legs, with a bowler hat stuck on the side of its head. His only qualification for running the huge hospital was that he was an ex-boxer, who once had been the bodyguard of the city boss. He said angrily, "Why did you guys throw me down? I promised Abe Ruef (the boss) I'd deliver this ward solid, and then you go and vote against me. You made a sucker out of me. All right, for the rest of your year here, I'll keep sticking it into you fellows good and plenty."

"But, Mac," I said, "we were brought up on the idea that here in America a man is free to vote for the candidate of his choice."

"No! When you work in this hospital, you vote as I want you to do. *You should have known that!*"

Actually, for the rest of that year, if we wanted his signature on a permit for an autopsy, he'd refuse us. If we asked him to OK a requisition for some much-needed drugs, he'd just glare at us.

A year later, when I was leaving, I dropped in on McQuaide and, holding out my hand, I said, "Come on, Mac, how about burying the hatchet?" "No," said he, "In my game of politics a man never forgives a slight, just as he never forgets a favor. I'll never forgive you for having voted against me last year."

These were the conditions under which we often had to work in those early days of medicine.

I never met William Osler in the flesh, and I heard him lecture only once, when in 1913 I was at Harvard. But he has always been my hero and my great teacher and inspiration. In

1905, I bought his *Aequanimitas and Other Addresses,* a book which was to have a great influence on my life. Osler re-enforced in me the idea that "medicine is an art, not a trade; a calling, not a business." As he said, "Often the best part of your work will have nothing to do with potions and powders, but with the exercise of an influence of the strong upon the weak; of the righteous upon the wicked, of the wise upon the foolish." In an old diary for January 23, 1906, I find a note showing that I was already wondering how I could so work and grow mentally and spiritually as to be of the most use *to humanity and to my profession.*

Osler impressed on his students the idea that their college education had been only a start—a beginning. In college a man should learn where to go in the library to find the information he needs. A physician worth his salt will keep studying hard all his days. "The all-important thing is to get a relish for the good company of the race in a daily intercourse with some of the great minds of all ages." "Many of you [doctors to be] will need a strong leaven to raise you above the dough in which it will be your lot to labour."

I learned from Osler that a fine physician should be a well-educated man, with much knowledge, not only of medicine, but also of general literature and the psychology of men and women. I was cheered by his statement that all doors will open to a man with the "Masterword, which is Work." I profited from his statement that everyone should live his life in "day-tight compartments," neither grieving over the mistakes of the past nor worrying about the problems of the morrow.

I have always believed strongly in Osler's injunction that everyone should "burn his own smoke," by which he meant that no one should grouse and keep telling people about his discomforts. In my many years with the Sierra (mountain-climbing) Club, I found that one of the most important of their unwritten laws was that no one should ever even remark to his neighbor that it was raining, that he was wet and cold and hungry, and that dinner was late.

I was much influenced by Osler's chapter on the joys of collecting the old medical books that are classics. This idea of his started me on a hobby that is still giving me pleasure. During some 40 years I gathered a large library, and eventually I owned most of the books written by the founders of American Medicine. As I traveled around the country lecturing, it was my habit to spend much of my time between trains rummaging in old book stores, and many were the treasures that I picked up in this way.

Other hundreds of treasures were found by looking through the many catalogs of old book stores that each month came to me from all over the world. I have derived much of my education from these catalogs. They list books which have been good enough to survive 50 or 100 years. I am convinced that any man who hopes to be not only a leader in his specialty, but a good and interesting teacher, lecturer, and perhaps editor, should know well the *history* of his subject's development.

I liked Osler's idea that a physician should so live that, eventually, he will become a philosopher. In many ways I soon did become a philosopher—each day helping some of my patients with their life-problems. Also, I learned from Osler the great value of imperturbability to a physician, by which he meant the ability to stay calm, cool, courageous and resourceful, even in the presence of great turmoil, and perhaps acute danger to the patient before him. It is a quality that is greatly appreciated by people, especially when things are going badly—as when the head of a family lies very ill after a stroke or a heart attack or a hemorrhage. The physician who, in such a situation, shows signs of bewilderment, indecision, fear, or mental paralysis, will not meet the needs of the patient and his family.

Once in my childhood I was impressed by signs of this imperturbability in the behavior of my father. As we were eating breakfast, a man galloped up on a lathered horse. Hurrying in, he said, "Doctor, get to my house as fast as you can; my wife is dying; you know where I live?" "Yes," said my father, "I'll get there as soon as I can," and with that, the man rode off.

My father called the yard man; told him to harness the horse, and then sat down and finished his breakfast. Then, seeing that the buggy was not yet at the door, he started changing some things from one little black bag to another.

Finally, my tense and excitable mother, unable to stand Dad's slowness and calmness any longer, said "Oh, Lu, Lu, how can you keep puttering around with those bags? Didn't you hear the man say that his wife was dying? Why don't you hurry?" My father looked at her quietly and thoughtfully, and said, "Well, Clemmie, if the woman is really dying, I won't be able to stop her, and if she isn't dying, there is no hurry."

During my internship, I kept learning much about human nature, and some of the lessons I have never forgotten. One day in December, 1905, a prematurely-aged street-walker who was perhaps 30 but who looked 50, applied for admission. Like many in her profession, she wanted to spend the worst part of the cold and rainy winter off the streets and in the hospital. She was thin and scrawny and uncommunicative, and so afflicted with the diseases incident to her business that I became nauseated when I had to treat her. She had drunk rather heavily, and in order to stand her contacts with the rough men whom she kept picking up, she had been taking morphine.

I thought her a very poor specimen of humanity, and hence was puzzled when, a few weeks later, I saw that in the women's ward, she had become the nurses' pet; she had been given bed No. 1, next to the desk, and she had been made head pantry-woman. This was the most coveted position, because it gave authority and enabled the woman to get better food than was served to the other patients.

Wondering how the nice nurses could be so chummy with such an awful creature, I asked them what they saw in her.

They said, "Don't you say a word against Lizzie; she may never cop a prize in a beauty show or be a deaconess in a church, but she is a wonderfully fine person, and good clear through. You just come and watch her some night after twelve when, as often happens, all hell breaks loose, and the poor lone little nurse who has to care for the upstairs ward as well as the downstairs one, is overwhelmed by the many calls made on her. Old Mrs. Murphy there in bed number 14 will wake and start keening over her boy who died years ago; then that foul-mouthed woman in number 16 will start cursing and yelling for a shot of morphine; that old woman in number 24, who is in her second childhood, will get up out of bed and start walking up and down the ward without anything on; that half-crazy one in number 8, in a nightmare, will start screaming that someone is cutting her throat, and then a dozen women will wake up and will all start calling for something or other.

"You'd think that some of the women who aren't very ill would get up and help the poor nurse, but, no; they just pull the bedclothes over their head and try to ride out the storm. But not Lizzie; she always gets right up and goes to work. With Mrs. Murphy she is gentle and kind; she brushes her hair for a minute and sings her a little Irish song, and soon Mrs. Murphy is quiet. In some secret way of her own she scares the daylights out of that demanding old devil in number 16, and shuts her right up. With those who are really suffering she has a remarkably kind and soothing way. To one she brings a glass of water; to another she takes an aspirin tablet; to another a needed bedpan; to another, with cramps in her legs, she will give a bit of rubbing with magic hands. Usually, within 40 minutes, the place is quiet again, and then after having given the nurse a cup of coffee, Lizzie goes back to her bed!"

I have never forgotten the lesson I learned that day. The terrible winds of adversity that had blown for years on Lizzie may have toughened her exterior and made her unattractive, but they had not changed materially the good, responsible, kind-hearted person who lived deep inside. The nurses had discovered that original Lizzie, and it was she whom they liked and respected, and accepted as a dear friend.

I learned from Lizzie what Jesus meant when He said, "There is nothing from without the man that going into him can defile him." I have always wondered what sort of woman Lizzie would have been if the good-for-nothing husband of her youth had not deserted her, and left her broken, drinking heavily, taking dope, selling her body for what little she could get, and hoping that the terrible life that she was leading would soon kill her.

Some may ask, "But, if she had so good a soul inside, why did she go on selling herself on the streets?" I imagine that she soon got down so low that no one would help her to get back up on her feet again. She was not trained for any job in either a business office or a home, and dissipation had so injured her appearance that few women would have liked to take her in, even as a scrub woman.

One day a big husky laborer came into my ward with the complaint that he had a frog hopping about in his stomach. He said he had gone to many doctors, begging for help in getting rid of the frog, but they would not believe him; they just laughed. In my youthful ignorance I thought it would be easy to cure the fellow by giving him an emetic, and while he was vomiting, to drop a palmed frog into the basin. When my old professor saw what I was planning to do, he shook his head and said, "It won't work; you cannot cure a fellow like that; you'll only waste your time."

But I had to learn this for myself, so I went ahead. My chum, who was an amateur magician, did a fine job of palming the frog and dropping it, and the patient was delighted. He kept saying, "I told them I had a frog, but they wouldn't believe me."

The only trouble was that next day he came back to say that I had been just 24 hours too late; the frog had spawned, and there were now a dozen little frogs hopping around in his stomach!

One day during the winter of 1905, when I was in charge of the receiving room, an old vagrant came in with lice crawling all over the outside of his coat and dropping off him by the dozen with each step he took. He begged me, for God's sake, to help him. He said he had gotten into his miserable state while living in boxcars where he couldn't bathe. He had no change of clothes, and hence he did not know how to get rid of the hundreds of insects which were eating him alive. His shoes were full of the dead bodies of hundreds of the cooties that he had trampled to death. He had applied at the City Emergency Hospital and other places for help but always had been quickly chased out into the street.

I had a hard time finding an orderly who would tackle the job of helping the man, but finally I induced one of the men from my ward—as a favor to me—to take the man out into the backyard, to undress him, to burn his clothes, and to sluice him off with a hose. Then we had to clip off the man's beard and every hair on his head and body. Down at the roots of the hair of his beard, the lice—two or three deep—were fighting to reach his skin! In a few days the fellow petered out and died, for no reason that we could determine, even at autopsy. In my medical lifetime, I have seen a few other vagrants with lice crawling on the outside of their clothes, but never did I see one whose awful state approached that of this unhappy man.

In the women's ward we always had some elderly woman with chronic ulcers on the inner surfaces of her legs, just above the ankles. Generally, we first "cleaned up" the ulcer; then we would cover it with skin grafts. One day when I had gotten an old woman's leg ulcers ready, I told her that, with her consent, we would perform the little operation the next morning. After a while she called me and asked how long it would take for her to get well. When I said, "Probably two weeks," she said she did not want to have the work done. Puzzled, I asked her, "But, why? Are you afraid?" "No," she said, "It isn't that. Don't laugh at me, doctor, but after nursing these ulcers for 20 years, I could not lose them that sudden!"

I marvelled at her honesty in giving me the real reason behind the choice to keep her big sores. Many a time since then I have suspected that a woman with some ache of nervous origin was hanging on to it because she "couldn't lose it that sudden."

One day in the hospital I learned how much sympathy and understanding can help a patient. In my ward there was a sweet Irish girl of 19 who had a terrible tuberculosis of a hip. To drain this, a surgeon had made two big cuts through the girl's hip muscles and down deep into the joint. Every day I had to pack these incisions with gauze so that perhaps the wound would "heal up from the bottom." I dreaded the job because what I had to do caused the girl much pain. One day, on my return from a week-end vacation, I found her running a fever because the foul dressings had not been changed. When I asked the nurses why the girl had been neglected, they said she would not let any of the other interns touch her. When I asked her why, she said, "Because *you* are sorry when it hurts me, and when you are sorry, I can stand the pain."

One morning when my Chief arrived I startled him by saying we had a leper in the ward. What had happened was that in came an old Chinese with a chronic "punched-out" ulcer on the bottom of one foot. Suspecting immediately that this might be due to leprosy, I pulled up his pajamas and, sure enough, there I saw some whitish patches, each surrounded by a narrow, dark ring. When I reached up to my lapel for a pin to see if the skin was without sensation (as it would be if the patches were leprous) the Chinese said, "No feel-'um; no feel-'um." With this, the diagnosis was made, and next day the poor fellow was taken to the local "pest house."

A year later my dear good friend, Dr. Robert Langley Porter, got me the job of taking care of this pest house. While I was there I saw a girl of 19 with a severe form of leprosy which had almost destroyed her eyes, and had caused some of her fingers and toes to drop off. She had a child by one of the orderlies; obviously a man who was not very particular in the choice of a love-mate!

When I started work at the hospital, some of my chiefs fired me with enthusiasm for certain types of strenuous treatment, and as a result I often gave ice-water baths to the patients with typhoid fever, or mustard packs to the patients with pneumonia. And then, one day, a wise old nurse said to me, "You know what we girls think? We think you are just wearing those poor people out. Why not let them rest and sleep? That might do them more good." I thought a while, and said, "You're probably right; I know that if I were the patient, I would want to be left alone." After that I never pulled very sick people around in order to give them a lot of examinations and treatments; I trusted to the statement of my wise old Professor, Dr. J. O. Hirschfelder, who used to say that for many illnesses the best treatment is *the blessed tincture of time!*"

One thing that soon perturbed me at the hospital was the tendency of a few of my chiefs to alter the original record of a patient so it would agree better with their theories or prejudices or desires. This behavior reminded me of the exhortation that Mark Twain once gave a group of reporters. With his usual mixture of fun and wisdom, he said that always when a man is sent out by his editor to gather some information, he should record accurately and honestly the facts as he heard them or saw them. Later, he could distort these facts to his heart's content, or his editor could re-write them to suit his particular bias.

I have thought of this statement whenever I have seen a physician erasing something from a patient's record because he refused to believe the statement of fact, or refused to accept the implications of the fact, or wanted the record to support an idea he had. To illustrate: if a man in my ward died after treatment with the favorite drug regularly used by one of my chiefs, he might say to me, "Don't file this case record for use in the paper I am planning to write because the man was too neurotic to be a suitable case for study." Usually, so far as I could see, there was no good basis for his having said this.

As a surgical intern, I hated to see one of my Chiefs being dishonest with himself. For instance, one day he crossed out my record of the fact that one of our patients had developed typical symptoms and signs of an acute new ulcer within a few days after the performance of a gastroenterostomy (a new opening out of the stomach designed to cure the original duodenal ulcer). The doctor, an eminent man, explained that he would not believe a word that that patient might say. But I could see no reason for distrusting the fellow, he seemed like a fine, honest man. I felt that what the patient had said should have been recorded in his history, exactly as he had said it. My impression was that my teacher's behavior was based purely on his great reluctance to admit that a gastroenterostomy was not a good operation for a young man with a duodenal ulcer. Actually, after some 25 years, the operation had to be given up except for a few special purposes.

Another time when I had recorded the fact that a mentally disturbed patient had told me that his brother, his mother, and his mother's sister were in mental hospitals, I was distressed when a chief of mine, who would not permit me to mention the word "heredity" in his presence, came along and angrily crossed out the note that I had made.

One of my teachers of surgery used to rather amuse us interns because he seemed so unconscious of the fact that he was not honest with himself. To show what he would do: whenever at an operation he found the gallstones he had expected, he would dictate to his assistant; "a stone-containing gallbladder was removed in the usual way." But when, on failing to find stones in the gallbladder of a woman whose abdominal distress was due to a depression, he would dictate half a page telling of a slight milkiness of her gallbladder wall, a slight thickening of the wall; one little adhesion between the gallbladder and the duodenum; a little rounding and softening of the edge of the liver; an enlargement of the lymph node draining the gallbladder; or a little hardening of the head of the pancreas. After watching our Chief do this a number of times, we interns knew perfectly well that this was his odd way of saying that he had opened a normal abdomen by mistake.

My feeling, even in those early days, was that if my teacher had been scrupulously honest with himself and with us—his assistants—he would have written "normal gallbladder," and let it go at that. The only objection to this would have been that such a written record would have left him open to legal attack if the patient had later wanted to sue him. At one hospital in which I worked in my youth, many an appendix was removed supposedly to cure the "vapors" of a neurotic woman. When it appeared normal to the pathologist who examined it with his microscope, he would write, "chronic appendicitis, grade i." He did this partly for legal reasons, and partly so that the surgeon would not have him fired.

While still in my intern year I did one of the most useful things I ever did in my life—which was to get many surgeons to stop their ancient practice of giving powerful purges to all patients before operations. They called this the *preparation of the patient.* I soon began to ask my surgical teachers why they gave everyone 10 grains of jalap, plus 10 grains of calomel, plus an ounce of magnesium sulfate, since the resultant weakening, dehydration, and exhaustion of the patient seemed often to be the cause of his postoperative death.

When they said the preparation was to clean out the digestive tract before an operation on the bowel, I said, "Begging your pardon, sir, that cannot be the reason, because you purge a woman just as violently before you take off her breast or remove her womb." Then they said, "It must be to prepare for the anesthetic"; but I showed them quickly that this wasn't the reason, because the anesthetists said they had no desire to have the patients purged.

Finally, to his great credit, my surgical teacher, instead of firing me as a nuisance, admitted that he didn't know why the patients were purged. Day after day I kept showing him that when some of the older and weaker patients came up to the operating room after a sleepless night on the toilet, they were so worn out that they were easily thrown into shock, and finished off by the operation. I also got my professor to admit that, in those many cases in which some emergency, such as a bullet wound, compelled him to open the abdomen of a person who had not been "prepared," almost always that patient had an unusually easy postoperative course.

I can imagine a European-trained physician having the horrors over the idea of an intern arguing this way with the leading surgeon in his college and his state, but my then chief, Dr. Emmett Rixford, was a "big" man, and we were friends, and so he never became impatient with me or tried to shut me up.

Then I went to the library, and after weeks of reading, I discovered that the practice of purging patients before an operation was a remnant of the idea of many primitive peoples that when a lad is to face any ordeal, such as torture incident to his initiation into the tribe, he must be *prepared* by purgation, fasting, vigils, and abstention from sex. In ancient Greece, a philosopher who was to debate with a man from another "school" first purged himself with the violent drug hellebore. This was to "rid himself of peccant (harmful) humors (supposedly important body fluids)."

In 1918 I published this evidence in a paper and soon many of the surgeons throughout the world gave in, and either quit preparatory purging of patients, or toned it down so as to make it less harmful, or they ordered only an enema. One day the then leading surgeon of Los Angeles told me how grateful he was to me because at last he had the answer to a question that for a long time had puzzled him—namely—why, when he operated on a famous movie queen did she always have a stormy postoperative course, while a "nobody" in the County Hospital, on whom he performed an emergency abdominal operation, was usually up and walking around in three or four days. With my evidence before him he saw that in his anxiety to get a good result with the movie queen he had purged her particularly thoroughly, whereas the other woman had not been "prepared" at all. Later, some of the abdominal surgeons who had done much operating in front-line hospitals during World War I, wrote to tell me how right I was—they said their operative patients (who rarely were prepared) did unusually well.

Recently, as I wrote this, I was saddened and disillusioned to get a letter from a friend who said that in 1962 he had had a kidney removed in one of America's greatest teaching hospitals, and before the eminent surgeon would operate, he ordered three powerful purges—one after the other! Nothing sticks harder or longer in this world than a stupid and useless practice. Even we learned physicians will sometimes fight for our right to follow some 5,000-year-old bit of stupidity.

Incidentally, during my first six months in the hospital I expected to be a surgeon, because that was what my father wanted me to be. But then I got "rotated" into a surgical ward, and discovered that I had very little interest in surgery. What most impressed me was my great and constant desire to get back to my *medical* patients, and particularly to the problems of diagnosis, which fascinated me. Accordingly, I wrote my father that I was sorry to disappoint him, but I was going to be an internist. I am glad that he accepted this decision of mine without any protest.

Ever since then I have been saying to medical students, "Don't worry about what specialty to follow; you are likely to find out which it is to be—when the time comes."

I soon learned that in those days all unconscious patients, when on their way to the County Hospital were well "rolled." I discovered this when I was visiting with the morgue-tender— my old friend, Tingley, a cadaverous-looking man who was dying of tuberculosis. The handsome young man who drove the ambulance came in, and Tingley said, "Heh, George; you missed it with that bum you brought in at ten last night; he had fifty dollars on him." And George said, "You're a damned liar; he hadn't a nickel on him!" When George had gone, I asked Tingley, "Where was the money?" and he said, "Look here; it was between the layers of leather in the old boy's shoes; he had ten five dollar gold pieces hidden there." What amused me was George's certainty that the man had no money *in his pockets!*

For months I had in my ward a sweet gray-haired old German tailor whom I came to like. He was dying of tuberculosis, and he was down to skin and bones. Because the tuberculosis had eaten into his voice box, every cough was torture to him. Finally, a day came when he started to die in earnest. He would stop breathing for a few moments and seem dead, but then he would take a deep breath and regain consciousness for a while. This went on for several days until the poor fellow, hardly able to stand the suffering any more, begged me to put him out of his misery.

That night I gave him a grain of codeine which I hoped would be enough to ease his pain so he could get some rest. Actually, he did *sleep all night*, and, as a result, he woke in the morning feeling like a new man. Because he had been conscious when I gave him his "shot," his gratitude to me was pathetic. After that I gave him a grain of codeine whenever he needed it to control his suffering, and as a result, he lived comfortably enough for several weeks. Then, suddenly, a big hemorrhage came and carried him off. This experience taught me a good lesson, which is that a sedative usually will not shorten a dying man's life, as his family so greatly fears it will. Actually, by lessening his pain, the drug will *lengthen* his life.

I had a number of good teachers, but the most brilliant of all was Dr. Emile Schmoll. I immediately saw that he was the ablest of my chiefs, and so I made a special effort to "work up" his cases for him. As a result, we soon became friends. He loved what we doctors call the art of "snap diagnosis," and was keen at it. A snap diagnosis is one that is made with a shrewd glance at the patient, and perhaps a couple of questions. Schmoll would take me out into the great corridor of the hospital where, while he smoked a cigarette, he would keep asking me, "That man with the queer limp—what has he got?" And I had to learn to tell the disease at a glance. It was splendid training for me. One day he was disgusted because I could not tell him what was wrong with a man who, when he walked, rose on one foot and then swung the other leg through a big arc.

"What's the matter with you?" said Schmoll. "He has a wooden leg!"

One evening in 1906 I was given some advice about graduate education which was to help me greatly. One of my best-beloved teachers was Dr. A. J. Houston. In his youth, he had had a hard time getting to Vienna, where he obtained his special training. Then for a time he had to work as a waiter in order to get enough money to get back to San Francisco.

I asked him how a young man like myself, unwilling to take any more money from my father, could get a graduate education. Dr. Houston said, "If you want it bad enough, just go after it; keep eternally after it; and remember: somehow or other you'll get it, and somehow or other you won't starve to death."

He proved to be right. I got the training, and I didn't starve.

In my intern days, studying almost entirely by myself, I learned so much about laboratory diagnosis that at the end of the year I was made an Instructor, and given the job of teaching "lab-work" to the senior medical students and the interns in the Cooper College wards. During the 10 months between July 1906 and April 1907, I did this teaching plus some residency work.

2

My Early Days
in Hawaii

RARELY DURING MY intern days I tried to figure
out what fate held in store for me as a doctor in the world
of men. And I could not help but marvel at how much our
lives are already decided by our ancestry, our origins, and our
inherited selves.

The study of heredity always fascinated me, perhaps in part
because my own family tree has such diverse origins. My
father came from the Spanish province of Asturias on the Bay
of Biscay. Because around 400 A.D. the Visigoths conquered
that part of Spain, many of the people are blond, energetic,
and hard-working—more like Germans than are the often easygoing peoples of the south of Spain.

Perhaps another reason I am tall and blond instead of short
and swarthy is that my maternal grandmother's people were
German. My great-grandfather was a vineyardist in the Moselle
valley, and my mother's father was a Dane.

My father's father must have been an able man because he
was the business manager for Don Francisco de Paula, the then
Pretender to the Spanish throne. My grandfather ran Don

21

Francisco's palace in Madrid, and the old Prince used to say that my grandfather was the only man in Spain whom he would trust with the keys to his wine cellar!

My mother's mother's people came to America years ago and settled down as pioneers in Minnesota. They had a strong love of music. One was trained in Berlin as an orchestra conductor, one was organist and choir leader in a big Chicago church, and one was Millie Potter, who in her day was a well-known concert singer.

I was very fortunate in that my father and mother were the outstanding members of their two family groups. My mother was interesting and attractive, a good conversationalist, a good writer, and always interested in self-improvement. Her passion was to train her voice, and in her later years, in Los Angeles, she was a soloist in a big church. I have a faint memory that when I was a child she drew lovely pictures for me. Her name was Clementina—my grandmother was especially devoted to her old Confessor, Father Clement—and I became Walter Clement.

My father—a distinguished-looking man—was short, blond, blue-eyed, and slight in build. He was not at all athletic, and walked slowly. He spoke and wrote well. He had only one all-absorbing interest—medicine. He was a general practitioner, sometimes working 24 hours a day—yet I never saw him tired. He was seriously ill only once in his life. One reason why he never tired may have been that no one could hurry him. Also, he was the most even-tempered man I ever knew. I saw him angry only twice. He was generous with Mother and us children, but very frugal with himself. He ate very little, he never touched liquor, and he never smoked. He was always kind to his patients, and so they loved him.

In 1883 my father owned a block of what is now downtown Los Angeles. Then the river went dry, and my father—unable to foresee the two huge aqueducts which now bring rivers of water hundreds of miles over mountains and through deserts—

said, "There never can be a city here because we have only a few wells." And so he sold the block, and in 1884 he went to San Francisco and enrolled as a student in Cooper Medical College to begin his training as a physician.

Studying was easy for him, if only because he had a wonderful memory. I was fortunate in that I inherited it.

In 1887, when my father graduated, he opened an office in San Francisco and rigged himself out in the regalia of a physician of those days: a Prince Albert coat, a "hard-boiled shirt" with a stiff collar and big stiff removable cuffs, a stovepipe hat, and a gold-headed cane! As a medical student he had grown the large full beard which was then supposed to be an essential part of a physician's outfit.

But few people came to his office, and soon my father's small reserve of funds was almost gone. Perhaps with the anxiety of all this, he began to run a little fever. Fearing that he might have tuberculosis, he went to see one of his favorite old professors. When this man heard his story, he said, "What you need is a sea voyage. It happens I am the physician for the steamship line that runs to Honolulu, and it also happens that the S. S. *Australia's* doctor has just jumped ship. So you are taking his place. You leave tomorrow!"

My father went to Honolulu and when he got there, he became friendly with the president of the Board of Health who offered him a job as a government physician such as was then needed to take care of the many natives—who of course had no money. Hence it came about that in 1887 the Alvarezes were on their way to Hawaii, there to live for the next 16 years.

I remember well our arrival in Honolulu, and I remember my father departing soon after on some ship. As the vessel pulled away from the wharf, my mother said, "Throw a kiss to Daddy," but I refused. I said it might fall into the water. A thrifty and careful child I was!

Waianae, on the island of Oahu, was our first home. It proved to be a small, hot, rainless, and miserable village where we—mother, father, my baby brother Milton, and I—had to

live in a very unattractive house built over an evil-smelling
filled-up old fish-pond. One day it was so hot we all of us went
up to a "mountain house" at the foot of Kaala, the nearby
4,000-foot mountain. I will never forget my thrill when, sitting
in front of a cowboy on his horse, I went up into the hills.
Today, after 75 years, I can still see that house and the yard
about it, and I can still remember my pleasure on inhaling the
several perfumes from the trees, and shrubs, and grasses. How
remarkable that, as a child of three, I was already enthralled
with mountains, which have been a joy to me ever since! I
strongly suspect there is something hereditary about this because, on my father's side, I am descended from mountainy
people who lived in the Cantabrian range—an extension of the
Pyrenees.

Fortunately, after a few months in Waianae, my father
was transferred to Waialua, a village on the west side of the
island of Oahu—a much more comfortable place in which to
live. My father then became responsible for the health of the
people living on a fifty-mile-long narrow shelf of land lying
between the mountains and the sea.

In sleepy Waialua we lived in a deserted building—a church
and parsonage under the same roof—which had housed an
Anglican mission. We lived in that old house for eight years,
largely isolated from the world. The Halsteads lived a mile or
two away. They were English, and the founders of the big
Waialua sugar plantation. But although they were friendly,
we seldom saw them.

There were a number of other Caucasians in our neighborhood, but not one of them *ever* called on us. They were all
strange persons who wanted only to be let alone. Most of the
men were "queer birds," or misanthropes who were rarely seen
by anyone. One was said to be an Oxford graduate. Another,
a Welshman, had a ranch which I don't think he ever left for
even a day; certainly I never saw him.

Up in the mountains was a solitary rancher named Galbraith. One day his horse threw him and broke his hip. All that saved him was that somehow or other he induced his dog to go into town and hang around. When Dad heard about the dog, he feared that Galbraith might have died, and went up to see. Dad found the man lying out on the ground in the cold rain. He had been so badly hurt he could not even crawl into his shack.

Next door to us was an Englishman named Hore who taught the children in the little Hawaiian school. He was married to a native woman. This is hard to believe: but he never once came over to see us! A half-mile north of us, in a lonely, unpainted, "haunted house" there lived a "remittance man," named Johnston. I never saw him. With him lived a white woman and a number of wild-looking, scantily-clad children who received no schooling. One night some old enemy called Johnston to his door and shot him dead.

The patriarch of the Hawaiian group next door to us was a gray-haired old man named Mokumia. He seldom wore more than a malu—a red rag around his loins. He lived with his sons and their families. They had a grass house of ancient type. Nearby they had a taro (elephant ears) patch—an area full of deep mud. Occasionally two of the sons would wade out into this mud up to their waists. They would pull up a few taro plants, cut off the big tubers, and boil them. Then they would put a number of these tubers on a big wooden platter about 4 feet long, and 2½ feet wide. Two men, seated one at each end of the platter, each with a stone poi-pounder in his hand, would mash the taro into a paste. This paste, when fermented, and diluted with water, made poi—the Hawaiian national dish.

With the poi, some bread-fruit, some mangoes, some raw fish (caught each day), and occasionally some pork or beef, these people lived well without much effort. They slept much of each day. No native would ever work in the canefields. A few would work on ships or wharves, or as cowboys on cattle ranches. They never would catch fish *for sale*. If they ever had a fish to spare, they were happy to give it to a relative or a neighbor, or even a passer-by.

Because of my very lonely childhood I was very interested when I heard Dr. Alan Gregg speak years ago about the difficulties of adjustment to life that a man is likely to experience when his childhood has been spent on a lonely ranch in the West, or in an isolated missionary "compound" in the Orient. As Gregg said, a child who is taught his three R's by his mother or his aunt misses many of the early democratizing influences that are to be found in a grammar school, and he fails to develop many of the "herd-loyalties of mankind."

As a result, what with his tendency to think independently and to disregard the less sensible mores of his community, he is likely always to feel as if he were an outsider. He may be a bit odd, and he may "never belong." Often during his life he will feel like a man on the outside looking in.

A child brought up in such isolation is usually old-in-his-ways. In Honolulu I met a boy who had spent his boyhood on a lonely ranch on one of the smaller islands of the Hawaiian group, living with his English father and a few Japanese sheep-herders. He was decidedly eccentric. Because of his years spent on the moors of the little island, he had the habit of opening a conversation with any acquaintance whom he spied on the street while still a block away! This sort of thing was all right on the island, but on the streets of Honolulu it was most embarrassing. Whenever the high school girls saw him coming, they would dive into a store or down a side street to escape his stentorian greeting!

Another Honolulu friend, brought up on a lonely ranch with only Hawaiian cowboys for his playmates, was a curious, odd, sad artist. Twenty years later, when I ran into him in California, he still was the same curious coot he had been in his youth. He had not married. His sister was also a strange, definitely unmarriageable, shy person. Their eccentricity was due probably to their inheritance from their odd parents, who left

England to "bury themselves alive" on a little-frequented spot on the island of Hawaii.

Although during my lonely years in Waialua I never became queer enough to take my place alongside of these odd friends of mine, my lonely upbringing probably did reinforce some inborn traits which tended to set me somewhat apart.

When I was about five my mother taught me to read. After that I devoured every bit of printed material I could find in the house. Unfortunately, there wasn't much. Because I was not allowed to go to the Hawaiian school or to play with the polyglot children in the neighborhood, and because my brothers and sisters were considerably younger than I, there were no playmates for me.

I so hungered for books that I begged my father to get me some, especially books about science. Eventually, he bought me one. Once I climbed up into the attic of our house, and imagine my thrill when I saw a big pile of books—a few hundred of them! I immediately examined every one, but oh, what a let-down! All but one of these books were dry-as-dust controversial volumes on Anglican high church dogma and ritual! I still marvel at the literary choice of that missionary who had come from England to bury himself alive—mentally—in a Hawaiian village.

I remember a day, perhaps in 1888, when Dad took Mother and me for a drive. As we were on the moor near the ocean, a toothless old crone—a Hawaiian woman who had been out on the reef fishing—came by carrying an octopus which she had caught and was taking home for dinner. The minute she saw us she had but one desire; like a true Polynesian, she wanted to give us the octopus. All the woman had on was the remnant of an old *mumu*—a chemise-like garment which covered her from the waist down.

The octopus, still alive, was crawling over her shoulders and breasts, and hanging on with its many suckers. The woman kept trying to pull it free so as to hand it over to my horrified mother! Fortunately, my father already spoke enough Hawaiian so that he could thank the old woman and tell her that octopus meat was taboo to American women. With this, she was satisfied. No feelings were hurt, and we drove on.

Interesting to me, illustrating how early my scientific way of looking at problems first appeared, was my behavior when, in my seventh year, my mother got out her old Catechism and told me to start memorizing it. I read it through and then said, "Mother, the men who wrote this were evidently sure about every statement they made, but how could they know anything of what goes on in Heaven? They just couldn't, and so I don't want to have anything more to do with this book." I must already have had a strong character because, although my mother had a strong will, she gave in; she admitted that the writers of the book had no proof for most of their statements, and so I never saw the Catechism again.

Another early sign of the scientist in me came when I started to take a sliver out of my finger with a pin. My mother, of course, said, "Oh, don't do that, take a needle."

"But why?"

"Because a pin is brass and a needle is iron."

Again, I asked, "But why should that make any difference?"

My mother could not explain any further, and for the next 40 years I kept asking many of the old women I met why one should never remove a sliver with a pin. They all agreed that a pin should never be used—because it was brass—but no one could tell me why. Old doctors I questioned on this subject were just as unable to give me an explanation.

Because I soon became convinced that I would find the explanation only in some old folk idea, I kept collecting and reading books on medical folklore. By the time I was 50 I had become satisfied that the only reason for using a needle and not a pin is that iron will keep away wicked fairies or elves who might get into the wound and cause it to fester. As we all know, an iron horseshoe over the door of a barn will keep the devil and the witches out.

Every "wise woman" and every witch doctor who ever lived

in any part of the world has known that the old gods, the fairies, the witches, and the demons have so feared or disliked iron that they would never go near it. Perhaps it was too new-fangled for them, having come into general use rather late—in some countries between 1,000 and 750 B.C., in others as late as 1 A.D.[1]

My father was a good companion because of his constant good humor, his love of fun, and his love of teaching. One day as we drove along in his buggy we passed a Hawaiian wearing nothing more than a brand-new denim shirt. My father said, "Look, Walter, someone gave that native a new shirt and he is so proud of it and so anxious to show it to his neighbors that he has rushed out without remembering to put on his pants."

One of my most vivid childhood memories is of going into a yard where my father had just cut some grass for his horse. The perfume of that cut grass delighted me so much that, even now, after 70 years, I can still see in my mind's eye, and with pleasure, the place under a tree whence the grass had been removed. Another perfume I learned to love in those early days was that of crushed fern fronds. Now, when I smell it, it takes me back to the days when the Hawaiians next door used to bring down from the mountains great armfuls of ferns to plait into garlands, or to use as a table for one of their *luaus*. To cook their food for the feast the men would dig a pit in the ground and line it with stones. They would fill the pit with wood and set this afire. When it had all burned down, they raked out the ashes and lined the pit with big ti leaves. Then they cut up their meat, sweet potatoes, and other foods into portions as big as a fist and wrapped these portions in ti leaves. After putting these packages into the pit, they covered it over with ti leaves and gunny sacks and poured in water which, on coming into contact with the hot stones, produced steam,

---

[1] This first bit of research of mine eventually was written up in 1936 as a Sigma Xi lecture on "The Impact of the Discovery of Iron on the Medical Thought of the Ancient World." It was republished in the *Transactions* of the Smithsonian Institution.

much as in a pressure-cooker. As a result, the food was soon
well cooked—tender, and with all its taste left in. The people
sat on the ground and ate without knives, forks, or spoons.
They stuck their fingers into the poi and then licked off the
food.

I loved to roam where grassland and forest met. There was
something about that forest, with its odors, its loneliness and
its eeriness, that thrilled me so much that I can still see it and
feel the joy and wonder of it all. Near a deserted ranch house,
my father and I found an old Hawaiian road paved with blocks
of lava. It led down into a wide place in the river valley where,
in ancient days, there was a village.

Moonlight picnics on the beach were a special treat. Moonlight in the tropics can be remarkably brilliant and beautiful.
There was always something soul-stirring about it. I loved the
beauty of the night, with the waves lapping up on the beach,
and the little crabs scuttling around.

I wonder if many other children feel as much joy in nature
as I did. So many of my vivid childhood memories are of the
beauties of nature—sunsets, storms, and the occasional brilliant
double lunar rainbows of Hawaii. I marvel now that while I
have forgotten so many thousands of events of those days of
long ago, I remember so vividly moments in which all I did
was to exult in the beauty of nature about me.

During the years in which we lived in Waialua, one of my
great pleasures each day was to watch the clouds forming and
re-forming over the nearby 4,000-foot mountain, called Kaala.
When I was 18 or 19, I climbed to the top of it and saw the
old volcanic crater filled with muddy water and moss-covered
trees. I remember my wonder at seeing for the first time the
remarkable giant-leaved plant, called the *á-pe-á-pe*. Later I was
to study it on the heavily wooded north side of Haleakala—
the huge extinct crater on Maui.

My medical education began in Waialua when I watched
my father going out on calls at all hours of the day and night,
often in the foulest weather. Many a time he would come in,

exhausted from a long horseback ride, only to find that he had to start right out again, perhaps back along the same road.

Often he started out on a hard journey knowing full well that he would never be paid. He was the only physician on the west and north coasts of the island of Oahu, and he never refused to go to see anyone who was ill. Sometimes the rains were so torrential that the tracks—which were then called roads—and the bridge at Waimea Canyon would be washed out. Then he could get through only on horseback, with his saddlebags behind him. Once, when crossing a river on his horse, the animal lost its footing, and all that saved me that day from becoming a fatherless boy was the skill of a couple of Hawaiian cowboys who promptly threw their lassoes around Dad's middle and pulled him out of the water.

A young man who plans to go into medicine has a big advantage when he grows up, as I did, the son of a fine doctor of the old school. As I drove about the countryside with my father, I learned what the life of a general practitioner is, and I became imbued with the idealism and the spirit of service of a fine physician. I imagine that in those days a certain stamp was put upon me—one that ever since has influenced my behavior and my ways of thinking about medical practice.

I was particularly fortunate in that my father was a man with a well-stocked mind, who liked to teach, and who taught well. He taught me the Greek and Latin roots (like *tele*–far, *micro*–small, *phonos*–sound, *scopein*–to see), roots from which so many of our scientific words have been made. He also introduced me to the Spanish language.

I can remember well the first operation at which I assisted. I imagine I was about seven at the time. A native who had been fishing with dynamite had hung on to the explosive too long, and had blown off his right hand. Dad had to clean up the bleeding stump and cover it with skin. He pulled the kitchen table out into the yard and put the man on it. The Hawaiian minister of the local native church gave the anesthetic—the first he had ever seen—and Mother and I were the nurses. After the operation the patient got up and walked home with his friends!

There was another operation I remember—probably because I was the patient. When I was five or six and was bathing with my father in the ocean, I slipped on some slimy seaweed. My feet shot out from under me and my head struck hard on a bit of sharp coral. The spicule of coral had made so big a cut in the skin of my left temple that Dad said he would have to put in some stitches.

On hearing this, I set up a howl, and I cried all the way home. Then Dad started sewing, and I can still feel that needle and thread going through my skin. When I found the pain was bearable, I stopped crying, and made no further protest. My father then said, "You see, Walter, you have now learned one of the most useful lessons that you will ever have to learn. Often the anticipation of evil hurts us much more than does the evil when it arrives."

I soon learned that when walking along a road I must constantly be on the watch for the wild cattle which occasionally were left behind by the native drovers. When crazed with heat and thirst, an animal which had been left behind would instantly attack a person on foot or on horseback, or even in a buggy. My life depended on my keeping my eyes open, because at any moment I might find such a steer dashing at me with intent to kill. Once I barely beat such an animal to a fence and, throwing myself on the ground, I rolled to safety. If I had been a bit slower on my feet or in my thinking, I would probably have been left a cripple with a smashed spinc or a punctured lung. One time I *did* get tossed into the air, and on another occasion my sister Mabel got tossed, but luckily neither of us was injured.

One day, when I was nine, I asked my father, "How did that black cow get into the school yard (next door)?" He said, "What cow?" and I pointed to what I thought was the animal.

"Why, that is a photographer with a tripod and camera and a black cloth over his head!"

Then, of course, Dad knew that my vision was very bad. As soon as he could get away, he took me with him to Honolulu in the light two-wheeled gig which in good weather he used for getting about the country. We went around the island and up over the *Pali*, or pass in the mountain range, and down to Honolulu. There I got my first pair of glasses.

Naturally, it was a wonderful adventure for me, and I still have some memories of it. I remember the huge tree—probably a redwood—which we saw cast up on the beach. It must have drifted some 2,000 miles from the coast of California.

I remember Dad's showing me the little plovers on the beach, and telling me that these young birds, unaccompanied by their parents, had flown 2,000 miles across the Pacific, all the way from Alaska. Today, 69 years later, scientists still have almost no idea how these birds can navigate so well, and how they know they must fly to eight little islands far out in the wastes of the Pacific.

I can still remember well the time, I think it was about 1888, when my father took me into the village of Waialua and paid 25 cents so I could listen to the first Edison phonograph. It was being demonstrated by a "traveling-man." Even with ear-phones like those of a doctor's stethoscope, I could barely hear the music, but it seemed like a miracle.

Early in my boyhood I developed a great interest in the tremendous influence of the mind on the body—an interest that is strong in me today, 70 years later. Occasionally I would hear my father telling my mother of a case in which a *Kahuna*, or witch doctor of the evil type, was "praying a man to death." Perhaps a young man who wanted to get rid of a rival for the hand of his girl would hire a *Kahuna* to do away with the fellow. As soon as the victim heard that he was being prayed to death, he would sit down on a mat, quit eating and drinking, and in perhaps ten days he would have it over with. My father would tell the victim that he had spells and charms stronger than those of the *Kahuna* but the native would always say, "No, *Kauka* (doctor), you are a *malihini* (a foreigner) and so you can't help me, no one can."

Once my father became a bit flabbergasted when he realized that he had unwittingly contributed to two of these witch-doctor killings. In Waialua there lived a six-foot-tall, coal-black ex-whaler from the Cape Verde Islands, a Portuguese, named Anton Lopez, with big gold rings in his ears. By marrying the daughter of the local chief, he had acquired a cattle ranch. One day he was complaining to my father that every so often a couple of Hawaiians would steal one of his steers and kill it in order to give their friends a feast. Twice Lopez' cowboys had caught the thieves red-handed, and twice Lopez had taken them to jail. But each time, when it came to testifying in court, his cowboys lost their memory. As Lopez' native wife told him, the reason was that the thieves had hired a *Kahuna* to promise the cowboys that "one peep out of them" and they would be prayed to death.

My father, who always had a quick sense of humor, said in fun, "Why, that's easy; all you need do is to pay the *Kahuna* a little more to pray the two thieves to death." "Wonderful," said Anton Lopez; "Why didn't *I* think of that?" And off he went. Ten days later he dropped in to say that the thieves were dead, and it had cost him only a cow and two pigs!

Eventually my life in that lonely village approached its end, and a new day dawned. I do not know what would have happened to me if this miracle had not come along—a miracle that took my father and all of us out of that primitive place and into a city with all its advantages.

In 1895 my father was asked by the Hawaiian Board of Health to see if anything could be done to help the lepers. I never cease wondering how the Board had the vision to see that Dad—an unknown practitioner in a small village—had it in him to do research.

To prepare for his new job Dad left immediately for Johns Hopkins Medical School in Baltimore where, for some six months, he studied bacteriology day and night under such great teachers as William Welch and Simon Flexner. Meanwhile, Mother, with us five children, stayed behind in our new home in Honolulu.

On father's return, he opened a little hospital for lepers in Honolulu, and in it built a laboratory in which he tried to develop a serum against leprosy. He devised a method for finding the bacilli (of leprosy) in suspicious-looking small anesthetic white patches of skin. He would snip off a tiny bit of the diseased skin, grind it up in a small mortar, make a smear on a glass slide, stain it, and with his microscope look for the red-stained germs.

On Saturdays and holidays I worked with my father in his laboratory. In the afternoons and evenings Dad practiced medicine, and soon had a large clientele.

The best part of my education during those years took place in the Public Library of Honolulu. The first thing I did on arriving in the city was to start taking out books. Before long, I was a pet of the kindly old librarian, and a few years later I was in charge of the place every evening during the dinner hour.

It was a wonderful privilege for a voracious reader like me to have the run of a good library. First I read widely in geology, paleontology, and evolution, and then I read much archaeology, travel, and general biology. I rarely read any fiction because there wasn't enough time left over.

School used to let out at 2 P.M., and the first thing many of us boys did was to hurry home and pull off our shoes. We, who from early childhood had gone barefoot, hated shoes. Next, a few of us would jump on our bicycles and would go to the Boat House on the eastern edge of the harbor where we would swim and perhaps go sailing. A friend and I built the first sailing catamaran (boat with a deck between two hulls) seen in Honolulu. After a swim I often went to the YMCA for gymnasium work and handball. On some days I would practice with the track team, running the quarter-mile and doing the high-jump. On an occasional Saturday, a few of us boys would go up into the jungle-covered mountains back of Honolulu. I was happiest when up in those hills.

Perhaps the best thing I did in my five years in Honolulu

was, by constantly exercising, to develop the big strong body which has served me so well ever since.

When I was a boy in Hawaii, talking to people who knew only a hundred words of English, I was learning a lesson that was to be invaluable to me later on in my life when I would have to take medical histories from illiterate immigrants, and still later when I would be writing a medical column for lay readers. When talking with non-English-speaking persons, I learned to use only the few words that they knew.

Interesting to me is the fact that back in 1895 I realized that my chum, whom we will call Bill Smith, had just taught me much about a certain fairly common type of human behavior. I was then eleven, and Bill was two years older. One day in a vacant lot we found an old battered milk can, and Bill said, "Look, a fire engine. We'll find four wheels for the truck, and another for the pump, and then I'll make an engine that will spout fire and smoke, and will pump water."

I could not see how we two boys without a lathe, a planer, and several other tools, also without mechanical skill, could possibly build such an engine, but Bill was older than I. I looked up to him and trusted him, as many a young boy looks up to an older one; and if he said he could make a fire engine, who was I to doubt him? And so for the rest of the week, every afternoon after school, we two searched through dumps and vacant lots until we had five decrepit wheels, and some axles and many odd scraps of metal which Bill said would be ideal for our purpose. These treasures we piled up in Bill's backyard.

And then, overnight, Bill lost all interest in the project. Without a word of comment or explanation he abandoned it, and put me to work making wooden swords and shields that we were to use in some knightly tournaments. What I now marvel at is that at the age of eleven I should have sensed the fact that for the rest of my days I would be seeing an occasional Bill Smith, bustling along with confidence to build or achieve something or other, when a moment's thought should have shown him that what he was planning was beyond his capability. Often I have watched someone, perhaps in the Capitol in Washington, setting up a committee to do something which he almost certainly couldn't do, and later didn't do; and I have said, "There goes Bill Smith and his fire engine!"

One evening, I think in 1899, I witnessed the old Polynesian ceremony of walking on hot stones. Early that morning a pit, perhaps 30 feet square, had been dug and filled with logs of wood. This wood was then covered with lava blocks, each perhaps 2 feet square and a foot deep. The wood was ignited and, as it burned down to coals, the rocks fell in so as to form a rough pavement.

A Tahitian "witch doctor" took a ti plant and, pounding it on the ground, uttered some incantations. Then, with his bare feet, he walked about on the stones. His god was supposed to be protecting him, but soon I got a hunch that the porous rocks were such good insulators that, while the under surface looked red-hot, the upper surfaces were only warm. This hunch of mine was then proved correct when a couple of American soldiers, on their way to the Philippines, pulled off their shoes and socks, and without the help of the half-inch of tough leather-like material which the witch doctor had on the soles of his (always bare) feet, they went walking about over the stones! The Tahitian, of course, was disgusted when the soldiers showed that there had been nothing miraculous about what he had done.

One day in 1901, shortly after I had graduated from High School, my Father took me with him for what was to me a great adventure—luncheon at the Royal Hawaiian Hotel. After the meal, my Father asked, "Well, Walter, what are you going to do next?" And I answered, "Am I not going to be a physician? I have never thought of anything else." My father was much pleased, and immediately started making plans for me to go to college in San Francisco.

3

My Medical
School Days

In September, 1901, my father and I sailed for
San Francisco where I was matriculated in what was then
Cooper Medical College, but now is the medical department
of Stanford University. In those days there were few medical
schools in the country which required of their matriculants a
pre-medical course, so my father thought I might as well go
from high school directly into the professional college, and
this is what I did.

Actually, I doubt if the lack of a pre-medical course handi-
capped me much; I easily made up for it later by reading many
serious books. In my years in a research laboratory, whenever
I wanted some special information in regard to some phase of
modern chemistry, physics, biology, statistics, or genetics, I
read rapidly on the subject, and soon had learned what I
needed to know. An educator might be interested in the fact
that the pre-medical studies which are hard and dull for many
students, were fun for me *when I needed them,* because I
then so greatly wanted the information I sought.

Many a student starting out in medicine asks me if, in order to succeed in life, he should graduate from a big-name school, and I say, "No." I have never felt any handicap because I got my basic training in a small "proprietary" school. If a man studies hard in college, and particularly if he does an outstanding job in his years as intern, resident, and graduate student, no one will care a hoot where he started, and certainly no patient will ever bother to examine his diploma.

When I went to college I knew that I was preparing myself for my lifework, and hence I buckled down and studied hard. Sometimes I said to myself, "Some day you may be in a lonely shack somewhere in the country, fighting to save the life of a young woman in a hard labor; or the life of a cowboy kicked in the head by a horse, and if then there is no other physician within miles who can come to help you, your patient's life will depend on your knowledge and skill."

Actually, during my three years in a mining-camp, a number of experiences like that *did* come to me. I can remember the night in a lonely house on a mountainside when I confined a huge woman who must have weighed over 300 pounds. As soon as the child was born, the mother started to bleed as if a knife had been driven into a large artery. I never saw such bleeding. If I hadn't known enough to double her womb over forward and hold it closed for 10 minutes, she would soon have died.

Throughout all of my four years at college, I would go down town to the YMCA gymnasium three nights a week where I would spend half an hour on the mats with the wrestlers, then another half-hour teaching a squad either simple tumbling or the simpler stunts on the horizontal bar. After this, I would race rapidly back and forth a few times in the swimming-pool, and would then go home to study until about 10:30. Putting on light tennis shoes, I would then run two miles or more along the quiet streets to Golden Gate Park and back. In this way I kept my "wind" in good condition for an occasional quarter-mile race. Each day was very full of lectures and studies.

On Saturday evenings, with the two chums with whom I lived, I often went to theater. We sat in the top gallery where the cost was usually either 10 or 25 cents. Because we could run up 6 or 7 flights of stairs and knew exactly where to go, we generally got to sit in the front row.

As I look back on my first year in San Francisco, I wonder that I, who was only 17 and away from home for the first time, never felt even a twinge of home-sickness. Fortunately, I have always been like that.

They say that little things tell much about a man, and hence perhaps I should tell here of something overly conscientious I did a couple of months after I started college. All my life I have realized that there is a bit of the idealistic old knight of La Mancha (Don Quixote) in me, and sometimes he has gotten me into much trouble. One cold night in 1901, I went to the Orpheum, and not being used to wearing a top-coat— I had never seen such a thing in Hawaii—I left my new one on the back of my seat. On getting to the street and meeting the cold air, I ran back for my coat—but it was gone.

Next day I bought another, but not feeling that I should penalize my father for my forgetfulness, I paid for that coat, saving 5 or 10 cents at a time, by walking 2 miles instead of taking a street car, or going without my lunch, or without a dessert. I kept an account of my savings until I had paid back what the coat had cost. I never told Dad what I had done. I am sure if I had, he would have said there was no need for such self-denial.

One of my first disillusionments came when, at the age of 19, I discovered that even young men who were preparing themselves for their professions could not be trusted to behave sensibly and to their own advantage. Today, of course, this observation would not surprise me in the least. When at the hospital, I started as a clinical clerk, I was so delighted with the new experience that I jumped into the work with enthusiasm, and each week studied as many patients as I could. But then came a committee of my classmates to say that the laziest men in the class had decided that a patient a week was all they were going to "work-up." If I were to go on preparing several cases a week, the professors would get ideas in their heads, and hence I was "to pipe down."

I just went ahead with my work. In 1905, when I became an intern, again, I ran into the "slow-down"; and again I marvelled that so few of my fellows cared to take advantage of the good courses of training our teachers were offering us. Later, after 1926, when I had been teaching graduate students for years, I was again saddened to find some men trying to avoid working up more than a few cases a day.

Because I studied so hard during my first six years of medical training, I had almost no social life, but I felt no need of any. I took Osler's advice and kept my affections pretty much in cold storage. Every other Sunday I would cross the Bay to Berkeley to call on the young lady, Harriet Smyth, who, in 1907 became my wife.

Even before my intern year, I had gotten sense enough to be dissatisfied with a number of my teachers because they were not observers or thinkers, but just "givers-out" of what they had read in books. I cannot remember that any one of them ever thought of learning medicine from patients as I already was doing with my little note book.

I remember asking my old professor why a man in our ward who evidently was suffering from locomotor ataxia lacked much of the textbook clinical picture of the disease. When I asked, "How does it come about that some people have such an atypical form of their illness?" my Chief put his hand kindly on my shoulder and, with a twinkle in his eye, said, "Alvarez: remember this: *the Good Lord just won't read Osler!*" In other words, he told me not to expect all my patients to present *all* of the disease picture that is described in the textbooks. I am now interested to see that, so early in my life, I saw what, centuries before, the great Leonardo da Vinci had seen, that experience "is more truthful than books"—it is "the instructor of instructors." I saw what I was learning from books might be

wrong, but what I was learning from listening to 100 patients
was sure to be right.

Osler used to say that the doctor who does not study books
is like a sailor who goes to sea without a chart, while the doctor
who studies only what is in the books is like a sailor who so
loves charts that he never puts out to sea! I have tried to be
like a sailor who, though well supplied with charts, spends his
life at sea, and there, for all his days, keeps studying the ocean
around him—in all its moods.

While a student "clinical clerk," I began to accumulate
interesting stories of patients. I remember a man who was so
extremely irritable that I remarked on it. He said, "Yes, doctor,
I am so damned irritable that sometimes when I wake in the
morning I slap my wife's face, and I say, 'There, that's for
nuthin'; now you just try and start somethin'.' " Ever since
then, whenever I give my wife a present which isn't for Christmas or a birthday, or an anniversary, or anything, I laugh and
say, "There, that's just for nuthin' "—and that is a little joke
between us.

4
Mining-Camp Doctor

IN 1907 MY father retired and offered me his practice in the large mining camp of Cananea, in Northern Mexico.

It was a small city, and did not even have a general hospital. Perhaps I should have "starved it out" in San Francisco where I was. But San Francisco was still in ruins, and all the medical school could give me was room and board and 25 dollars a month! In those days, men who loved science were expected to live on nothing.

In Cananea I came to know much about the lives of the very poor, and how generously they help each other in times of trouble. Often when I made a call and the man of the house found he hadn't a dollar in his pocket, he would turn to his best friend and say, "*Compadre*, you pay him," and the *compadre* would pay me. Many of these simple folk were so good and kind that I came to love them.

When I started my practice in Cananea, I was impressed with the way in which most of the Mexicans traced their illness to a day when they "washed their hands and face at the same time and caught a cold!" One of my patients with a smashed hand used to come in every day for a dressing. I

43

noticed that his other hand was getting dirtier and dirtier until a crust started to cake and peel off. After some six weeks, he asked if I thought it would be safe enough then to wash the dirty hand! I thought quickly and said, "Yes, but only if we put some protective medicine in the water." My "wisdom" about this pleased him very much.

I soon saw that if I was to practice among those people I must become acquainted with their medical folklore. Otherwise I would often make them think I was terribly ignorant of "the essentials of medicine."

My experiences in Mexico taught me to recognize hysteria at a glance. I came to know the disease well because it was so very common. Hardly a week passed but I was called to see a woman in what the people called an *ataque* (attack). A man would come running to say that a woman was dying. Hurrying along after him, I would be taken to a house where on a bed lay a woman, apparently unconscious. Every minute or so she would go into a sort of convulsion in which she would thrash about and pull toward her four men, each of whom was hanging on to an arm or leg.

There would be a lot of neighbors looking on, very interested in the show. Several would be in the room, and more would be watching through the windows and doors. Usually I found that the patient, born excitable and perhaps a bit psychotic to begin with, had had a row with someone. She had worked herself up into a rage, and had then gone into the spell.

The first patient of this type really had me worried. The crowd expected me quickly to quiet her, but how was I to do it? My books and teachers had not prepared me for this embarrassing situation. I knew that the local doctors either threw cold water on the woman or gave her an emetic. But I feared that if I used either of these methods she would later hate the sight of me, and that would not make for good public relations!

Because I knew that the people all thought the woman was having a *heart* attack, I decided that, in order to satisfy them, I had better listen to her heart. So getting out my stethoscope,

I applied it to her chest wall. When she kept thrashing about, I said (in Spanish), "How do you expect me to listen to your heart when you are making such an infernal racket?" With this, to my great relief, she quieted down. I kept on listening for several minutes while I motioned to the woman's mother to get rid of the onlookers and to close the windows and doors.

When I stopped listening to her heart, and the girl tried to start up again, I said firmly, "No, no more. You have had enough." And with this she quieted down. I then gave her a sedative, and left with everyone satisfied. After that, I never had any trouble with *ataques*. I stopped them all in a few minutes with the help of my stethoscope. I have never seen this remarkably useful technique described in any medical textbooks!

Many other hysterical girls and women whom I saw were suffering from trances ("playing possum"), or blindness, or marked bloating so that they looked 7-months pregnant, or they were numb and unable to feel anything in a limb, or they seemed paralyzed from the waist down. I saw so much of this sort of thing that years later, during my Mayo days, the minute a woman came into my office, perhaps whispering or limping in a peculiar way, or shuffling her feet, or walking with her body bent far forward and twisted so that she was looking upward, I knew instantly what was wrong.

One day I was treating a Mexican woman suffering from "paralysis" of a lower limb. She said that when her house was struck by lightning, a "ball of fire" came into the room and, running from her foot up to her abdomen, paralyzed the limb. I took a small electric battery and told her that I would drive the electricity out of her leg by reversing its direction. I started at her groin and stroked the limb with the electrode, moving it down to her foot. With this, she got up and walked, and was well.

During those years in which I was constantly studying hysterical women, I learned that if I was to talk one out of her spell of paralysis I must not have the least doubt as to the nature of her illness. Then if I was to get her to *stay well* for a while, I must either sell her the idea that it would be more fun to be well, or I must give her the idea that she had already punished someone—or herself—long enough.

In the Mexico of 1907 a woman would never think of taking a bath for 40 days after a child was born to her. This period of time was called the *dieta,* or period of diet and regimen. Accordingly, when some 10 days after my wife's first confinement she had a shampoo, and went out on the front porch of our house to dry her hair, a crowd gathered to watch her drop dead! To their great disappointment nothing happened, and they finally dispersed.

In 1908 I was foolish enough to buy an automobile. It was so poorly made that I just could not make it run on hilly roads. It had no top and no windshield and—worst of all—when we were out on the hills the brakes might not work! I bought the car in Douglas, on the American side of the Line and, *without even a 10-minute lesson in driving,* I started to take it along the desert tracks to Cananea, some 100 miles away. My wife and I—with our five-month-old daughter—hadn't gone 20 miles when the engine quit and left us stranded. Fortunately, a friendly railroad repair crew took pity on us and took us into town. In those days there were no filling stations and no garages. I bought gasoline in 5-gallon tins from a hay and feed store! I had to get the company manager's chauffeur to work for me in his spare time when the engine had to be overhauled. At the end of six months I was glad to give the car away.

One day I was called to a mountain shack where I had a hard struggle to save the life of a girl of 19, who was in labor with her first child and was going from one convulsion into another. She was in that dreaded state called eclampsia. There was no hospital available, and the nearest physician was miles away. I told the young husband to go into town to get help for me, but all he did was to go on a drunk. The girl's mother, like many Indian women when faced by a great emergency, became paralyzed. She sat down on the floor, threw her apron over her head, and went into a sort of trance. The nearest neighbors were some distance away and I did not dare leave the girl alone while I went in search of a couple of women who could help me by holding the girl's thighs. There wasn't even a bed in the shack, only a canvas cot with the bolt lost from one end. Imagine a husband so shiftless that he would not take the trouble to find a bolt or a stick of wood for one end of a canvas cot! I gave the woman enough anesthetic to quiet her convulsions. Then, with the help of forceps, I brought into the world a live baby. The mother also lived, and was none the worse for her experience.

I used to take care of the beautiful blonde wife of a tough old rancher. How she happened to marry such an unpleasant fellow I never could understand.

One night I was summoned to the ranch to confine the woman with their sixth child. Because the first five had all been girls, the man was determined to have a son. As the night wore on and the child was slow in coming, I sat talking with him. He was drinking tequila, which is strong stuff, and like many unpleasant men the more he drank the more nasty and belligerent he got. About midnight he staggered into his room and returned with a big .45 revolver. Placing it on the table beside him, he said to me, "Damn you, doctor, if you bring me another girl, I will put a bullet right there between your two eyes!"

In spite of his threat, I just went on chatting with him, as if I hadn't heard him. Gradually I moved my chair over beside his, so that if he reached for the gun I could hit him with everything I had. Then, noticing that he was getting sleepy, I got a better idea, and kept encouraging him to go on drinking toasts to his new son, and to the mother of his son—until he passed out. Then a couple of the servants and I carried him to his room and put him to bed. Later, the child was born—as I remember, a boy—and I went home without the promised bullet-hole between my eyes!

Incidentally this man was much disliked by his fellow

ranchers because he was so "nearsighted" that he could not always distinguish between his neighbors' calves and his own and, as a result, he was often putting his brand on someone else's calf! Eventually, one of his friends became so annoyed over these frequent unfortunate mistakes that he waited for him behind a tree by the side of the road, and blew a big hole through him with a blast from a shotgun.

Much happier was my memorable experience one glorious moonlight night as, in a humble one-room house of a miner, I waited until four in the morning to help bring into this world a pair of twins. What delighted me so much that I have never forgotten the experience was the song of the mockingbird in a tree beside the door. I have always loved the song of the mockingbird, but this one was a virtuoso who kept imitating the notes of all the local birds. Then, for a while, the bird would talk to himself and chuckle a bit, as he thought over some important events in his life.

The most interesting patient I saw during my days in Mexico was a tall, handsome man of 55—sad-looking, haggard, and prematurely aged. He complained of what he called heart attacks which, night after night, threw him into a panic and deprived him of sleep and rest. Because I could not find anything wrong with his heart, I told him to call me the next time he went into a spell. Accordingly, the next night he called me at 2 A.M. and I went to his home. There I was met at the gate by a big, well-armed watchman who, after tying up two savage dogs, let me into the house. I found my patient in bed surrounded by guns. In a scabbard within easy reach of his right hand was a sawed-off shotgun. To his left was a rifle, and on one of his pillows lay a big revolver. So far as I could see, all that was wrong with him was that he was in a nervous chill due to fright. I asked him what he was afraid of, but he would not tell me; so I gave him a sedative and left.

A few days later, when an old prospector came in to see me, I asked him if he knew what was worrying my patient. He said, "Sure I know. He has plenty to worry about. This is the story they tell around here: Years ago two cowboys discovered a big vein of rich copper ore back up there in the canyon. They promptly registered their claim in the local mining office. But soon there appeared some armed men who drove them off. The first court appealed to by the cowboys gave them back their property, but much litigation followed, and finally the judge of the Supreme Court of the State ruled in favor of the claim-jumpers. That judge is now your patient."

With their funds exhausted, the cowboys gave up the fight. But before leaving town they sent word to the judge that some night they would surely return, and then he would find himself looking down the barrels of their guns. They would then take him out into the hills, where, after the custom of the old Apaches, they would broil his feet over a slow fire. Obviously, the lawyer, although always well guarded, had gone to pieces under the strain of never knowing what day the cowboys might show up and get him. No wonder he spent his nights going from one paroxysm of fear into another!

Probably the last thing a storyteller would think of for a plot would be the case of a man who eloped with his mother-in-law! And yet, once, this actually happened. One day my father was consulted by a distraught Mexican woman who said she feared her husband had been kidnapped. When my father found that the man was only a clerk on a small salary, he reassured the woman, pointing out to her that kidnappers never bother with clerks.

My father asked the woman if, on the day of his disappearance, the man had gone to work as usual, and she said, "No." That morning he had done a most unusual thing. He had taken a bath, dressed in his Sunday best, and had put some of her perfume on him! My father asked if at that time anything else curious had happened, and the woman said, "Yes, my widowed mother who lives with us also disappeared." A few days later the two honeymooners returned, crestfallen and shamefaced. They had eloped, but after running out of money they had had to come back home!

5

I Get My Special Training as an Internist

ONE OF THE happiest days of my life came in the winter of 1909 when I received a letter from my former teacher, Dr. Emile Schmoll, asking me to return to San Francisco to work with him.

Because the next three years were probably the most formative in my life; because they fitted me for my career as a consultant in internal medicine; and because Dr. Schmoll rescued me from my intolerable situation in Mexico, I will stop here for a moment to tell how my "miraculous escape" came about.

In 1906, as an intern in the big San Francisco City Hospital, I happened to befriend and help two people. One was a kindly, gray-haired old Irishman named Foley, who at the time was suffering great pain in one of his feet. Because I had "taken a shine" to the old fellow, I asked Dr. Schmoll to see him, and see if he could give him some relief. Fortunately, Schmoll quickly recognized gout; he gave some colchicine, and in a few days, Foley was up and showing me how to dance an Irish jig.

Then he said, "Look, for years I was coachman to Mr. N. (one of San Francisco's millionaires) and he has the same pain

I have. So, quick, give me a pass, and I will go out and take him to see Dr. Schmoll." Foley was right; Mr. N. *did* have the gout, and soon, he too was relieved of his pain. As a result, in the next few months most of the gouty old feet in the Pacific Union (millionaires') Club were hobbling their way into the office of a doctor who, until then, had been unable to get a practice. In the next five years the wealthy and prominent patients that Mr. N. and his friends referred to Dr. Schmoll built up for him such a fine clientele that he began to need an assistant, and then he thought of me who, he was kind enough to say, had been his favorite intern.

But one of Schmoll's several peculiarities was that he would practically never write a letter, and hence, in 1909, someone had to put him in touch with me. This someone was a little roly-poly redheaded merry Irish girl—Georgia Bustin, a nurse in my ward who, when she developed a bad heart lesion, was pretty discouraged. I got Dr. Schmoll to help her, and for the next ten years he kept her alive and well enough to work. It was she who, in October, 1909, told my old Chief that she had heard that I wanted to get back to San Francisco, and it was she who then arranged for my return. How much more difficult my path through life would have been if I hadn't had the good fortune to help these two very friendly immigrants from the Emerald Isle!

I often mused, however, over the fact that if, in the years from 1904 to 1909, I had not used my spare time to become an expert in laboratory and X-ray work, Dr. Schmoll would not have sent for me because I would not have been able to do the work he wanted done. Men often say, "That fellow had good luck." True, he did; but still he would never have been given the fine job if he hadn't prepared himself by hard study to do the work.

Soon after going to work in January, 1910, I was taking histories, examining patients, and helping my Chief in the Clinic in which he worked in the mornings. I spent all my spare time in the medical library.

I quickly learned to perform the then new Wassermann test for syphilis, and soon the money I earned for doing this work for several physicians was adding much to my income, and making life more comfortable for me, my wife and our little daughter.

In two years, my Chief and I became so busy we had to move to larger quarters, and I became his partner. It wasn't long before Dr. Schmoll and I had one of the best consultant practices in California. Although it is not always easy for a young doctor to work with an older man, especially with an eccentric and excitable person such as my brilliant Chief, it is a wise thing to do. It will save him from wasting much time during those long lean years which can be so trying and perhaps demoralizing if he starts alone in a big city.

Dr. Schmoll was a bachelor about 40, a tall, stout man, a Swiss Jew who walked in a peculiar ungainly way, holding his head to one side. In his early days he was usually good-humored, full of fun, an interesting talker, well-read in many fields, a *bon vivant* and a *gourmet*, with a capacity for making interesting friends.

Because my Chief would not write letters, I helped make our big consultant practice possible by writing all of the reports to the physicians who had sent us patients. Then I had to go even further; I started writing Dr. Schmoll's love letters!

I remember well the first one I wrote. A gushing divorcée of 40 or so—a patient of ours—who evidently thought it might be a good idea to pick up a wealthy bachelor, wrote my Chief a "come on" letter. Dr. S. glanced at it, and gave it to me saying, "You answer it."

"But what sort of a letter should I write?"

"Oh, just write her a cheerful letter!"

So, imitating my Chief's handwriting, I wrote her a mildly affectionate letter.

Back came a perfumed missive saying, "Oh, Dr. Schmoll, you don't know how happy you have made me. To think that you, a great big man, should have stopped in your terribly busy day to write such a sweet sweet letter to poor little me has filled my heart with joy (etc., etc.)"

I have often smiled as I thought of that correspondence—wondering just how angry the lady would have been if she had ever learned that I had written the letters that had warmed her heart. She came to the office a few times to see what she could do in the way of ensnaring my Chief, but he was wary, and saw to it that he was always so busy that I had to take care of her. With this, she gave up and quit coming.

Another handsome woman did much better with a simple approach; she just remarked to my Chief, "Five hundred dollars a month would keep me very comfortably!"

My three years with Dr. Schmoll was a time of great mental growth. I worked hard to add much to my knowledge of laboratory diagnosis; I kept reading and rereading Wood's big textbook on the subject until it fell to pieces in my hands. I had to work hard also to keep up with the big advances then being made in X-ray work. I had to make films of the teeth, which, in the beginning, without specialized apparatus, was a very difficult job. In those days I had even to cut and wrap the little dental films, because no company was as yet selling them.

From my Chief I learned a great deal about the then-new science of dietetics, and soon I was calculating the caloric and other values of diets. Dr. Schmoll was one of the first men in the United States to reduce people's weight with a scientifically designed low-calorie diet. The idea was so novel that one day a not overly-bright society woman made the mistake of thinking that the diet was like a bottle of medicine, to be added to her regular diet! When, after a week, she came in weighing several pounds *more* than before, Dr. Schmoll roared, "You *must have eaten* more than the food I prescribed"; and the woman said, "Of course, I have also eaten my regular meals!" This story so amused the woman's relatives and friends that it quickly spread all over the country.

Dr. Schmoll was the most brilliant "snap diagnostician" I

have ever known. I remember the day a man came in and Schmoll, noting a glass eye, asked, "Was that eye removed for a little black tumor?"

"Yes," said the man.

"Now you have pains all over?"

"Yes."

Turning to me, Schmoll whispered, "Black cancer all over him."

And he was right. The man was soon dead.

One day a boy came in with his mother, and Dr. Schmoll remarked to her, "You nearly died in labor with that boy."

"Why, yes," said the woman, "but how could you possibly know that?"

Turning to me he said, "Look at that unusually deep, old forceps scar over his left eye."

One day Dr. Schmoll said to a patient, "You have polyps (small, soft nodules) in your nose, and chronic asthma; and for years you have been dropping a blackish silver-containing drug into your nose."

The man, astonished, said, "Goodness gracious, you're right!"

Schmoll said to me, "Look at the wide bridge to his nose, listen to his nasal voice, look at his bluish skin (filled with silver from the drug); note his barrel-shaped chest, his 'spade-shaped' finger-ends, and his contracted neck muscles in front —all signs of an old asthma."

One day a woman came in and instantly my Chief said, "Old exophthalmic goiter, and still a fibrillating heart." (A fibrillating heart is one in which, in the auricles—the two small chambers at the top of the heart—the muscle is not contracting as a unit, but each fiber is quivering separately.) Such fibrillating is common in cases of long-lasting toxic goiter. When I was puzzled, Dr. Schmoll said, "Look at that scar of a goiter operation peeping out from under her string of pearls, look at those shiny, rather frightened eyes, also, note her dark reddish skin, that tremor of her hands, and that irregularly irregular pulse in the side of her neck." It was irregularly irregular because the fibrillating auricles at the top of her heart were not supplying the ventricles (big pumping cavities) with the regular beat.

Dr. Schmoll was always doing that sort of thing. When walking out to luncheon with me, or while seated in the restaurant, he would say, "Look to your left and see the woman with myxedema (marked by a puffy, dull-looking face due to a loss of function in the thyroid gland). Or he might say, "Look at that man, he once had a Bell's palsy (paralysis of half of his face); or "Look at that pale-skinned man who has either pernicious anemia or a severe form of kidney disease."

After a while I began to try my hand at this sort of diagnosis, and when occasionally, I "hit the bull's-eye," I derived great pleasure from the practice of the art.

One day I found in my office a friendly old fellow whose complaint was that he was "too tired even to go fishing." He had been thoroughly examined by three able physicians who, when they could not make a diagnosis, asked me to see him. Following in the footsteps of my Chief, I just said to the man, "On this hot July day, what are you doing with those big winter galoshes on your feet?" And he said, "Oh, doctor, I am so cold." Because he did not have the pudgy look of most persons with a complete loss of function of the thyroid gland, my able friends had failed to think of myxedema. Because they hadn't noticed his galoshes or thought of what his wearing them should mean, they had failed to make a ridiculously easy diagnosis. When I gave the old fellow big doses of thyroid substance, he quickly perked up, warmed up, and felt fine.

A snap diagnosis that surprised even me was one I made one day when called in consultation to see a woman of 35 with some curious distresses for which a thorough examination had shown no cause. The impression I gained from my first glance at her was so strong that I took a big chance and said to her physicians, "She has a tumor of the pituitary (the very important growth-stimulating gland at the base of the brain)."

Because my friends were incredulous, I said. "Let's go to the X-ray room and get a lateral film of the head." When the film was lifted out of the clearing solution, there, sure enough, at the base of her skull was a *sella turcica* (the bony "Turkish saddle") much distended by a pituitary tumor.

The doctors then all said at once, "But, Al, how did you do it?" What had struck me forcibly was that this small woman had the big forearms of an athletic man—something I had never noticed before. Usually, a pituitary tumor produces a big nose, a big lower jaw, big hands and feet, and perhaps a raucous voice, but in the case of this woman, the excess of growth hormome coming from the gland had made only one big change in her, and this was in her forearms.

The fanciest bit of snap diagnosing I ever attempted was done just as a stunt to show some graduate students what can sometimes be accomplished. The X-ray man chose a chest film full of abnormalities. I was able to guess that the roentgenogram was that of a woman about 50, rather tall and thin, frail, and a Catholic. She had had several children. In her youth she had some tuberculosis, and possibly a mild polio. She once had a pneumonia with empyema. She could have been thrown once from her horse. She probably had a moderately high blood pressure with some arteriosclerosis, and she had suffered at times from arthritis. She used sometimes to go out with a brother or husband to shoot pheasants.

How could I guess so much—and so much that happened to be correct? I explained. The thin bones and the size of the breasts showed that the film was that of a woman. The fact that the breasts were hanging down suggested that she had had several children. The marked calcification (filling with lime) of the rib cartilages in front suggested she was over 45 and frail. (Such frailness with calcification has been shown in statistical studies.) The length of the thorax showed she was tall and thin, and the narrow "costal angle" made by the ribs and cartilages as they spread out from the lower end of her breastbone, suggested again that she was often sickly (also shown statistically). The medal on a chain around her neck indicated Catholicism. Calcified scars in the lungs and on the side of the neck showed that she had had tuberculosis. One arm a little smaller than the other suggested an old polio. A scar on one rib, marking where a tube had gone in for the drainage of pus, showed she probably had had a pneumonia with subsequent empyema. A healed fracture of the collarbone suggested a fall from a horse. The somewhat enlarged left ventricle (large pumping chamber) of the heart suggested a high blood pressure, and a calcification of the arch of the aorta—the big artery which comes out of the heart—suggested a tendency to hardening of her arteries. A marked roughening of several of the vertebrae where the ribs joined the spine, showed a tendency to arthritis, and three birdshot in the muscles of one shoulder suggested a hunting accident.

During my years with Dr. Schmoll, I kept constantly learning medicine—some of it from books and journals, but much from my daily study of symptoms as they appeared in people. At the end of each year I would sum up in my diary the new skills I had acquired, and usually then I would marvel at all the facts that a young physician must store away in his mind if he is to be a good diagnostician, a good physician, a good teacher, and a good consultant.

In 1912 a favorite "fashionable diagnosis" was "intestinal autointoxication." When a nervous woman felt tired and toxic and below par, and suffered from headaches, she was likely to be told that she was absorbing poisons from foul material in her large bowel. This explanation sounded so reasonable that most persons were well satisfied with it. But I always doubted if it was correct, and one day I knew it was *not* correct.

That day, after luncheon, my Chief came in looking the picture of dejection and misery. He said that because of a blinding headache he was going home and to bed, and I was to take care of the patients as best I could. A few minutes later I heard him out in the hall whistling merrily as he walked back to the office. He came into my room and said, "After I left you a few minutes ago, it occurred to me that because of an emergency call early this morning I forgot to do what I always do. So I went and attended to the matter; and now, here is the astonishing observation. *Before I left the men's room* my headache was gone, together with my feeling of depression and my indigestion. I was trained as a biologic chemist and I am sure there is no poison that could have been removed from my blood that quickly. Evidently what was wrong was a depressing effect on my brain produced by the distention of nerves in the lower end of my bowel."

I agreed with my Chief, and told him that I myself had had many similar experiences in which I had obtained immediate relief from abdominal distress and headache, just as he had.

This conversation started me on a series of studies in which I soon showed that some highly sensitive persons could develop the symptoms of "autointoxication" when the end of their bowel was packed *with cotton!* This proved that the distress in the head could be due purely to pressure on the nerves in the rectum—if the person was *sensitive enough.* No such distress is produced quickly by constipation in the case of the average, somewhat insensitive person.

I showed next that in the case of constipation, in certain persons, symptoms such as hiccup, belching, gurgles running up the gullet, a feeling of pressure up against the midriff, a little nausea, flatulence, a feeling of abdominal distress, and even abdominal pain, can all be due to ripples starting in the distended and hence stimulated segment of bowel, and running back up the digestive tract to the throat. Whenever I have been constipated, and these symptoms have distressed me, they have stopped the instant the constipation was overcome. Eventually, I gathered and wrote up so much evidence against the idea of "autointoxication" that most doctors stopped making this diagnosis.

All my life I have had a tendency, if time was available, to go on questioning a patient about his or her symptoms long after I was satisfied as to the diagnosis. Why? Because I wanted to learn all I could about the natural and biological history of the disease. I wanted to learn from the patient what were the triggers that brought on his attacks, or if he had learned any secret of avoiding his spells of acute illness, or of shortening them when they came, and each day I kept recording the information I obtained. I always carried a little loose-leaf notebook in my pocket, and with this I obtained the information which went into many of my scientific papers. Also, with it I learned much of what I now know about medicine. With the help of my notes I learned from many hundreds of patients when it pays a person to part with teeth, tonsils, an appendix, or a womb—and when it does not pay.

I became so interested in what is now called *psychosomatic medicine* that on November 12, 1912, before the San Francisco County Medical Society, I gave my first paper on the subject. The doctors were so pleased with the idea that they gave me an ovation. Ever since that day much of my time has been spent studying the influence of a disturbed mind on the body.

A good example of the type of nervous illness that has fascinated me ever since is to be found in the case of a young woman of 35, who came to me with a fever of 101°, which she had been running for four years, ever since her marriage. Because of the abdominal pain that accompanied it, she had had three surgical explorations of her abdomen. A fourth operation convinced me that there was no disease in her abdomen. I found that her troubles were all due to her indecision about getting a divorce, and when her sisters talked her into leaving her husband, she became well.

Later, when she returned with her old symptoms, and I found they were due to indecision about what to do with an unsuitable beau, all I had to do was to make up her mind for her, and again she was well.

In those early years of my practice, I had learned that a confession of sin made to a physician can be just as effective in clearing the mind and body of distress as is a confession made to a priest. One day a nice-looking, well-dressed married

woman of 50 had become angry with my Chief when, after
finding no cause for her chronic abdominal pain, he had tried
to dismiss her and send her back to her home in one of the
big old Bret Harte mining towns of California. When she refused to go, he turned her over to me.

Soon, I was asking her why she looked so unhappy, and
after sizing me up for a minute, she said, "I think I can talk to
you." Then she confessed that, in order to put her gifted and
adored son through an eastern university, she had run a fancy
house of ill fame. When that job was done and over with, and
she had had time to think, she had become overwhelmed with
the conviction that she had become so sinful and foul that
if the people on the street knew what she had done they would
divide and let her pass.

Because of my many human and anthropologic interests, I
got to talking with her about her problems in running the
"House": how she had handled the graft, how much she had
had to pay the police captain, how she had handled the problem of the pimps, how and where she had obtained the girls,
how she had kept them healthy, how she had dealt with her
doctor, how she had handled alcoholics and gangsters when
they came into the place, and so forth. The next day we had
another interesting chat on the problems of running a "house"
in a mining camp, and then she picked up her things and
started to say good-by.

Puzzled, I said, "Wait a minute; we haven't yet talked about
your stomach-ache."

"Oh," said she, "that's all right; it's all gone and I really
feel quite well."

"But," I asked "why are you well?"

"Because you like me!"

And it was true. I liked the woman, and the fact that I felt
no dislike or disgust satisfied her that she was forgivable, she
was not a pariah; and no longer did she have to feel sick with
shame, loneliness, and unhappiness.

In my medical confessional the most remarkable story I ever

heard was that told me one day by a sad-looking woman of 45 who came to consult my Chief and me about her ill-health, her indigestion, her insomnia, and some pains here and there. After a thorough examination had failed to show anything physically wrong, I asked her why she was so unhappy. After crying a while, she said that many years before, a handsome lawyer had been trying for months to get her pretty but very selfish and ambitious younger sister to marry him. When the sister finally told the man she would never accept him because he wasn't rich enough to suit her, he became so angry that he said to my patient, "Let's you and me *show her*; let's us get married." Because my patient really liked the man, and very much wanted to be married, she snapped him up.

After the wedding they went to his lodge for their honeymoon. A few days later the younger sister, having decided that she really wanted the man, came to the cottage to take him away. He was delighted with her idea, but not knowing exactly what to do with his bride he decided that, for a while, the two women would sleep together with him in his big bed! Finally, after twelve years of this, when my patient had become a nervous wreck, her sister decided she had had enough and left.

When I asked my patient why she had put up with the situation for so long, she said she was too weak-willed ever to stand up against her domineering husband and her steely-hard sister. For the first few weeks she had wanted to hang on to her legal rights, and later, when she found she was pregnant, she felt she just had to stay on because she could not go out to face the world alone. When two more children came, she felt all the more that she would have to stay.

If that isn't a curious story, I do not know one when I hear it!

In 1912 my acquaintance with some mentally disturbed members of two distinguished California families started me on a life-long study of the inheritance of equivalents of psychosis. In one family there was great ability in some of the members, but there were spells of insanity in one sister, another sister was a stout woman with a retarded intelligence, another sister was a recluse who could not make up her mind about anything, and a brother had made a mess of his life.

In the other distinguished family that much interested me, the first person I saw was a woman of 30 who came to consult me about a mentally retarded daughter. When I noted that the woman herself was a bit psychotic, I asked her about her family. I found that she had a handsome and brilliant but asexual sister, and six big, fine-looking brothers, one of whom was a periodic drinker—a "lost week-ender." The father was a very able and much respected man, but his brother was a red-nosed, skid-row type of alcoholic.

Also at about this time I saw a quick-tempered man who looked to me like some epileptics I had seen. He complained of terrible headaches. I asked him if there was epilepsy in his family, and he told me that his brother was in the State Epileptic Colony. When I treated him as an epileptic, he got well! It was he who introduced me to the idea of carriers of epilepsy without seizures—an idea which in the last 15 years has been very helpful in my practice.

These interesting families started me watching out for, and keeping records of, the type of case in which the grandfather was perhaps in a mental hospital, his son was perhaps an alcoholic, and his grandson was just a good-for-nothing. I kept studying such families for years, and eventually wrote a book about them.*

While practicing with Dr. Schmoll I began to notice something which I had not heard about in college—that many "chronic" complainers do not have any localized disease that can either be cured by medicine or removed by surgery. Many a person—and often a frail-looking one—seems to have been born to be uncomfortable, with "poor materials built into his or her body." I early sensed that many of these persons are doomed to live out their lives in weakness and frailness and

* "Practical Leads to Puzzling Diagnoses: Neuroses that run through Families" (1958).

sickliness. Any cold or little infection can lay them low for weeks, and rarely can a physician make such a person over into a strong, robust and uncomplaining hard-worker. Many will have no stamina, and for all their days will complain bitterly about some scratch or little bruise or a pimple. Many will always have the "habit of illness." When inducted into the Army, most men of this type promptly "crack up" and have to be sent home. It isn't their fault; it is the fault of an inherited frail body or troubled mind. These are the people who, as Osler once said, you will have to keep helping as long as they live.

I remember well a tall, thin, always tired and sickly young man of this type. My deep interest in his problem started me on a lifetime of study. His mother and sister were tall, thin, and frail, just like him. For a while his sister was mentally disturbed—and later I found that many constitutionally frail persons have psychotic relatives. Recently, I saw this old friend and patient of mine. He is now in his sixties—a thin, gray-haired man—still frail and ailing. I take my hat off to him because he has always had the guts to keep earning his living. It is sad that he has never felt strong enough to take on the responsibilities of marriage.

In my efforts to get a better understanding of this type of illness, I did much reading in physical anthropology and on the relation between physical build and mental capacity. I read everything I could find on fatigue. Eventually I came to the conclusion that constitutional inadequacy is more likely to be due to a peculiar brain than to a peculiar body. Some of these patients are highly intelligent and able, and some are well built, but they cannot stand up to much strain. In 1942, after two years spent in organizing my thoughts on this problem, and polishing and re-polishing a paper on inadequacy, I published it in the *Journal* of the A.M.A.

I later had as a patient a handsome and interesting young woman with a syndrome somewhat like that of constitutional inadequacy, but a bit different, and apparently related to her mild manic-depressive psychosis. I called it *asthenia* (a lack of strength). The woman often had so much distress in her abdomen that she had been operated on six times—all to no avail. She could hardly go out to dinner with friends because, as was the case with Charles Darwin, the least break in her routine would send her to bed for several days—weak and nauseated. The most important fact about her illness seemed to me to be that from time to time she would become so depressed that she would have to retire for a while into a mental hospital. Now, in her sixties, she writes me that she is still frail, she is still occasionally having her abdomen explored surgically, and she is still occasionally taking refuge in a mental hospital!

In 1959, after a lifetime of reading about Darwin and his forebears and children, I wrote an article showing that he had almost exactly the type of asthenia which I had studied in the case of this young woman. Whenever he had supper with a few old friends, he would lie awake all night, and would vomit and shiver all the next day. Curiously, if he ate with his family, he had no trouble. To me, the all-important point in Darwin's family history is that two of his uncles, a brother, a cousin, and four of his own sons were depressed. Charles Darwin himself, for a year and a half, was so badly depressed that he could not work, and could hardly read.

I am ashamed to say that, in my own case, I have been a poor diagnostician. I had an allergy for years. I suspected it was a food allergy but I did not systematically search for its identity until I was close to 50. It caused me so much suffering that it is a wonder I was able to do my work. The "offender" turned out to be chicken. The reason why I was so slow to recognize my allergy to chicken was that when I ate this food in the quiet of my home it gave me little trouble besides some mild abdominal pain, flatulence, and nightmares. But when I ate it at a convention, where I was tired or tense from speaking, I got a diarrhea, sometimes severe, and often I had to walk the floor for half the night with severe abdominal pain. Because of this I blamed all my troubles on fatigue and nervous tension. Yet when I quit eating chicken I became a strong healthy man.

By 1910 I was already reading many books and articles on digestive diseases and, particularly, digestive physiology and digestive neuroses. I imagine that one reason I went on into the study of gastroenterology was that Dr. Schmoll and I had many patients with digestive troubles, and I had plenty of indigestion myself.

During my years with Dr. Schmoll I came to see ever more clearly that my interests were centering in the *diagnosis of chronic abdominal diseases*. I never was much interested in patients with *acute* illnesses, and when I was at the Mayo Clinic I never had a hospital service.

Because by 1913 I sensed that some day I was going to be a teacher of gastroenterology I started reading widely on the history of the subject. I wanted to know how knowledge had developed in this field of science, and who were the great pioneers. Also, I felt a need to read every article I could find in several languages on the minute structure and function of the digestive organs and the nerves that supply them. I could not depend on the sketchy and often incorrect information to be found in textbooks.

Fortunately, I learned early that when I was devising an experiment I must see to it that the question I *thought* I was asking of Nature was actually the question I asked. The trouble is that Nature answers truthfully the question one asks—not the question one thinks one asks. To illustrate: one day I failed in a bit of research I had attempted. I had sent into a hospital a redheaded woman of 50. When her "special" arrived and proved to be redheaded, the head nurse was apologetic, and said that since "redheads commonly do not get along well together," she would immediately ask the registry to send someone else. I said, "Wait a bit; let's do a little research on this old folk-idea; there may be nothing to it." The next day the two redheads were so chummy that I said, "You see, folk-lore ideas are often wrong." But a couple of weeks later, as I was bending over the patient listening to her heart, I noticed that, for a quarter of an inch next to her scalp, her hair was gray! Evidently, then, when I had thought I was asking Nature if two redheads could get along well together, actually, what I had asked was, could a woman with dyed red hair get along with a natural redhead?

I soon realized that if I were ever to be the sort of physician and teacher I wanted to be, I would have to learn to read rapidly in several languages. I already could read Spanish and French easily. I could understand medical Italian well enough, if only because I had studied Latin for four years. What I lacked was German; and so in 1912 I began to study this language. Many and many an evening I read German articles and books, with a teacher by my side to help me over rough spots. In 1916 he said, "You can now read medical German faster than I can," and he left.

Also, I soon saw I would have to learn when not to waste my time reading articles by men who were either devoid of clinical wisdom, or stupidly verbose, or able to fool themselves into thinking they had done some research.

A busy scientist must learn to "skim" and to read by paragraphs. My old German teacher, who read word by word, could never understand how I could glance at half a page in a German book and say, "We won't read that because the man has nothing to say there that interests me." I fear that no one who reads slowly and with difficulty can ever hope to gain an encyclopedic knowledge of his branch of medicine. He just won't have the time. A busy physician has only a few minutes a day for keeping up-to-date, and hence he must use this time for reading the best articles and chapters of books. Furthermore, most of his information must be derived from good abstracts or summaries of articles. Every month I read many book reviews in order to find the volume I should be reading.

I soon realized how fortunate a physician is when he can

and will give his patients a clear and simple understanding of what he thinks their trouble is, or tells them what is hopeful about their condition, or what he plans or hopes to do in the way of treatment. Dr. Schmoll's words were so technical, his speech so thick and Germanic, and his patience so short, that few lay persons could learn much from talking to him. As a result, many of his patients, after leaving his office, would come around to my door and ask, "What did my examination show, and what did Dr. Schmoll think about me?" Then I would explain, in words of one syllable, and in doing this I made many friends who later went out of their way to help me start my own practice in San Francisco.

Unfortunately, quite a few physicians today *pride themselves* on their ability to use long technical words. They will always say "cerebro-vascular accident" for a "stroke," and "urticarial wheals" for "hives." They make me think of the time in 1667, when Professor Christian Thomiseus of Leipzig had the temerity to lecture in German—instead of Latin—and for this was expelled from his university!

Nicholas Culpepper (1616-1654) similarly offended the Royal College of Physicians of England when he translated— from the Latin—the London Pharmacopoeia (the official list of drugs), and described these drugs in the English language.

I agree with Dr. William Bennett Bean that many of us physicians who write in a ponderous way, using long and obscure words, are fooling ourselves into believing that we know a lot, when really we don't. This is particularly true of the psychoanalysts.

As "Boss" Kettering once reminded me, too often the explanation given by a teacher does not explain anything. One day in his youth Kettering was disturbed because his teacher seemed perfectly satisfied with the statement that we can see through glass "because it is transparent!" Young Kettering wanted to know what is peculiar about the arrangement of the atoms in glass that allows the waves of light to go through.

I always believed my Chief was wrong in thinking that by

translating a patient's complaint into Greek, he had thrown a great light on it! When a psychotic girl came in weighing only 78 pounds because for months she had refused to eat, my Chief was satisfied when he said she had *anorexia nervosa*. But, young as I was, I saw that he had merely said *in Greek* that she had a nervous lack of appetite. Because we doctors are so satisfied with the words *anorexia nervosa*, even today it is a rare physician who notices that many girls of this type are typical schizophrenics. But even the man who says the girl is "schizophrenic" has done little more than to express in Greek the recently popular, but probably meaningless, theory that the girl has a split personality!

I remember occasions when my Chief fooled himself in still another way. Once, a purblind and partially paralyzed young woman came in and we made the diagnosis of multiple sclerosis. Dr. Schmoll, like many other physicians, thought that having given a name to the disease, we could look in a book and see how to cure it. But, of course, we couldn't cure it. Even today, half a century later, no one can cure it.

It would be bad enough if we doctors just fooled our patients. What is sad is that so often we fool ourselves! As Osler used to say, it is bad for the doctor when he "can fool himself to his heart's content all the time." Early in my career I learned that even some able physicians can never do research of any value because, like many psychoanalysts today, they start their study with the conviction that they know what the answer is going to be.

My Chief used to give a woman a medicine and tell her to take it for a week, and then report. When she returned, he'd fix her with a menacing eye, and say, "You're much better, now don't you deny it!" Under these circumstances it was only a very courageous, or honest, or stubborn woman who would keep maintaining that her symptoms were unchanged. Obviously, any paper on a drug action that my Chief might write could not have much value. And yet, I am sure he had no idea that he was fooling himself. He was quite naive in the matter.

Ever since my years with Dr. Schmoll I have worked hard trying to learn to write well and clearly—in simple English, and in short sentences. I am sorry to say that after half a century of writing in all spare time, the job seems to be just as hard as it ever was. My only comfort is that that master of lovely prose —Robert Louis Stevenson—confessed shortly before he died that for him, writing was still as difficult as it had ever been. Ernest Hemingway also, even just before he died, kept re-writing and re-writing.

Early in my life I realized that some skill in public speaking could be a tremendous asset to me. In those early days, practically all doctors droned along, reading their papers without paying any attention to the audience. Hoping to learn how to do better than this, I read a book on public speaking, and learned that what is essential is that the speaker have a strong desire to pass on to his audience some information which he feels is interesting and important; also, he must *give it* with enthusiasm.

Then, one hot day in June, 1911, at a big medical meeting in Los Angeles, after hours of listening to doctors who had been *reading* apathetically, I saw a man come up onto the platform—a man who obviously was filled with enthusiasm about a discovery he had made—and who was highly desirous that all of us share his interest. He had no paper; he just talked and showed us some charts. As was to be expected, even those of us who had been drowsing, sat up and watched and listened. The man was the late Dr. Francis Pottenger, the great expert on TB, who later became a good friend of mine. I immediately said to myself, "I am going to learn to talk like that, even if the effort nearly kills me." Since then I have always *talked* from a few notes in my hand, and I think usually with some vigor and enthusiasm.

In my early years I suffered terribly from stage fright. While at a meeting waiting for my turn to speak, I would be ill, my heart pounding, my body shaking. I became cured of this when I started lecturing to medical students. I then said to myself, "You darned fool; surely you know immensely more about this subject than those lads do, so why should you feel at all self-conscious before them?" With this, I lost all of my uneasiness, and it never came back.

I learned early that when presenting facts, it is very helpful to present verbal pictures. As the Arabs say, "He is the best speaker who can turn his listeners' ears into eyes." To illustrate: many a physician, in giving a case report, will start out saying, "A man of 50, of normal weight, with a normal white count, a hemoglobin of 85 per cent, etc."—and his audience will drowse; but let him get up and say, "A vice-president of a big corporation got up clumsily out of his chair in the reception room and started to walk into my office with short, shuffling steps. He said he was 50, but he looked 70. He was so slowed-up, and there was so little animation in his face, that no one would have hired him to run a popcorn wagon. He talked thickly out of one side of his mouth. He had a little egg on his chin, and some gravy down the front of his coat! A few questions showed that he had had some 'little strokes.' "

A picture like that grabs the interest of one's listeners, and the mental picture of that patient tends to stay with them for years.

I am glad that in my early years in practice I learned to say often to patients and consultants, "I don't know what is wrong." This behavior was good for the development of my mind and character, and it made many friends for me. Osler taught that to say, "I don't know" is much better than to beat about the bush. Often an intelligent patient has said to me, "I like your courage and honesty in confessing your ignorance, and now I am going to stay with you until you say you know what is wrong. And then I'll believe you."

In my youthful days, when I had to deal with a millionaire, I was inclined to be awe-struck and ill-at-ease with him. But one night I was so well cured of this fear of the wealthy that I never suffered from it again. What happened was that, around midnight, my Chief asked me to make a call on one of the wealthiest of our California millionaires. I remember going up to the door of one of the biggest "palaces" that then lined Pacific Avenue. After I had rung for a while, the butler came over from the servants' house, took me up an imposing stairway, and then back through a long dark hallway to a great big, poorly-lit room.

There, all alone in a canopied bed, sat a little old man who I soon saw was "scared to death." He thought he was about to die with a heart attack, and he particularly dreaded dying all alone with no one to keep him company. As I remember, he had a wife and daughter, but they were in Europe. His son was playing polo somewhere. I wound up feeling so sorry for the lonely old fellow that I stayed for an hour trying to cheer him up. I hated to leave him alone again in that huge dark house.

Since then, I have come to know well a number of millionaires, nearly all of them odd characters. There was one multimillionaire patient of mine who, everyone agreed, was a very unpleasant man. He barked at most people and bawled out his employees until they came to "hate his guts." His wife and children could not stand him, and left for distant parts. But there was a nice side to the old man that I liked, and so for 40 years we remained good friends.

Another crotchety and violent-tempered old millionaire who came to me with a bad reputation had such a kindly soul hidden away inside of his rough exterior that, when I found it, we came to like each other. Originally, he came to me to say that when he "blew his top," as he often did, his face would get red, his blood pressure would shoot up to 220 mm., and he would feel as if he were going to have a stroke. He finally became so frightened over these spells that he told me he would do anything I might ask of him if it would only prolong his life. When I said he would have to quit his tantrums, he said, "Oh, doctor that is a big order." Finally, after thinking a while, he said, "All right, I'll do it."

Six weeks later his secretary dropped in to tell me that the old man had been very good, but on that day he had nearly exploded. A couple of dishonest men had come in to sell him a ship, and when he found where the "gyp" was his face got red and he started to rave. Then, suddenly, he stopped and roared, "Quick, get the hell out of here; *I can't afford to be mad at you."*

A hundred times since then, I have used this story with great effectiveness in helping choleric men to control themselves. They all agreed with me that they could no longer *"afford* to get mad."

I will never forget the strange-looking cousin of a famous millionaire who was an odd hypochondriac of the type who takes his temperature several times a day, lives on nuts and fruits, reads "physical culture" magazines, takes a half-dozen vitamins each day, and never marries because he feels he would not have time or energy enough to spend on a wife.

When my chief asked what was the trouble, the man said his anus was too tight. So Dr. Schmoll gave him a relaxant drug and told him to report in a week. When the fellow came back, Dr. Schmoll said in his usual way, "You are better!" But the man said no, his anus was still too tight. Dr. Schmoll asked, "How do you know it is too tight?" And the man said, "I stick my finger in, and it grips it firmly." Dr. Schmoll, whose patience and temper were always short, roared at him, "Get down on your knees there, and thank God it grips tightly; you'll be in an awful fix if it ever stops gripping!"

In 1912 I became very interested in the news then coming out of Europe to the effect that, with a good roentgenoscope (X-ray screening apparatus used in a darkroom) one could watch the stomach and bowel at work, and could see a peptic ulcer or a cancer. Realizing quickly how valuable such a technique could be, I talked my Chief into going to Vienna and there studying under the famous Dr. Holzknecht. Also, I got him to bring back a big European apparatus for roentgenoscopy.

For a while after it arrived—in late 1912—I was delighted with what I saw on the screen, but soon I was distressed because I could not understand so much of what I saw of the movements of the stomach and bowel. As weeks passed, I felt more and more the need for learning more about the laws underlying the mechanical workings of the digestive tract.

Late in 1912 I noticed a big change in my Chief. He was much more irascible and unreasonable than ever before. I am ashamed to say now that I did not then make the correct diagnosis of a beginning psychosis. This man, who was destined in a few years to go insane, started out in life with a tendency to eccentricities. As a result, when he began to slip into a psychosis, all that his friends like me could see was a greater tendency to eccentricity.

During the very trying last four months of my life with Dr. Schmoll, I kept asking him if there was some tragedy in his personal life that was distressing him terribly and making him so irritable. But he kept answering that all the trouble was with me—that I "was going crazy!" Eventually, the strain of trying to keep the peace with him became too great, and I had to leave. Four years later he had to be committed.

I have always regretted that I did not then have wisdom enough to realize what was happening to my Chief.

Time and again through the years my inability to see eye to eye with an honored Chief bothered me. It made me wonder if there was a defect in my character which kept me from becoming a devoted and loyal disciple. But now, as I look back over my life, I can see why I was not made to be a devout disciple. No matter how much I might like and respect my Chief, if I saw that on a certain point he was mistaken, my loyalty to him could not blind me to the fact.

On leaving Dr. Schmoll, I went to Boston where I wanted to learn from Dr. Walter B. Cannon, the great physiologist of Harvard, all I could about the movements of the stomach and bowel. He was the first man in America, in 1896, to use the newly-discovered X-rays for studies of the movements of the digestive tract.

After I had quizzed him for a while, he said, "You are obviously so anxious to secure information that I would suggest that you go into my laboratory there and try to get for yourself the answer to perhaps one of the many questions that are in your mind. I will show you how to study the intestines of an anesthetized animal with its abdomen open under a bath of warm saline solution, and with that, you can go ahead." What a wonderfully generous and trustful act that was, for Dr. Cannon to take into his department a young physician of whom he knew nothing, and who had come to him with little more recommendation than his obvious curiosity and desire to learn!

Instantly accepting Dr. Cannon's offer, I took off my coat and went to work. I started trying to learn something about flatulence—about the ways in which the several common gases are absorbed from the bowel. I began by injecting 10 cc. of oxygen, carbon dioxide or nitrogen into a short segment of a rabbit's small bowel. Then I would note with a stopwatch how quickly or how slowly the gas was absorbed.

In a few days I noted something that I had not started out to study. I saw that when I injected any type of gas into a segment of the *upper part* of the small bowel near the stomach, the muscle contracted immediately and powerfully, and it kept working hard and rapidly, trying to push the gas on down through the bowel. When I injected the same amount of gas into the *middle part* of the bowel, the segment was less sensitive and reacted less to the distention; and when I injected the gas into the *lower end* of the small bowel next to the colon (large bowel), the segment showed little response to the stimulus. It might even let the gas lie quiet for several minutes at a time.

I saw quickly that what I had found was a gradation in the irritability of the gut, running from the upper to the lower end. Soon I found another similarly-graded difference—one in the rate of rhythmic contraction of the muscle. In a rabbit this rate was about 17 per minute near the stomach, and 10 per minute low down near the colon. Later I was to find several more of these related gradients.

When I showed my notes to Dr. Cannon, he instantly agreed with me that I had run into something far more important than what I had started out to study (a fine example of serendipity), and he advised me to drop the study of flatulence and to learn as much as I could of the "gradients." He reminded me that in 1884 Dr. Walter Gaskell of England had observed such a gradient in the rhythmic activity of the muscle of the heart, and this had supplied a very helpful explanation for many facts about the progress of the heartbeat. As Dr. Cannon said, what had been of such great value in the field of heart physiology should prove of equal or greater value in understanding the downward progress of waves in the bowel.

I gladly followed Dr. Cannon's advice, and thus it came about that for much of my lifetime I devoted about half of each day to the study of intestinal gradients and the ways in which waves and ripples tend to travel up and down the stomach and the bowel.

A fortunate outcome of my trip to Boston was the gaining of a dear friend in the person of Doctor Cannon. One day he showed up at the laboratory with a grin that suggested to me that he had a story to tell. When I asked him what had happened, he said his little boy had just shown that he was going to be a scientist. "He evidently has the requisite desire for accuracy and a scientist's willingness to repeat his work." What had happened was that the evening before, when at his mother's knee, he had made a mistake in the Lord's prayer and had said, "Now damn it; I'll have to start all over again!"

Another morning when Dr. Cannon came in, I found him in a blue and discouraged mood—something unusual for him. When I asked what the trouble was, he said, "Today I feel like hiring someone to kick me around the block for trying to be a physiologist. Today, physiology is mainly biochemistry, and I am no chemist, my main training was in biology. I feel now as if I am being left so far behind in my field of science that I ought to quit trying to keep up."

In my youth and ignorance, I said, "But, Dr. Cannon, you surely have done so much for physiology that you could even afford to lie abed all day for a while and let the other men catch up with you."

"No," he said. "Some day, when you have many achievements to your credit, you will have learned that *what you have done* gives you but little joy or comfort. It is only *what you want to do* and hope and plan to do that interests you." And later I found that he was so right. Today, I have no interest in the hundreds of papers I have published; but I am anxious to get at the writing of several papers and books that I have planned, and for which I have gathered hundreds of facts. Only the work that lies ahead interests and delights me.

In 1931 I was happy when I was chosen to represent all of Dr. Cannon's students in speaking at the Celebration at Harvard—the Jubilee of the twenty-fifth anniversary of his professorate. My life was so enriched by his friendship; we kept corresponding until a few days before his death.

Men of science, when writing an autobiography, often tell about the great impetus in a certain direction that they got from one of their teachers. I wish I could do this, but I cannot. Even in the case of Dr. Cannon, I was not a disciple in the sense that I picked up one of his problems and carried on with it; I found my own problem.

Even Dr. Schmoll did not much direct my interests or change me. I developed my own interests, and when I left him I did not practice as he did.

I should add here that although in my San Francisco days my work was hard and strenuous and demanding, I had some play along the way. In 1911 and 1912 I started going with the Sierra Club into the magnificent high mountain country of California. Some 180 members would walk from 10 to 25 miles a day along the trails; during the four weeks we would climb a number of peaks, and at night, in our sleeping-bags we would rest on the ground.

As I have said before, I have always been happiest when up in the mountains. It seemed to me that I came nearest to "living" while I was on those Sierra Club "high trips." I had time then to do some thinking about life. In all, I had 13 such outings: one into Glacier Park, and one into the Canadian Rockies around Mt. Robson. On my last trips my sons, Luis and Robert, went with me.

6

A New Beginning
in San Francisco

WHEN I RETURNED from Boston, my savings were so nearly used up that I wondered how I could start practicing in a city as large as San Francisco—on a shoe string. Then came a friend, Dr. Carl L. Hoag, an able young surgeon. He said he also wanted to start a practice and he would be glad to share office expenses with me. So we rented space. He used the office between two and four; I used it from four to six. For two and a half years my practice did not grow at all, and each month I just made ends meet.

During this time one of my old teachers—a fine man—offered me a good partnership in a city some 40 miles from San Francisco. It would have put an end to my financial worries, but it would have meant the end of my researches, also my idea of a state-wide consultant practice, and so this time I took the "right turning at the fork in the trail" and decided to stick it out where I was.

But then, at the end of 1915, when I was becoming discouraged, suddenly more people began to crowd into my office than I could easily take care of. After that my problem was to save enough time out of each day for my research work and my reading and writing. In 1913 I had fitted up a little laboratory, and had gone ahead with my physiologic studies. Very fortunately, toward the end of 1914, The Hooper Foundation was created in San Francisco, and then Dr. George H. Whipple, the Director, gave me the laboratory facilities I so greatly wanted.

Most of the time I was studying the movements of the bowel in animals, but sometimes I made similar studies on men and women. Drs. Fletcher Taylor, B. K. Freelander, and I would study the progress of food and its residues through the human bowel by each day getting some medical students to swallow a capsule containing 50 tiny colored beads, and then counting these beads as they came away.

Once I went over to San Quentin prison with my friend, the great anatomist Dr. Herbert Evans, and there, within a few minutes after a young murderer was hanged, I obtained bits of muscle from several parts of his stomach and bowel. I took these to my laboratory, where for the next five days they kept contracting rhythmically. This seemed uncanny, in view of the fact that their owner was dead and buried.

On finding some elderly women with a big abdominal rupture which left little but skin covering the stomach, I obtained records of the waves running down the stomach and bowel. Also, I learned much about the activity of the human gut by studying two men each of whom had had a hole made—for feeding purposes—in the upper end of the small bowel. Through this hole I would put tiny balloons which went on down the bowel while connected through a rubber tube to a recording mechanism. I made electrocardiogram-like records of the movements of the human stomach, sometimes at an operation. Many of these studies were new to science and had never been made before.

Along the way, I did much statistical research to determine what is normal blood pressure. In 1917, while examining a number of draft evaders, I found many of them in poor health, with a high blood pressure. This so surprised me that I searched the literature and found that high blood pressure was not then supposed to occur in young men.

On learning that for many years the doctors in the Student Health Service of the University of California had been recording the blood pressures of the entering freshmen, I obtained permission to analyze 15,000 of these measurements. In order to learn something about the pressures in children, I taught some of the physical education teachers in the San Francisco schools to make the necessary measurements, and they soon supplied me with hundreds of data. From all these figures I learned that high blood pressure commonly begins in children and young adults. In the years that followed, I published six papers containing what, so far as I could ever learn, were the first reliable standards of blood pressure, based on records of persons chosen pretty much at random, and not of persons chosen because their pressures had been found to lie within limits previously assumed to be normal by life insurance medical examiners.

As I tried to analyze my mass of records of blood pressures, I soon saw that I needed some knowledge of statistical practices. Accordingly, I bought the four best books then available on the subject, and absorbed their contents. I also went to Baltimore to talk over my problems with Dr. Raymond Pearl, the great medical statistician. He was delighted to find that "at last a clinician was getting interested in statistical methods." Soon we were good friends.

Occasionally, during the years that followed, I tried to work out ways of measuring blood pressures in rats and other small laboratory animals. My hope was that some day, with them, I might study the heredity of hypertension; but I never found time in which to tackle this project, nor could I ever talk any young man into helping me with it.

In my office each afternoon, as was my custom, I kept learning much medicine from interesting patients; and I continued to make some statistical studies with the help of my little notebook, which was always with me.

I will never forget the lesson taught me by the first patient who, in 1913, came into my office. She was a woman of 40 with a "misery" in her abdomen which, after some study, I decided was due partly to her overly sensitive nervous system and partly to her frequent distresses, trying to live with a difficult husband. When I found she had no "organic disease," I told her that I doubted if any treatment would ever entirely stave off her discomforts. Later, she returned to tell me *for my own good* that a surgeon had instantly sensed that her distress was due to a "chronic appendix." He had removed it, and she was well. Although I could not believe she could be "cured" that easily, I thanked her for contributing to my education.

After a while she came back to say that, when her "misery" had returned, she had consulted another surgeon who had surmised that the fault was all in her gallbladder. He had operated on it, and she was well. Again, I thanked her for teaching me something, and again she left in a friendly mood. In three months she returned to say that when her "cure" hadn't lasted, she had consulted a urologist who had found a movable right kidney, and had sewed it up in place (an operation now largely discarded). When his huge bill came, her husband "blew his top," and with this her old distress came back—worse than it had ever been.

This time the lady said she had learned her lesson. She admitted that her husband's tantrums had had most to do with producing the flare-ups in her abdominal discomfort, and she thanked me for having been the one man who had never tried to make money out of her. For years after that she was a good and devoted patient. Strangely enough, the other day, after 48 years, I heard from her again, and she said she was still having her old abdominal discomfort!

It was fortunate for me that, so early in my medical career, I learned something which I am sorry to say, is not always

remembered today; this is that *abdominal pain* is often produced by some disturbance (emotional or physical) *up in the
brain*. When I was an intern I learned to recognize the very
painful "gastric crises" of late nervous syphilis, but it was
many years before I came to see how commonly somewhat
similar crises, often with retching, are due to migraine, epilepsy, psychoses, or hysteria. After 1955 I wrote several papers
on this type of pain.

Many a time when my students just could not believe that
a pain in a patient's abdomen could be due to something
wrong in his brain, I used to tell them of the fine old doctor
I saw once with pain in the pit of his stomach, so severe that
the most probable diagnosis was a cancer of the pancreas.
Then he died, and at autopsy his abdominal organs were
found to be perfectly normal. He had died of a tumor in his
brain.

A young woman who taught me much about abdominal
pain coming from the brain was a lovely person of poor nervous heredity who, until she was 30, was an efficient office manager. Then a man who made his living by cheating women
"borrowed" all of her savings, ostensibly to go and get a
divorce and come back to marry her. He took her money, and
she never saw him again. After this terrible shock and disgrace,
she never could work. She developed a constant and very distressing pain in her right side—a pain which was not relieved
by either an appendectomy or later the cutting of all the
sensory nerves which leave the abdominal cavity. Eventually,
she went into a depression and committed suicide. Her abdominal pain evidently had come out of her brain.

How interesting that Plato warned physicians not to try
to cure the body without at the same time helping the soul.
And the great Michel de Montaigne told of a man who, a
few days after having given a dinner at his home, "bragged
in jest—for there was no such thing—that he had made them
eat of a baked cat; at which, a young gentlewoman, who had
been at the feast, took such a horror, that falling into a violent

vomiting and a fever, there was no possible means to save her."

Another one of the patients who came into my office when I first opened my doors taught me a very good lesson which helps me still today—49 years later. His story demonstrates how every physician ought constantly to be learning that some of the accepted medical practices of his day are not good, and should be either given up or used only in occasional cases. This patient was a little tailor, suffering from a duodenal ulcer. His symptoms were so mild that I shouldn't have sent him into a hospital, but in 1913 I did what I had been taught to do with every ulcer patient, and that was to hospitalize him and keep him in bed for a month on a milk-and-egg-yolk diet. When I dismissed him, I assumed, as was then the custom, that I had cured him!

When some months passed and the man paid no attention to my bill, I looked in on him and learned that, on his return home, disaster had hit him so hard that his ulcer had come back—much worse than it had ever been. The man he had left in charge of his shop had decamped with, not only the list of his customers, but all of his bolts of cloth—and his wife! I felt so sorry for the poor fellow, and so ashamed of the awful mess I had gotten him into, that I would like to have helped him financially, but unfortunately, at the time, I was about as broke as he was! After that, for the rest of my medical life, I rarely hospitalized a patient because of an ulcer, and when I did I always warned the man that no matter how well cured he might seem to be, when he went back to his desk, piled high with accumulated work, his ulcer might flare up and growl at him again.

A nice-looking woman of 35, a gifted and clever but poorly adjusted business woman, could never be taught to keep living sensibly enough so as to maintain good mental and physical health. She could be charming, but she had little self-discipline, and little sense when it came to leading a well-ordered life.

The important point—so typical of such people—was that every time I thought I had gotten her "on her feet," she would come tumbling down again. For years urologists had kept treating her for a pain that was supposed to be in her right kidney, but which, actually, was coming out of her stormy brain. Several times she had a chance to marry advantageously, but each time, at the last minute, she backed out because she felt she was entering a trap. Perhaps she knew in her heart that she was too independent, undisciplined, and self-centered ever to make a good wife for any man.

One day when she came into my office, I noticed an impish grin on her face, and asked her what sort of "hell" she had been up to. She said she had been to see her psychoanalyst, and for some reason or other, the Devil had gotten into her, and had put her up to filling him to the eyebrows with just the sort of "crazy" theories that he loved. As she said: "After years of 'analysis' I have come to know well the mental processes of these people, and hence with my fertile imagination, it was no trick at all to spin a marvellous yarn about all sorts of bizarre and passionate sexual desires for my father, which supposedly I could remember since I was a year old. My analyst took full notes on all this 'awful bilge'; he loved it, and said he would use it as the basis for his special address before the next Psychoanalytic Congress in Europe."

One day, when I heard that for nearly a week the woman had been vomiting steadily, I dropped in and found that, as usual, she had become badly frightened—this time over some letters about something wrong with her income tax. When I asked her why she hadn't gone to see what the trouble was, she said she had been too scared to go. So I went to the Federal Building, and soon found that all the young lady owed was $3.85. I paid this, and then telephoned her that Uncle Samuel was appeased and happy. With this, she began eating voraciously, and in a few days she was back at work! The last I heard of her a few years ago, she was living in a big city hospital—the fate she had dreaded most.

Another patient was the wife of a Nevada miner who one day struck a big vein of silver ore, so rich that it quickly made him wealthy. Soon he was being invited to the homes of well-to-do mining friends. However, he saw that his wife, whom years before he had picked up in a "House" in Reno, was in need of culture. So he paid a decayed gentlewoman—an old patient of mine in San Francisco—to "make a lady" of her. One noon, some weeks later, as the two women were having luncheon in the Court of the Palace Hotel in San Francisco, the miner's wife suddenly pointed to a large, bediamonded woman at a nearby table, and said, "Well, for crying out loud; if that ain't Carson City Lil; why, I once worked in her House; I wonder what the goddamned old bitch is doing here. Oh; excuse me for pointing!" Obviously, the pupil's manners were well on the way to improvement!

Around 1917 everyone who consulted a physician, even for an ingrowing toenail, was likely to be told, "Go and get all of your devitalized teeth extracted." Because it seemed to me that this was a fad from which we physicians should be recovering, I asked some 200 people who had each had several perfectly serviceable teeth removed, what they had gotten out of their sacrifice. Had they been cured of their arthritis or stomach-ache? And soon I found that few had gotten anything except a dentist's bill. Hence in 1919, I wrote a "Protest against the reckless extraction of Teeth." I think this paper eventually did some good.

Later I made another statistical study to find out how often an *adult* got any benefit from the then very fashionable operation of tonsillectomy; and, again, I found that most of the persons out of the 251 studied received no benefit—unless they had been suffering from acute attacks of tonsillitis. After I went to Mayo's I questioned many people who had had a "chronic appendix" removed, and found only a very small percentage had been helped.

As I worked hard in my research laboratory I kept putting out many technical reports on the behavior of the gut. By

1925, I had published 75 papers. This work brought me election to membership in a number of research societies, such as the American Physiological Society, the Society for Experimental Biology and Medicine, the Society for Pharmacology and Experimental Therapeutics, the Society for Clinical Investigation, the Central Society for Clinical Research, etc. I was pleased to receive these honors, because they suggested that my research work was being accepted by men well trained in science.

About 1915, I published in the *Journal* of the American Medical Association a couple of articles summing up my laboratory researches, and throwing light on the production of symptoms in the cases of patients with indigestion. I think they had an influence on the medical thinking of that time.

In 1920, dear old Dr. Jimmy Case—a pioneer in X-ray work, and then president of the American Roentgen Ray Society—invited me to give the first "Caldwell Lecture." I will always be grateful to him for this because it helped to give me national recognition.

After the lecture, a man with bright black eyes came up to me and said, "I am Paul Hoeber, the medical publisher, and starting with that lecture as a foundation you are going to write a book for me." From that day forward until he died Paul was one of my closest friends. I promptly wrote the book which we called *The Mechanics of the Digestive Tract.* In the next 26 years, this book went through four editions, each larger than the previous one.

In May, 1922, I became well-known overnight because of a story I told at the meeting of the American Medical Association. At that time most of the physicians in America were beginning to realize that many men with a peptic ulcer had a lifelong series of flare-ups ahead of them, and hence were not likely to be permanently cured by any type of treatment.

At St. Louis, the A.M.A. arranged for a symposium on the subject, and the biggest church in the city was packed with doctors who came to hear the talks. After two of the leading physicians and two of the leading surgeons of the country had left the impression that they could *always cure* an ulcer, I was asked to start the discussion. With my knees shaking together, I went up on that platform wondering what on earth I could say in a few minutes that would sum up the impression I felt the crowd had gained, that is, that they hadn't been told all of the truth. And then there popped into my head just the story I needed.

I said that whenever any one of my friends, either medical or surgical, told me he could *cure* all of his patients with ulcers, I liked to tell him the story of St. Peter and St. Paul, who came down to earth to look about them and report to the Lord. After lunch they shook dice to see who would pick up the tab. Peter shook the box carefully, mumbled a few words, and rolled out five sixes. He looked at Paul, as much to say, "Well, that settles that." But Paul took the dice, shook them very carefully, mumbled a few words, and rolled out— five sevens! And Peter said, "Now, Paul, no miracles between friends!"

With this, the doctors roared with laughter, and in a few days the story was being repeated all over the country.

An excellent story of this type was told many years ago by my old friend, Dr. John Finney of Johns Hopkins, after a young surgeon had reported some nineteen consecutive operations on the brain—*without a death*. Because in those days the mortality from brain operations was high, everyone in the audience knew that what the man had done had been to report an unusually long run of good fortune, much like when black keeps showing up again and again on a roulette wheel.

Dr. Finney said that he was glad to congratulate the doctor, but he could not help thinking of the window washer who fell off the ledge. Fortunately for him, at that moment a wagon full of hay was passing, and the window washer fell right in and bounced out unhurt onto the sidewalk. A friend who was lounging there said, "Well, Sam, from now on you got to be mighty keerful, 'cause you done used up all yo' luck!"

I never liked the consultations of the old type, in which I would meet the family physician, listen to what he had to say, examine the patient, and then retire to a room to tell the doctor what I thought. If only because the patient was paying me, I felt he had a right to receive my honest and frank opinion. In the old days most doctors thought that medical etiquette demanded that the consultant's first and main duty was to back up their diagnosis, and perhaps save them from criticism when they had made a bad mistake.

Because I could not bring myself to do this sort of thing, I never got a consultant practice in San Francisco. When I disagreed at all openly with a certain type of doctor and said so, that was the last time he ever called me in. When I asked a few old-time professional consultants how they had managed for 30 or 40 years to keep their practice, they admitted that they had always protected the doctors who had called them in.

Occasionally I found a physician whose honesty I greatly admired. After I had examined his patient he would say to me, "Go ahead and talk to the family right here; if I have been mistaken, so be it. I called you in because you know more about this type of illness than I do, and I want your help and guidance."

Incidentally, I have always loved the story a dear old doctor from Georgia told me about a consultation he once took part in. He told of an ailing old "Colonel" in Georgia who had agreed to accept a consultation with a physician who would run down from Johns Hopkins University. Shortly before the great professor arrived, the testy old patient called his butler and said, "Look, George; you know how these consultations go: the professor will come in and poke me here and there; then he and old Doc will go into my den for a drink. They'll talk over their golf scores; then they'll figure out what I am to be told, and then the professor will come and tell me a cheerful yarn. But I am not going to pay $1,000 for that. While they are in the den, you stand around and keep your ears open, and when they are gone you come and tell me exactly what they said."

So later, George came, and the Colonel started asking about the condition of his heart and his other organs. All went well until it came to the question of his kidneys, about which George was vague. As he said, "They just argued and argued about your kidneys." "But what," said the Colonel, "did they finally say was wrong with my kidneys?" "They didn't say, sir; they said the autopsy would show what's the matter with your kidneys!"

After 1923 I received a half-dozen offers of an associate professorship of medicine, but turned them all down. The salary offered was always so small that my family and I could not possibly have lived on it; and besides, with the many administrative and teaching duties that go with a professorship, I would have had even less time for my beloved researches.

In 1924 I tried to accept a "full-time" associate professorship of research medicine, but since the salary was only $4,000 a year, I had to earn my living—seeing many patients late each afternoon. Within a month I found that the strain of trying to do this was too great, and so I gave up.

About this time I was offered a full-time editorship, and later a lucrative position as head roentgenologist in a big hospital, but I refused these offers because I was determined to stay in either physiology or internal medicine. Once I was offered a professorship of physiology, but luckily I turned it down. The man who then accepted the place soon was blocked in his every move by the other people working in his department. They ganged up on him, and eventually forced him to resign.

In 1924 I was elected to full membership in that Valhalla of professors of medicine—the Association of American Physicians. As I remember, its membership was then limited to some 200 clinicians and research workers in the U.S.A. and Canada.

Along the way, I began to get requests to write articles for medical textbooks and encyclopedias; also articles on medicine for monthly magazines and for a chain of newspapers. Even in those days I saw the great need for someone to explain medicine to laymen, and I wished I could help; but I knew that I could not do it and hope to stay in the good graces of the medical profession. To show how bad the situation was 40 years ago, I got called on the carpet by the local medical society because, when a reporter went through the Hooper Foundation—a state-owned institution—and asked for some idea of what was being done there, I told him. In spite of the fact that I had first gotten my Director's permission to do this, I was censured!

Many years later, when I thought it would be safe for me to write some booklets on medicine for laymen—if I did it *anonymously*—my "friends" found out what I had done and were very angry with me—so angry that they saw to it that the local bookstores stopped selling the booklets.

It is no wonder that a number of my older friends—leaders of the medical profession—kept urging me never to speak to a reporter. For a while I took their advice, but when I saw that this made for bad public relations, I changed, and always thereafter went out of my way to help the men of the press to get their story. I will admit that in the old days, when most reporters had no medical training, some of them, with their great desire to turn in a front-page story, got me into very embarrassing situations. Fortunately, today, a newspaper of any size has a well-trained science writer with whom I can chat freely.

In 1919 I began to attend the meetings of the American Gastroenterological Association, and each year to give a paper. In 1926 I became their president, and then, with the help of Paul Hoeber, Sr., I quickly got the society out of debt. I put the "old-timers" into an "honorary" or emeritus status, and with the help of the ablest members, I reached out into the fields of physiology and surgery for research-minded men interested in the digestive tract, and built a new and much more scientific "Gastro" Association. This work showed me that the businessman's contempt for the "impractical scientist" is not always justified. I could be a good businessman when I had to be.

Almost every year I went East from San Francisco to some of the big medical meetings, not so much to listen to the papers as to meet the leaders of my profession, and to ask them about many things. On my return home, my wife used to say, "You are a new man, full of new inspiration and enthusiasm."

I thought I had more or less "arrived" when, in one week I saw patients from Los Angeles, Spokane, San Diego, and China. A Scotch banker from Shanghai amused me because, when I found only a hypertension and advised two medicinal highballs before dinner, the man was so delighted he almost shouted, "Doctor, will you put that in writing? My wife belongs to the W.C.T.U." I put my prescription in writing, but it did my patient no good because his wife maintained that there had been some collusion!

One evening, about this time, when I thought I was beginning to get "pretty good" and fairly well-known, I had an experience which had a salutary effect on me. Not far from my home there lived a very wealthy, but decidedly uncultured woman. One night about ten, she came pounding on my door, begging me to come quickly to save her daughter "who was dying." I grabbed my emergency bag and hurried after her into her big palatial home. There, lying on a rug, kicking and screaming and biting herself, was a tough-looking hoyden. The minute she saw me, she started yelling, "Send that doctor away; I won't have him; I tell you I won't have him;" and the mother said, "Shut up." When the girl went on yelling, "I want *my* doctor; you send for *my* doctor," the mother said,

"Shut up; at a time like this you take any goddamn thing you can get!"

In 1916, when my name began to mean something in San Francisco, an interesting thing happened—a few ambitious men tried to use me for their purposes. The first man, a very busy general practitioner, came one afternoon with two patients for me. Taking me aside, he said that he much wanted to confine his work to surgery. He said, "Look, if you can talk even one of these two patients into letting me operate on him for something, I'll have two more men for you tomorrow, and two more the next day." During the next few weeks, in came three other physicians of the same stripe, who made much the same proposition. Obviously, I was not going to engage in any such nefarious business, and so I never saw the men again.

The great difficulty with some of the surgeons of this sort is not that they want money. They so love to operate that they would gladly spend the day operating, *even on patients who could never pay*. Also, many surgeons have one great ambition, which is to have the longest "list" (of operations for the day) chalked up on the blackboard on the operating-room "floor."

One thing I learned was that when I called a consultant I must choose a man, not because he would send me back a patient in return, but because he was the sort of able and honorable man I would choose to take care of my mother, or my wife, or my child. There are several reasons for a young doctor's being honest in this matter. Let us say that when he has to refer a patient for an operation, he calls an incompetent surgeon, just because the man will send a "case" back to him, or will split his fee with him; some of the lay people and physicians in the town will soon know what he is doing, and their unpleasant remarks will do him harm.

When he refers a woman for an operation, she will ask her lay friends and a doctor or two about the "surgeon." If she hears good reports of the man, she will go to him with confidence; and then, if she is well treated, and gets a good result, she will be grateful to the internist who sent her. But if everywhere the woman asks, she hears, "I never heard of him," or "He's not much of a surgeon," she will be angry, and will have no more to do with the young man who made the referral.

Also, if the young physician wants to become one of the leading internists in his city, he had better start right off referring his patients only to the best surgeons, orthopedists, obstetricians, gynecologists, and other specialists in the town.

In my early days in San Francisco, the top consultants to whom I kept referring my patients already had their special friends among the internists, and hence rarely sent me back "a case." This did not bother me. Three good things happened: one, the people I referred were grateful to me for having found for them the best doctor available; the second, I soon had the privilege of a happy friendship with the top group of consultants in the city; and third, when a patient was referred *to me* by someone, and then kept asking prominent physicians or surgeons about town if I was "all right," they said I was.

I will never forget my embarrassment one day when I made the very mistake that I am now decrying. What happened was that one of my woman patients telephoned me to say that during the night she had a miscarriage, and she thought she needed a curetment. I referred her to a certain general practitioner who for a long time had been trying to limit his practice to gynecologic surgery. He had been so helpful to me during my first few years of practice after 1913 that I much wanted to show him I was appreciative. I felt sure that he must be competent enough to perform a curetment (I could easily have performed it myself).

Unfortunately for me, I had forgotten that my patient had been a head nurse before her marriage, and was still chummy with several head nurses in the city. When she called them to see if Dr. X. was all right, they said they neither liked him nor respected him. With this, the woman went to another man, and I lost her friendship—also the friendship and respect of her family and her friends. This taught me a lesson, and after that, I tried never to recommend a man merely because he was a friend.

In 1916 I made a bad mistake in failing to follow up a good hunch. I mention this here only to show how when a man is too busy to think he can overlook a great opportunity.

I remember well the Dutch woman whom I saw about 1914, as she passed through San Francisco on her way home from years of life as a missionary in China. She told me that when she went down to skin and bones with pernicious anemia, and her American physician felt hopeless, her old Chinese nurse said, "I can cure you if you will take our ancient remedy." This proved to be a thick soup made of liver. The woman ate this every day and soon was fat and well. Perhaps I should have reported this, but I didn't, largely because, in medicine, one must never draw conclusions from the cure of *one* person.

Early in my medical life I learned that commonly, if one goes ahead and does something that needs to be done, no one objects; but if one asks permission, and is refused, then the opposition is likely to become adamant. One day in came two nuns, the younger one—the patient—suffering from severe menstrual difficulties. After taking the history, I asked the older nun if it would be permissible for me to make a pelvic examination. She said she did not know, but would ask the Reverend Mother.

In a few days the Mother Superior telephoned that she was putting the question up to the local Archbishop. Later, when the Archbishop refused to decide the matter, the question was referred to the head of the Order in New York, and eventually, the Superior there wrote that the answer was, "No."

I then asked the Superior in New York if the examination might be made by a woman physician, and finally permission for this was granted. Ever since then, whenever a nun has come into my office for an examination, my nurse has had her undress and get up on the table like everyone else.

And in 40 years, there has never been one question or protest about it!

Often in my early years I was impressed by the fact that certain physicians have enough strength of character, or vividness of personality, or "magic" power to enable them to cope with "difficult," eccentric, or mildly psychotic people—and especially, hysterical women.

Sometimes a curmudgeon has to be handled in some vivid way that perhaps interests him or somehow causes him to bow to the wishes of a physician. To show what I mean: one day a friend said he was bringing me his old tartar of a father-in-law. As he said, "Like many an Irishman, he is sweet and dear on the inside, but with most people he is very rough on the outside. Forty years ago, when he arrived in this country, he was found to have 'consumption,' and so went to Colorado. He became a 'Nature man,' lived out of doors without a top coat or a hat, ate only vegetables, and 'cured himself.' Ever since, he has hated doctors because some said he would die.

"The other day when my wife went to visit him, she found him recovering from a pneumonia. Because he treated it after Bernarr MacFadden's fashion, with a fast, he is now very thin and weak, and so she brought him home with her. The only reason he has consented to see you is because Shirley is expecting her first-born any day now, and we do not want her to be troubled with anxiety."

That afternoon, when the old lawyer came in, I chatted with him a while about the efficacy of a fast in curing a fever, and then, with a smile, I said, "But Mr. O'Brien, for a man who is a rigid vegetarian, wasn't it a bit inconsistent of you to go on a pure meat diet, and a cannibalistic one at that?" He looked at me, surprised, for a moment, and then a grin broke over his face, and he said, "By God, you're right; I never thought of that." Then we made a deal—I promised not to give him any medicine or any orders, and he agreed for the sake of his daughter and the unborn baby to stay for a while in a hospital, and to eat the food given him. Each of us kept his side of the bargain, and so we got along fine.

Another time I saw a spoiled and hysterical girl of 18 who, for two years had remained on a couch, with her widowed mother a slave to her. Seeing that the girl had no interest in getting well, I told her to go on home; I wasn't interested either, and had no time to waste on her. But I went ahead for a few minutes to paint a word picture of what her future was to be—without beaux, without a husband or a home of her own—just a dull, stupid life on a couch. Worse yet, yhen her old mother died, she (the girl) would be "buried alive"— alone in an apartment. Then I painted a picture of how much more fun she could have if she would get up and go back to school and college, and to a normal social life of dances and week-end parties.

After crying a while, she begged me to help her. Then she got up from her couch; she started eating, and she eventually went to college. Fattened up, she was a pretty girl. As she said, several doctors had failed to help her because she needed to be shaken out of her complacency. What startled her was to find a doctor who would have nothing to do with her unless she showed some desire to get well. Actually one of the biggest lessons I had to learn after I started practice is that one cannot cure anyone against his will. For several reasons many people need their disease; they use it to control or punish someone, or to get out of some unpleasant duty.

One noon, when I was lunching with a physician, a big handsome man came by. I glanced at his large, magnetic black eyes and said to my friend, "What a wonderful quack that man could be." And my friend said, "What an intuition you have: a while ago that man discovered that he has a remarkable ability to cure nervous women by the 'laying on of hands,' and so that is now his occupation."

Years ago I knew a surgeon who had this same remarkable ability to influence women. He had that "look" in his eyes, and he could quickly give a woman the impression that he had fallen for her in a big way. Because he was born overly shy, he compensated for this by being terribly profane with practically everyone. But for some reason, profanity coming from him did not offend anyone; in spite of it, his woman patients adored him.

One day he was asked to see the wife of a prominent Anglican bishop. She had gotten into a fine room in the plushiest of the local hospitals, and she loved it there so much that she wouldn't get up and go home. The family doctor became worried because he just couldn't talk the woman into going back to her dull husband in his dreary "palace." So the doctor asked the surgeon to come and see what he could do. The story, as it was told to me by the woman's nurse, was that the surgeon came, looked over the record, quickly examined the old lady's heart, and then, for a few minutes, in his subtlest and most charming way, acted as if he had fallen in love with her.

Then, with the merriest twinkle in his eyes, he said, "Look; you goddamned old bitch, you don't need that bed any more than I do. You're not sick; you are just bored stiff with that prosaic old bishop of yours. So, come on now! Get up out of there, put on your clothes, and go home!"

She did exactly as she was told, and then, for the rest of her days, went around town telling everyone how she loved the surgeon for his "cute ways."

Often in the office, as I have tried to put some sense into a neurotic, opinionated, unpleasant, or whiny woman, I have failed to get anywhere. I just could not get her to listen to me. Instead, she wanted to do all of the talking. I then quickly dismissed her because I never had any time to waste.

Often, in such circumstances, I thought of Charles Darwin who, one day in a pet shop, met a man who was buying a monkey to train for an act on the vaudeville stage. When Dar-

win heard the man say to the owner of the shop that he
would pay several times the current cost of a monkey if he
were allowed to take home a lot of them over the week-end
and then, on Monday, to bring back all but one, Darwin
asked, "But how can you tell that quickly which monkey can
be trained and which cannot?" And the man said, "That is
easy; I can train the monkey who looks at me and listens to
me." It is the same with patients in a doctor's office.

I used to marvel at some of my doctor friends who, in spite
of the fact that they had more patients than they could comfortably handle, were often grumbling because, as they maintained, some doctor had "stolen a case from them!" I used to
say to these men, "You ought to thank and bless the supposed
thief; perhaps because of him, one evening a while ago you
were able to go home at ten instead of ten-thirty!"

When my friends used to grouse about patients being
stolen from them, I used to laugh and say, "I am so lucky in
that no one ever *stole* a patient from me; many of my patients
just walked off because I did not please them, or I could not
cure them. When I cannot help a patient I am often relieved
when he goes elsewhere; it saves me from embarrassment and
from wasting time."

I used to feel sorry for some of my friends who had enormous practices, and I would swear to myself that I would try
hard never to get one. What a curse it can be! I am thinking
now of a dear old friend of mine who, until a stroke cut him
down, every day saw patients for some 18 hours out of each
24. Once when I went to his office to see him for a minute,
one of his nurses let me in the side door while another was
taking his last patient out by the back door. What astounded
me was that when I came in, my friend was resting his head
on his desk, and some 30 seconds after his last patient had
left, he was snoring! That is how tired he was. I could not
bear to wake him, so I tiptoed out the back way.

Another friend of mine with a huge practice became so
tired that, as he said, he went around in a daze. He got so

irritable and grouchy that his nice wife had to leave him. Then he began to get little strokes, and soon he was dead—in his fifties.

Oscar Wilde expressed this so well when he said that in this world some of us get what we want, and that is our punishment! Osler used to say, "Of all men in the profession, the 40-visit-a-day man is the most to be pitied. Too often he is lost beyond all recall; he is lost 'by mental death.' He needs to pray the prayer of the Litany against the evils of prosperity. The Psalmist said, 'He gave them their hearts' desire, but sent leanness withal into their souls.' "

When my practice got too big for me, I was worried. Some of my friends said, "Put up your prices and scare most people away." But I would not do this.

Other friends said, "Cut your visits down to 10 minutes each," but this I would never do. It would have meant practicing very bad medicine. One day in my office I was puzzled when a young woman whose history I had just begun to take, jumped up and started for the door. I said, "Wait; why the hurry?" In another 10 minutes she rose again, picked up her gloves, and started to go. Again I said, "Wait; I haven't yet gotten enough of your history." Ten minutes later, when again she got up to go, I asked, "What is the matter with you?"

Then she explained that for years she had worked for a very busy doctor, and her job had been to go into his consulting room every 10 minutes to take out the patient who was there and to bring in a new one! She assumed that I worked in the same way!

One thing I was determined I would never do, and that would be to save time by just *telling people* what I thought was wrong, as many psychoanalysts do to end the hour. One day I learned how unwise it is to do this when one of my teachers took a chance and *told* a woman that her abdominal discomfort was all due to adhesions left by her appendectomy. When she said, "But, no, doctor, that can't be, because

I had these pains for a year before that operation," my pompous Chief was so outraged at the lack of respect shown for his great eminence and authority that he stalked angrily out of the room.

I always hate to see any such sign of arrogance in a physician. I have known many a doctor who was so touchy that no patient was ever allowed to question what he had said. Naturally, this refusal to listen to a patient's objection must have led to many serious mistakes in diagnosis. I remember an occasion when I was asked to see a woman who was on her way to the hospital for a surgical exploration of her abdomen. She said, "Doctor, I fear your colleagues did not get my history correct; they all got the impression that I have abdominal *pain*, but that is wrong; what I have are spells of *nausea* with a *headache*, and some *abdominal soreness*." When I took another and more detailed history, it became clear that what the woman had was a severe migraine, and hence she did not need an operation.

The most beautiful example of the sort of stupid mistake a physician can make when he *tells* his patient right off what is wrong, was made by a doctor who believed that every woman should have many children. When he was consulted by a handsome, well-dressed woman of 40, and learned that she had no children, he bristled at her and said, "I know your type well. You spend most of the morning dolling yourself up; you play cards in the afternoon, and you live a stupid indoor existence. What you need is to get out of doors, and to get some excitement into your dull life." As the woman said to me later, "I did not bother to tell him that my husband is head of a gang of men who smuggle Scotch whisky across the Canadian border. Most nights I sit in the car with him, holding a sub-machine gun across my knees, watching out for highjackers!"

With all my hard work, I tried to stay close to my four children, and we took many trips in the car up into the mountains or down by the sea. We all had sleeping-bags, so sometimes we would sleep out under the stars. It is not always easy for a very busy doctor to stay close to his children. Often he must seem somewhat inaccessible to them, or unloving, if only because of his constant preoccupation with his patients and with his reading and writing.

Sometimes in those busy days in San Francisco I used to feel that I had to criticize some of the things that we physicians were doing. I felt it was my duty to do this, and that if I did not speak up, at some later date I would be ashamed of the fact that I had remained silent. As Abraham Lincoln said, "To sin by silence when they should protest makes cowards of men." Sometimes it is "base to sit dumb."

On several occasions—on principle—I stood up just to be counted as one of those few physicians in my state who was not fighting the much-needed Workmen's Compensation laws.

The man who runs athwart the current of his time is bound to gain some unpopularity, and most of us hate to be unpopular; we would much prefer to be known for our genial good nature. But we must remember that only the man who never does anything outstanding can go through this life without running into opposition, dislike, and bitter criticism.

We have to remember that "A turtle can never get anywhere unless he sticks his neck out!" I would have much liked to be always popular, but I did not care to buy my popularity at the price of remaining silent when I felt that someone should speak out against certain unwise, purely commercial, or heartless types of medical practice.

After 1920 I kept wishing I could find some institution that would give me a laboratory and just enough money for me and my family to live on. Each month I kept watching the medical journals, looking for some place to which I might go—but I never heard of one.

And then, late in 1925, I had the good fortune to be invited to give a number of lectures in Salt Lake City and Pocatello. At the final banquet, my good angel saw to it that I was seated beside Dr. William Braasch, a member of the

Board of Governors of the Mayo Clinic. When he learned from me that I was unhappy in San Francisco, and anxious to make any move that would give me more time for study, he went back and told Dr. Will Mayo, who promptly invited me to join the Staff of the Mayo Clinic. One glance at the letter that came, and I said to my secretary, "Goodby, I am going!"

One of the pleasantest memories I have of the days when I was leaving San Francisco is of the farewell luncheon that a number of my friends in the two medical schools gave me when I left. There were several very kind speeches made, but I particularly remember a few sentences out of the summing-up talk made by Walter Boardman, Professor of Medicine at Stanford. He said, "Walter, there are men who, if they had risen to prominence as fast as you have done in the last 10 years, would have brought on themselves envy and jealousy, but you have not excited any such ill feelings, because we all know that what you have won has been gained, not at the expense of any one of us—your competitors for a consultant practice—but by the hardest sort of work in the laboratory, the library, and the clinic."

Because of these affectionate words, I left that luncheon with feelings of humility and warmth in my heart, and gladness because in this world what are most worthwhile are not money and honors, but the esteem and good will and affection of the men who know if one's work has been good and honest. They know also if, while climbing up the ladder, the man has not soiled his hands on the rungs, and has not kicked down men who were climbing beside him.

7

Mayo Clinic Days

On FEBRUARY 1ST, 1926, my family and I arrived in Rochester, Minnesota, and I went to work in the Mayo Clinic. My first months were particularly happy because every day I was learning something at the several seminars and Staff meetings. I could so quickly and easily get answers to the many questions that were in my mind. Often all I had to do was to talk to a colleague who was an authority on the particular subject that was then interesting me. Sometimes, in one week, I would see so many people with the same rare disease that I could quickly become well acquainted with its clinical picture.

For instance: in 1926 there were so many patients with exophthalmic goiter always walking about the streets of Rochester that even our observant laymen, on noticing the bulging eyes, the dark red skin, and perhaps the operative scar on the woman's neck, could instantly make the diagnosis.

My good friend Dr. Alfred Kinsey once told me that when his little boy began to show signs of exophthalmic goiter, he had a hunch what was wrong, because he had watched a relative suffering from the disease. Because the local professor of pediatrics hooted at the idea of a small boy's ever having a toxic goiter (actually it *is* very rare in a child), Dr. and Mrs. Kinsey took the boy to Rochester. There, a small girl in the hotel promptly called out, "Hey! You with the poppy eyes! You'd better go have your goiter cut out!" She had made the correct diagnosis in an instant, when a teacher of pediatrics had failed! I remember when a newsboy made this diagnosis and astonished a much-traveled patient as he got off the train at Rochester. His examination at the Clinic showed that the newsboy was right.

Every Wednesday morning at Mayo's I attended Dr. W. C. MacCarty's seminar in which a number of us would review the histories of the men and women who that week at operation had been found to have an abdominal disease other than the one that had been diagnosed. Then we would try to figure out wherein the "diagnostic mill" had failed to function accurately—why a mistake had been made, and how a similar "slip-up" could later be avoided.

Every Wednesday night our able pathologist, Dr. H. E. Robertson, reviewed the essential points of the several autopsies of the week, and from these "clinical-pathological conferences" I learned much. I hated ever to miss one. And every day in the Clinic I kept learning much from consultations with my able colleagues.

At first I saw only a few patients, largely because there was no space available for me in the then old, over-crowded Clinic building. I had to take histories while seated at a tiny table in a busy hallway! I felt better about this when, one day, I called on my good friend, the head of another large clinic, and found him working under big sewer-pipes in the basement of his over-crowded building!

My mornings were spent in my laboratory in the basement of St. Mary's Hospital, where I worked with a number of assistants, who had come from the ends of the earth to work with me. We labored hard, and in one year published over a dozen research papers. Dr. Arnold Zimmermann and I made the first movies of the actively-moving stomach and bowels of anesthetized rabbits, with the abdomen open under a bath of warm salt solution. For the next year or more these movies were shown at all major medical meetings.

With George Little, our chief mechanic, I designed and built an X-ray motion picture machine, which performed perfectly. I recorded the passage of waves up and down the bowels of animals, and I studied the behavior of the bowel, weeks after its nerve supply had been cut off and allowed to degenerate. I wanted to know something of how the nerves work in the digestive tract of man.

In Rochester the men were very kind in inviting me to join a dozen clubs of various kinds, but I had to decline, largely because I had neither the liking nor the skill, nor the time for hunting, fishing, golfing, and card playing. In order to do the many things I wanted to do in medicine I just had to keep most of my spare time free for study and reading and writing. But in isolating myself, I realized that in many ways, I must have made myself look like an "odd duck."

I made many good friends in Rochester, but few bosom chums. This isolation was largely my own fault—I was too bookish. Another difficulty was that in a small clinic city, if I was to keep out of trouble, it was absolutely essential that I keep my mouth shut. I heard much gossip but I could not repeat it and prosper.

My life was always most interesting, if only because "the world and his wife" kept constantly coming through Rochester. Many delightful people came, not only from the four corners of North America, but from all over the world. One day my wife and I had in our home for luncheon a Chinese, two Australians, two Canadians, a South African, a South American, and one or two physicians from the United States. In all, we entertained each year over 600 persons, and this was a joy for people like us—living in a small city of some 35,000 inhabitants.

It was a good thing also for our children to meet many

famous people, and to find that usually the greater the man, the more approachable he is, and the more at home one almost immediately feels with him. I remember the evening when my old friend Paul DeKruif was in our home, and our daughter Bernice, then 14, whispered, "Daddy, do you think he would come down to the High School and talk to our journalism class?" I said, "Go ask him." And I remember his booming answer, "But, dear, what will I talk about?" I remember also, a few minutes later, the charming picture of the great big man and the young girl walking down the street together, hand in hand—having a grand chat!

One evening my wife and I learned something about entertaining the "great." The day before Christmas I was chatting with one of the most distinguished generals in the U.S. Army Medical Corps—a big handsome man with many rows of service ribbons on his coat. Because of his eminence, I felt sure he would be spending Christmas Eve in one of our "great houses;" but I asked anyway, and learned that everyone had thought that someone else was taking care of him, and hence no one was. Accordingly, I invited him to our home, and he gladly accepted. That bitter cold evening my wife and I put together two card tables by the fireplace; we had a happy dinner there with much good conversation, and then the general came out into the kitchen with us and helped me wipe the dishes, as my wife washed them.

Later we received the sweetest letter from this much-traveled man, saying that many a time he had dined in state, he had dined with kings; but never had he enjoyed a dinner more than the one that was served on card tables by a crackling fire.

Every morning I was in my office at eight. Especially on Mondays, over 1,000 new patients might come streaming into the Clinic buildings. They would be registered and each assigned to one of the several "Diagnostic Sections." In most of these Sections, the doctors tended to specialize, as in heart disease, or diabetes, or allergy, or diseases of the lungs, or stomach, or bowels. Thus, I, in a "stomach section," saw many a patient with a bad heart or bad lungs. But in most such cases, if the problem was at all puzzling, I would quickly call a heart or a lung consultant and turn the patient over to him. One of the wonderful features about practice in the Mayo Clinic is the ease and quickness with which a doctor can call a consultant; also the honesty and the openness with which the consultations are held—always in the presence of the patient.

After being registered, a patient who (unless he is bedfast) stays in a hotel or a boarding-house, is assigned to a Fellow—a young physician who, after finishing his internship and residency, has come to the Clinic to work for 3 years as a graduate student of the University of Minnesota. This Fellow takes the first history and makes a physical examination. Then one of the men of the "Permanent Staff" consults, and perhaps OK's the orders made for laboratory and X-ray work. When this work is done and he sees the patient again, he may re-take the history and re-examine the patient, and perhaps with this he can make the diagnosis. If not, he orders more examinations or tests. Later he may consult with someone, or he may arrange for an operation or some special treatment, or he may dismiss the person. Then, in many a case, he dictates a report to the patient's home physician.

Each patient gets one bill, which is never excessive. Close to a third of the patients, because of their financial problems, are given all the time they need to pay their bill. No one has ever been sued for payment, and no one has ever been turned away because his purse was empty.

One thing I have always loved and admired about the Mayo Clinic practice is that there has never been any buncombe in it—no carrying-out of long treatments that are not needed; no operating on people who do not need an operation, and no ordering of tests just to run up a big bill. Actually, there were times when Dr. Will and Dr. Charlie called the Staff together, and begged us to try always to hold down the size of the bill—particularly for people who had but little money. One day Dr. Will was distressed when he found that a poor young tenant farmer, who had come in with a mangled hand, had had three expensive transfusions of blood. As Dr. Will said, a husky young chap like him could almost certainly have recovered without the help of the blood. Some salt solution in his veins would have worked about as well.

Another time, Dr. Will called a meeting to discuss the foolishness and unkindness of ordering great numbers of tests which, with a little thought, could have been "done without." Our Fellows used often to order dozens of tests without much thinking—perhaps because in their University hospitals they had been allowed to do this, or even taught to do it. As Dr. Will said, it is not honest to take money for unneeded tests. Eventually, a regulation had to be passed to the effect that tests asked for by a Fellow could not be made until each order had been approved by a consultant.

Naturally, for an ardent student of disease, like me, it was wonderful to see so many patients, and particularly those many who came because their trouble was so rare and puzzling that their home doctors could not guess what it was. Each day was full of diagnostic challenges which I greatly enjoyed. Soon I was taking particular pleasure in helping patients who I found were ill only because of a great sorrow, or a great strain of some kind.

Typical was the story of the banker who had been traveling about the United States consulting eminent physicians in an effort to find out what was causing the pain in his abdomen. After much study, one of my associates dismissed him with the statement that there was "nothing the matter with him." Naturally, the man was disappointed and outraged. Then, while strolling past a book store he saw my book in the window, *Nervousness, Indigestion and Pain*. Thinking he might learn from this how to make his own diagnosis, he went in and bought a copy.

Later he came to my office and told my secretary he just had to see me and tell me that as soon as he had read the first chapter, a great light had dawned on him. It had never oc-

curred to him before that his pain could be due to some distressing emotion, but as he looked through my book he saw
that it could. Suddenly, the thought came to him that he never
felt the pain when he was away from home—at a bankers'
convention, on his ranch, or on his fishing preserve; and then
he realized that the minute he went home and stuck the key
into his door, he would get it.

I asked, "What is your wife like?" And he said, "She is a
good woman, but she is always looking down her nose at me.
She had a college education, and I didn't finish high school.
She was born up on the hill, and I was born below the railroad tracks. So she tells me I am common. She does not like
my English, or my table manners, or my friends. At home she
won't let me kick off my shoes, and she won't let me smoke
in the living-room. She won't let me bring my poker-playing
cronies in the house. She always manages to keep me tense and
uncomfortable."

"Well, you now know how to cure your stomach-ache; just
keep away from home."

"That," he said, "is precisely what I am going to do. From
now on, I am going to live alone on my ranch."

One of the patients I saw in 1926 found himself faced with
such a strange problem that, in my mind's eye, I can still see
the poor old fellow. He was a man of sixty who for most of his
life had run a general store in a small town in North Dakota.
When some indigestion began to bother him, he went to a
doctor who had just bought an X-ray machine, and didn't yet
know much about it. When the films of the man's stomach
showed a big indentation, the doctor diagnosed an inoperable
cancer.

When the man came to Rochester and showed me these
films, I laughed and said, "That isn't a cancer; that apparent
deformity is produced by the pressure of your spine on your
stomach." As the man continued to look sad and apathetic,
I asked, "What is the matter? You should be registering joy
and great mental relief!"

"Oh, Doctor," he said, "I don't know what I am going to do; I am in an awful fix. When the doctor said I would soon be gone, I gave the store to my son. All I saved out was some money for a trip to Rochester and a funeral! The townspeople were so kind and so wonderful to me; they all came down to the railroad station to say goodbye to me; and now they do not expect ever to see me again. I just can't go back! It would be such an awful anticlimax. I do not know where to go!"

One day I had another strange experience with an unusual patient, and learned something from her I had never known before. I learned that Saint Peter must make pelvic examinations on very proper maiden ladies whose main claim to the right to enter heaven is that they always kept their virginity. What happened was that a very wealthy and very proper old maid came up from South America for the removal of a large tumor of her womb. A few months after her return home, I was surprised to have her come in again. She said that she had returned just to get from me a certificate to the effect that the loss of her hymen had come about perfectly innocently during her several medical and surgical examinations. She had discovered her loss when, on her return to Lima, her prissy old Spanish doctor had checked her over and had been horrified to find that an extremely important little portal had become somewhat dilated. When I asked her what she was going to do with her certificate, she said that, of course, it was going with her in her coffin to be presented in due time to St. Peter. I had never before realized that the Saint or some deputy of his at the gates of Heaven must perform pelvic examinations on all would-be entrants who claim to be "virgo intacta!"

Although my quarter-century at the Clinic was the most fortunate and productive period of my life, I must admit that occasionally I ran into trouble with a few of my associates, and a few committees made up of men who doubted the wisdom or advisability of what I wanted to do. Often I must have appeared to them as an *enfant terrible*. Certainly I was not the quiet, retiring, and conforming man who is most likely to get along comfortably as a simple cog in a great machine. I was too full of ideas for doing something new.

I never wanted "to rock the boat," but sometimes I blundered into doing this if only because, when I arrived in Rochester, no one told me of all the many unwritten laws and "feelings of personal rights" around the place—"rights" that must be respected. Some of the men at times tried to block what I was doing, usually, I think, because they were not convinced that I was right in what I was reporting, or because they feared that what I wanted to do would injure the medical standing of the Clinic, or it would make enemies for the place.

My occasional troubles in getting along with a few of my colleagues were not typical of just the Mayo Clinic; I found them everywhere I went—in university departments and in big hospitals. Everywhere I visited I heard of clashes of personality; conflicts perhaps between the "often-publishing" research workers and the "seldom-publishing" non-research men; or between the quiet, non-politically-minded research men and the "pushers" who loved authority and wanted always to run things, or who were jealous, or "ornery," or "difficult," or dog-in-the-mangerish, or too fearful of losing their rights and prerogatives.

I am happy to say that I never "had words" with the few men who occasionally opposed me or my ideas. In our personal dealings we were always friendly, and I never became angry. This was no credit to me—it was just a way of life which I inherited from my easygoing father. I have always loved Joseph Hall's statement that "A small injury shall go as it comes, a great injury may dine or sup with me, but none at all shall lodge with me."

What helped me to be forgiving was that I had sense enough to see why some men, if at all human, would have to resent my presence in their department; they not only hadn't invited me in, they had not even been consulted about my coming; and so I could easily understand why some of my activities produced in them feelings of annoyance or insecurity. I was sorry that they did not feel they could trust me when I said I would never reach out for powers not yet granted me.

I just could not get them to see that my coming did not constitute any threat to them. All I wanted was to be left alone to work and study and learn; I very much did not want anyone's job or anyone's patients. I did not want to be head of a department; I did not want even a hospital appointment. I guess my associates' trouble was that they just could not imagine how a man could have as little ambition as I claimed to have. I was full of a desire to work, but the work I wanted to do was in research and not in administration.

Everywhere I went in medical schools and clinics I found that a man who does not quickly fit into a well-recognized groove in an organization is bound to run into trouble. As my old associate Dr. McVicar used to say, "Walter, for God's sake, either fish or cut bait. You want to do both!" One of my troubles arose from the fact that in my mornings I worked as a physiologist in my laboratory, and afternoons I worked as a consultant on the Clinic "Floor." Naturally, the physiologists said I was a clinician, and the clinicians said I was a physiologist!

Furthermore, a man will surely have trouble as I did if, when something urgently needs to be done, he does it without waiting until two or three committees have discussed it at length and decided to block it.

As I traveled about, hearing of the difficulties encountered by able men in many institutions, I thought often of what my great hero, Sir Francis Galton, once wrote. He told how, in South Africa, the lions used to pick off and pull down just those oxen that were fearless enough and independent enough to *graze away from the herd.* In a land where the grass was deep and lions were numerous, practically all of the cattle, while grazing, felt comfortable only when gathered in a circle with their rumps together and their sharp horns facing outward.

But in every herd there were one or two oxen, brave enough

or independent enough or perhaps foolish enough to graze off away by themselves. Naturally, in doing this, a steer ran a great risk, because a lion, sneaking up behind, could jump on his back and break his neck. Because independence with courage is apparently inherited, and because the lions destroyed most of the *brave animals* early in their life, there could never be many born into a herd.

Galton became much interested in these cattle with the independent-grazing habit because, while exploring in the desert, he used heavy carts pulled by perhaps ten pairs of oxen; and the biggest problem of the carters was to find two *"lead animals"* with enough courage to walk ahead, especially when the scent of lions was in the air. The average ox—like many an average man—*would never lead*; and the minute it became frightened, it would turn back and snarl up the team by trying to hide itself between the two lines of animals.

But here is the important point. Early in their life in South Africa the Boers discovered that the only animals that could ever be trained to be leaders were just those rare brave ones that *would graze away from the herd*. Because of this, the Boers always watched for these particular cattle, and prized them highly.

I think of this story whenever in an organization I see men sneaking up behind the lead-ox type of man with plans to pull him down. Being attacked is the price many an able man must pay for being fearless, independent, progressive, willing to lead, and willing to graze away from the herd. Many men in this world will always refuse to accept responsibility—because they don't want to lead and they don't want to make decisions; they are too afraid of the criticism that would follow a mistake; they just do not want to "face the music" that would follow the making of an error in judgment. A man who is "going to the top" must have guts enough to risk making many a mistake.

A few times in my life I have learned how dangerous it is for a man to receive much praise. A physician in an organization can get into very embarrassing trouble when a number of fellow practitioners write in, praising him for something he has done or is supposed to have done. High praise of a man is bound to cause some of his less energetic and less successful colleagues to feel outraged; and when this happens, they tend to gang up on him, and to try to get rid of him. David learned this in Israel some 3,000 years ago when the plaudits of the people for the Goliath affair all but cost him his life. King Saul became so jealous and annoyed, and came to feel so insecure, that he kept sending soldiers to find David and kill him. One day, it was only with the help of a clever and devoted wife that David was able to evade the soldiers and get away.

Often a successful researcher's detractors will bring against him the most unreasonable accusations, such as that he is gathering unto himself all of the credit that ought to go to the men in his department. They will become convinced that in some underhanded way he is taking advantage of them, and "he is skimming the cream off of their work." No wonder then that they resent his presence among them, and no wonder that they try to push him out.

Some 100 years ago that great surgeon, Dr. Marion Sims, the founder of gynecology, described how many confreres treat an innovator when honors come to him. First, for a while, his associates just ignore him; they act as if they had never heard of him or of his work. Later, when perhaps scientists all over the world begin to express appreciation of what he has done, his opponents speak up to say that he is all wrong; and finally, when almost everyone has accepted his discovery, the objectors say that it was nothing new—it was well-known many years before!

An adage that many a highly successful man must early learn and get used to is that "When you want to beat a dog, any old stick will do." This saying has often occurred to me as I have watched an able man taking a verbal beating for having done a splendid piece of work. Take the life of Linnaeus—the great organizer of the science of botany. On one

Dr. Walter C. Alvarez at his desk in Chicago.

Photograph by Austen Field

Dr. Alvarez' father, Dr. Luis F. Alvarez.

Dr. Alvarez' mother, Mrs. L. F. Alvarez. This photo was taken in 1915.

Taken in Waiahua, this photograph shows Dr. L. F. Alvarez seated in the buggy with his children, Milton, Florence and Mabel. This was taken about 1892 when Walter Alvarez, standing at the horse's head, was eight.

Taken on Dr. Alvarez' first trip into the Sierras in May, 1905. From left to right: "Happy" Reed, William Smyth, "Judd" Harris, and Walter Alvarez.

Dr. Alvarez about 1920 in San Francisco.

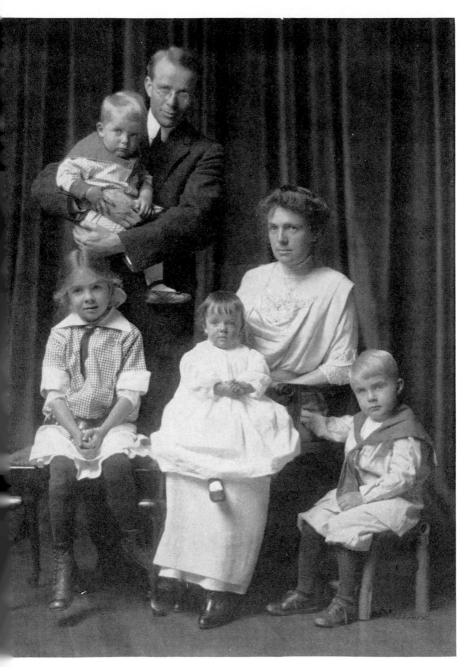

Dr. and Mrs. Alvarez with their children in 1915. Dr. Alvarez holds Robert and seated from left to right are Gladys, Bernice and Luis.

The Hooper Foundation, 1917 to 1918. Left to right, top row: Prof. Karl F. Meyer (Director after Dr. Whipple left), Charles Hooper, Irving McQuarrie, etc. Left to right, lower row: Miss Foster, Mrs. Frieda Robscheit Robbins, (*unidentified*), George H. Whipple (Director), Professor Ernest Walker.

Dr. Alvarez at the Mayo Clinic.

Walter Alvarez in his office in Chicago. To his left on the wall are two of his awards. Top, the Friedenwald Medal; Bottom, his Certificate of Honorary Membership in the Royal Society of Medicine.

Photograph by Austen Field

Dr. Alvarez being interviewed in 1955 at the offices of the *Courier-Journal* and *Louisville Times*. The owner of the *Journal* said that never in his life had he seen a number of editors stay to listen to someone being interviewed at closing time.

Mrs. Harriet S. Alvarez.

Dr. Walter Alvarez and his wife, Harriet in Honolulu in 1961.

occasion jealous associates who wanted to pull him down and have him imprisoned, attacked him because he had shown that plants have two sexes! This discovery was regarded by the small men around him as so reprehensible that only Linnaeus' friendship with the king saved him from serious trouble.

Oliver Wendell Holmes once said that "doctors are the best-natured people in the world, except when they get to fighting each other."

With my wide reading in anthropology, I have been interested to see that in many primitive tribes a man can easily lose his life if he becomes too famous as the group's best hunter or warrior. Then the Chief and the Shaman will get so jealous or fearful that they will bring charges of witchcraft against him, and will quickly have him executed.

As I intimated above, occasionally I got into hot water because I had broken some unwritten law of the Clinic men. For instance: every man in the Clinic had been given some division of the body, or some disease, or group of diseases that constituted the province in which he might do his research work. This was a good idea insofar as it enabled a man to become an expert in some one field of medicine. But it was a bad idea when it encouraged a mean cuss to insist that an able associate must stop investigating a problem on the borderline of the field which the mean man thought he owned. And it was particularly bad when the "Watch Dog Committee" sided, as they were inclined to do, with the dog-in-the-manger.

Several times I got into serious trouble with The Committee. For instance, while working in the "stomach section," I kept seeing hundreds of women who asked for a gastroenterologist because, with their frequent attacks of retching and abdominal pain, they thought they had "stomach trouble." When I found that all they had was an atypical and hence puzzling form of migraine, I started to study these forms and, after a few years, I wrote a paper based on my notes on some 500 cases.

I was then told that migraine belonged in the field of the

neurologists, and hence I could not publish my paper. I insisted that since I was seeing 20 or 30 of the migrainous women to the neurologists' one, I ought to be writing up at least the common abdominal symptoms of the disease. Eventually, I broke the rules and just went ahead and published the paper. Then, in order to avoid further trouble, I put aside for 25 years the big pile of notes I had made on some 2,000 more case histories of migrainous people. It wasn't until around 1956 that I got around to publishing a half-dozen papers based largely on the migraine studies I had begun in the early 1930's.

I wish all committee men who now compel the research workers in their institution to stay in one narrow rut would remember that insulin was discovered by a country surgeon who got an idea and followed it up. Obviously, the drug should have been found by a physiologist—but it wasn't! Penicillin was found first by a bacteriologist. Years later it was isolated and purified by some chemists. Still later, it was made in bulk with the help of techniques borrowed from the brewers. The sulfa drugs were found by Gerhard Domagk—a chemist. Perhaps these drugs *should* have been found and developed by professors of pharmacology—but they weren't!

Pasteur's life is the best illustration of what great gifts can come to the world when a man of genius strays from one field of endeavor to another. As we all know, Pasteur left his field of chemistry to found the sciences of bacteriology and immunology. With this work he changed the whole face of medicine. If he were here in America today, the committee of his institution would quickly order him to go back into his chemical laboratory and stay there!

Often the only way I could learn something new about the functions of the digestive tract was to go out searching into other fields—like the fields of anatomy and physiology, and sometimes into the field of veterinary physiology.

The most digusting phenomenon that often comes out of this feeling that research workers *own* their field, and poachers on it will not be tolerated is that which one commonly observes

when a group of mean small men in a specialty keep trying
for 30 years or more to punish an intruder—by taking care
never to mention his name or the valuable discovery which he
once made in their field. The worst example I ever saw of this
mean type of childish behavior was the refusal of a professor
of medicine ever to permit anyone in his department to use
insulin! According to what his residents told me, eight years
after the discovery of this invaluable and life-giving drug this
mean small boy in professorial cap and gown was still refusing
even to have Banting's name mentioned in his presence!

Once, long ago when an old friend of mine—a professor of
physiology—was commissioned to write a summary of that day's
knowledge of the emptying of the stomach, he made no mention in his article of what was by far the best planned and best
executed piece of work ever done on this subject. It was performed in my laboratory by a brilliant young roentgenologist,
Dr. Cesare Gianturco, who used my X-ray movie machine
and along the way got a little help from me. We used an ideal
(motion-picture) technique in which the animal was wide
awake, frisky, happy, and digesting a meal, and without the
usual anesthesia, and surgically opened abdomen, or balloon
in his stomach, or a tube running down his gullet. When I
asked my friend, the professor, why he hadn't done Gianturco
the courtesy of at least criticizing his work, he said (as I knew
he would) that Gianturco and I were not full-time physiologists. We weren't full time "members of the union" so we had
to be punished.

Once or twice, especially in my first years at the Clinic,
when I ran into annoyances I thought of going back to San
Francisco; but then I said to myself, "No; there is no bed of
roses anywhere. In so many ways the Clinic is a wonderful
place in which to work, with every advantage, so why leave?"
Perhaps also it is true, as Mark Twain used to say, that a certain number of fleas are good for a dog! One thing I fortunately learned early in my life is that when harassed by
someone, I must never waste any energy getting angry, or

trying to strike back; *a man is never so poorly employed as when defending himself!*

As my readers can guess, I often had reason to dislike a committee. I have always loved the statement that a camel is obviously a horse that was designed by a committee! I am like the man who said he would respect committees more if he ever found one that had produced a great picture, a great symphony, or a great poem. Thank goodness, only once did the "powers that were" trust me enough to put me on a committee! I never was a "safe" man; I never played poker with the right people, and I never cared to learn anything about politics.

I never have heard it mentioned that many committees are dominated by one conservative and savage old grouch who is so sarcastic and offensive in debate that no peace-loving man cares to tangle with him. If anyone suggests a new and promising change in the work of the department or the institution, the grouch says, "We tried that 20 years ago and it was a flop"; and that settles that.

Many a time in the old days when it came to my ears that an important committee had spent an hour discussing some peccadillo of mine—such as writing up the results of years of research, the value of which the committee men did not appreciate, or my having been written up in *Time* magazine, or my having seen many more patients a day than I had been told I might see, or my having written anonymously some books to help laymen understand their illnesses—I felt like going to the group and saying, "Why can't you fellows devote your time to some useful purpose? Why waste so much of it fussing at me?"

All throughout my years of writing, I kept having difficulties with committees, especially editorial committees. I had the worst times with young women who thought it their duty to rewrite almost every sentence in my articles and editorials. They always tried hard to make my work sound "more scientific" by putting in a lot of long Greek words—replacing my "hiccup" with "singultus," or my "belching" with "eructation," or my "urinate" with "micturate." I remember the time when a girl in an editorial office completely rewrote a paper by that master of powerful and delightful prose—Dr. Raymond Pearl. I wish I had been present when Dr. Pearl exploded; I heard later that the fireworks were brilliant.

Another trouble I had with some editorial assistants was that they wanted me to write by rule—perhaps seeing to it that no sentence ever ended with a preposition. Of late I have asked such editors to ponder over Winston Churchill's note to the woman who thought she could improve his magnificent prose by moving a preposition into the place where her high school teacher had said it should go. He wrote, "This is the sort of arrant pedantry up with which I will not put!" An eminent Harvard professor used to insist that in my chapters in Oxford Medicine I should never insert an adverb between the two parts of a compound verb. This caused some of my sentences to make me feel—as I read them—as if I had walked into a glass door that I hadn't seen was there.

What has bothered me much about many editors has been their insistence always that I "pussyfoot." Many an article of mine has come back to me from some editorial office with every strong sentence blue-pencilled, and every statement that did not follow the "party line" ripped out. Time and again I have had to tell the editor or his assistant that if I had always consented to the emasculation of my prose, with the deletion of every strong sentence that someone feared would cause comment or make for me an enemy, my writing would never have had any influence on American medicine.

Once when I much wanted to impress physicians with the need for their more quickly diagnosing cancer of the stomach, I decided that the best way in which to stir up their interest would be to show them what a disgracefully poor job of diagnosing gastric cancer had been done *on themselves* by the last 41 physicians seen at the Clinic with the disease. In 20 of these cases the doctors had waited an average of 12 months before doing anything about their symptoms. One eminent stomach specialist suffered a year with pain typical of gastric cancer before he came to see me and was X-rayed. Another physician suffered 2½ years before getting a diagnosis! A physician who lost 40 pounds waited a year before he got examined!

One of the editors who saw my manuscript demanded that I delete everything that would suggest that I was criticizing the diagnostic ability of the doctors. Obviously, this would have left-the article pointless. Not only would the Cheshire cat have disappeared; even its grin would have been wiped out; so I published the paper as it was.

The most awful "storm" of all was kicked up by a paper of mine on *abdominal ticklishness in women!* In 1913, when every afternoon I had to palpate the stomachs of people standing back of my X-ray screen, I found only a rare woman with an abdomen as ticklish as that of a boy. Becoming curious about this, for years I kept making notes about every decidedly ticklish woman whom I found. Finally, when I wrote a paper about these odd women, and mentioned the fact that in love-play it would be somewhat of a handicap for a women to have a very ticklish abdomen, my medical friends went into such paroxysms of horror that I yielded to their entreaties, and left the paper in my files, where it still is! How prissy we doctors can sometimes be! I can remember when a medical editor did not want me to mention sex or homosexuality in his august columns!

Very remarkable also was the "fit" many of my friends had when I turned in the manuscript of a paper I had written on those many persons who are ill because they feel "caught in a trap." My friends were so distressed over this paper that I gave in and put it away. When, a few years ago I took it out and published it, the response from the medical profession warmed my heart. Teachers of medicine all over the country are still writing in to ask for reprints, and to say how much they love that paper, which "much needed to be written."

Here are a few items from it to show how harmless it was.

One day I saw a girl who, because of her failure to eat, had gone down to skin and bones. I soon learned that her illness had begun when her half-crazy, sex-hating mother in Los Angeles had insisted that the girl give up her good job in Salt Lake City, dismiss her fiancé, and come home. The mother had taken to her bed with the unwarranted conviction that she was dying, and she insisted that the daughter stay and take care of her until the end came.

What with the girl's worry about her beau, and her dull stupid life in a darkened room where her mother read the Bible all day, the girl's nerves had gone to pieces. I immediately got her father to promise to set her free, and to let her go back to her fiancé and her job. When he agreed to do this, the girl started eating and gaining weight. During the next few years she kept writing to me to thank me, and to say she was well, and happily married.

Another entrapped person was a lovely woman of 35 who had a "touch" of "hereditary" syphilis presented to her by her "gay-dog" of a father, and another was a beautiful girl who felt trapped by a bit of Negro blood presented to her by her great-grandmother. Another felt trapped because she was illegitimate, and many were trapped by a mild epilepsy or a mild psychosis. These girls were too honorable to marry without first telling their beaux about their handicaps, but always, when the man got the news, he left!

Fortunately for me, in my many years at Mayo's, the Editors-in-Chief—from Mrs. Maud Mellish, to Richard Hewitt, to Lloyd Potter, and to my good buddy James Eckman—always came to my rescue; they chased away the young ladies with the blue pencil, and along the way, they became my dear friends.

Perhaps I can best close this discussion with that wise and charitable statement of Thomas à Kempis, "Be not angry that you cannot make others as you wish them to be, since you cannot make yourself as you wish to be."

When I began working in the "stomach section" of the

Mayo Clinic in 1926, I found that every man in the department had already been assigned some organ or disease as his
field for special study. Accordingly, I had to ask, "What is
there left for me?" And my associates said, "The digestive
neuroses. You can have them all. We don't want them. We
don't like 'neuros.' It takes too long to make anything out of
their stories."

The subject of neuroses suited me perfectly. Thus it came
about that for the next 25 years I studied the problems of thousands of patients with stomach-aches for which no abdominal
cause had been found. Soon I showed that usually in these
cases the diagnosis can be made only with the help of a care-
fully-taken and well-interpreted history.

Naturally, as the years passed, and I saw all these people
with neuroses, migraine, "nervous breakdowns," little strokes,
hysteria, mild and seizureless forms of epilepsy, and mild psychoses, my major interests changed, and soon I found myself
spending most of my time trying to help people, not with
ulcers or cancers, but with nervousness, worry, and fear. Before
long I was writing books on gastrointestinal neuroses.

Along the way, seeking help, I went into the library and
read widely on mental and nervous troubles. I particularly enjoyed the books and articles written by the older psychiatrists
—men of great wisdom, like S. Weir Mitchell of Philadelphia,
T. A. Ross, the great research psychiatrist of England, Austen
Riggs, Abraham Myerson, Stanley Cobb, Hervey Cleckly, and
others. They became my teachers and my heroes.

Soon I was spending much of my time teaching my students
to watch out for the thousands of persons who came complaining of aches and pains, but who really should have been telling
stories of great sorrow, unhappiness, overwork with fatigue and
insomnia, worry, strain, feelings of guilt, or feelings of distress
over an inability to make an important decision.

A married woman of 45 came 1,000 miles just (she said) to
have her gallbladder removed. She was much annoyed when
I did not immediately send her into a hospital for the opera-

tion, and much more annoyed when I told her that not only were her symptoms those of a neurosis, but the X-ray study had shown her gallbladder to be normal. For ten days I verbally wrestled with that women; I, asking her what had gone wrong in her life, and she saying, "Go on and get my gallbladder out." As I pointed out to my assistant on the first day, there must have been something wrong in the woman's sexual life because she had asked me if, with her examination, she would get a Wassermann test for syphilis.

On the tenth day she gave in and told me that her troubles had started when a woman had come to her door to say that her (my patient's) husband was a bigamist and her children were illegitimate because the man had never bothered to get a divorce before marrying again. This woman then blackmailed my patient into giving her $5,000—to keep her mouth shut. The husband admitted his guilt, but said, "Pay no attention to Alice; she always was a bluffer!"

Sometimes I got to thinking that I was pretty good in suspecting the presence of such unhappy stories, and then getting the patient to confess; but sometimes I would run into a case in which I found that I had failed badly.

For instance: I failed to help a stout, fortyish, prosaic-looking farmer's widow whom I certainly never suspected of having any love problem. Because she complained of abdominal pain, I had to check her carefully to rule out a cancer. Twice she came, and twice I sent her home with the admission that I did not know what was wrong. Then I received a letter from her telling me what had been wrong. She had been too ashamed to tell me that her trouble was that ever since her husband's death she had been constantly distressed by her great hunger for sex. She had hoped that I would ask her about the subject because then she would have had the courage to ask me if there wasn't some sort of an operation that would give her peace and relief. "Each time you failed me," she wrote, "and so I wasted my money."

A frequent trouble I had with many of my nervous patients

was that it was hard to help them when I could see them only occasionally. I had to tell them that most of the time by themselves they would have to fight their fears, worries, and feelings of illness. As Shakespeare said, "The patient must minister to himself."

Some of my patients amused me much, and many of them pleased me with their signs of great gratitude. Two of my most grateful patients were notorious gangsters who, strange to say, I came to like. One of them, a well-known citizen of Chicago, was so very grateful for the removal of a painful gallstone that he kept begging me to commit some crime so that through his friends he could quickly and easily "get me off"!

The other man kept asking if there wasn't someone whom I would like to have "bumped off." He assured me this would be done quickly and without any expense to me! All I was ever able to get him to do for me was to have a parking ticket "fixed"!

In my years at the Mayo Clinic I never came to feel that 'I belonged.' When talking to an audience about some Clinic practice, I unconsciously would say, "*they*" do so and so, and not "*we*." Dr. Will Mayo sensed this, and with his usual homely wisdom and kindliness he tried to comfort me.

He said, "Don't worry, Alvarez; a rat has to live in a strange garret for a good many years before he is accepted as one of the gang!"

Around 1930 I had the pleasure of having as an assistant a brilliant young woman, Dr. Frances Vanzant of Houston. Together we wrote six research papers, mainly on the gastric juice. One paper was on the technique of diagnosing with a computer. In the 1930's I spent much time studying food allergy, also the—to me—always fascinating syndrome of the "little strokes." These strokelets, rarely causing any paralysis, but often some mental deterioration, are exceedingly common in the later years of many persons, and they have most to do with the aging of many of us.

Although I did not begin to lecture about these little

strokes until the early 1930's, I came to know them well in the years from 1901 to 1911, as I watched a series of them slowly pull down and kill the brilliant college president who, in 1907, became my father-in-law.

Later I discovered that Osler had known the syndrome well, and had written briefly about those people "who take longer to die than they did to grow up." In the years following 1930 I wrote a number of papers describing the several groups of symptoms commonly produced by these little strokes. I am happy to say that general practitioners and lay people all over the world quickly accepted this work. Many doctors knew the disease well, if only because they had seen it develop in members of their own families.

When I first described—at a medical convention—the slow, steplike mental death of some of the people who keep having little strokes, a number of fine old family doctors came up to the platform and said, "How could we have been so stupid as not to recognize the nature of this very common disease? Why, right now in our town, we must have dozens of patients petering out in that way—dying at the top like an old tree."

My old friend Dr. James Kernohan, one of the most experienced brain pathologists in the world, has often told me that the commonest lesion he keeps finding in brains (removed at autopsies) has been a series of little black spots which represent plugged-up tiny arteries (little strokes).

In 1931 my wife and I went to Europe and traveled through Ireland, England, France, Spain, Switzerland, Germany, and Austria. I had delightful visits with professors in Oxford and Cambridge, and one Sunday night I had dinner at "High Table" with the Dons at Kings College at Cambridge. We all met in a big room where each of us put on a cap and gown. Then we filed into a big hall and stood for a few minutes around the "High Table," which was on a floor perhaps 10 feet higher than the floor below, where the students dined. A student scuttled rapidly through a long grace in Latin, and then we sat down. Around me I found a number of famous professors whose names are known all over the world.

Later, in London, my wife and I had an interesting dinner with Dr. and Mrs. Ryle. He was a fine idealistic man—one of England's best internists and stomach specialists. He had his office on Wimpole Street, which is much like Harley Street— a row of ancient residences, each full of the offices of specialists. What surprised me was that about 8:30 P.M., after the last patient had left, a table was brought into the *waiting room* which was then converted into the *dining room!* Imagine such a thing happening in a big city in the United States!

While I was visiting with one of my good friends, a professor of comparative anatomy at Oxford, he told me that in his work he dissected animals that had died in the London Zoo. One day he got a message saying a lioness had died, and if he wanted the entrails, he should come and get them. So he picked up his specially-built suitcase, with its metal lining that could be screwed down until it was watertight, and left for the City.

Before returning home he checked the suitcase at a hotel, while he ran an errand for his wife. He then picked up the suitcase and took the train for home. On arriving, he ran up to his laboratory to leave the material in the refrigerator. When he opened the suitcase he was astonished to find that the baggage man had given him a case that looked like his, but wasn't; it contained the robes and regalia of a Grand Master of the Masons!

For several days my friend kept in touch with the baggage man, and watched the papers for a "personal," but the grand master never peeped; he was not going to go on trial in Old Bailey as a trunk murderer—not he! My friend said he would have given good money to have seen the face of the Grand Master as he opened that suitcase!

On our way through Ireland, just for fun, I climbed up onto the top of Blarney Castle, and with a man sitting on my legs, I leaned far out backward and kissed the Blarney Stone. I do not know yet if it improved the quality of my compliments, as it is said to do.

In Vienna I sat at luncheon with Franz Lehár, the composer of "The Merry Widow." He was then a striking-looking man with a head of thick gray hair. I was surprised to see how quiet he was and how little inclined to chat. My greatest joy in Vienna was to go to a Hungarian restaurant where the Gypsy music was delightful.

After returning from Europe I went down to Mexico to speak at a meeting of the Mexican Medical Association. The meeting was held in what was said to be the oldest university building in the New World. The next day a friend drove me over to Patzcuaro, perhaps the most deeply religious town in a deeply religious land.

There I had a touching experience. I was strolling through the market place; it was a "feast day" and on every side there were gaily decorated booths where little articles of native manufacture were offered for sale. Some of the booths were filled with the cheapest of toys; little carts made of baked clay, much like those that are found in Mesopotamia in the graves of little children who died 5,000 years ago.

Walking just ahead of me was a Mexican Indian, in his white cotton suit, his floppy straw hat, his colorful *serape* over his shoulder, and his straw sandals on his feet. Holding on to his left hand was the cutest little black-eyed girl about five years old. She kept saying in Spanish, "Papacito (dear little father) please won't you buy me one of those little clay carts: I want one so much," and each time the Indian would say so sadly, "Dear little darling of my heart, I can't buy one because I have 'ni un centavo'—not a cent of money."

On impulse, I reached up to the woman in the nearest booth; I gave her the needed 35 centavos, and got one of the little wagons. Then, walking up silently behind the child, I slipped the toy into her chubby little hand. She just grasped it without looking back to see whence it had come. The father also did not notice what had happened because at the moment he was looking in another direction. The two just walked silently on up the street.

Later that afternoon I heard people saying that a miracle had taken place that day in the holy city of Patzcuaro; a little Indian girl had prayed to the Blessed Virgin of Guadalupe for a clay cart, and behold, her prayer had been granted, and she had found the toy in her hand!

Through all my years at Mayo's I helped scores of young men to get their training in internal medicine. I did this usually in an informal way: perhaps just by showing an assistant how I would go at the problem of studying a particular patient; what tests I would order, and particularly—how I would take a long *history*, and then interpret it.

Some few of the more earnest students would ask if they might be in the room when I checked upon the history, or when I told the patient what had been found and what I thought he should do to get well. The best Fellows always, when a patient with an interesting problem was dismissed, went to the man's history sheets to see what their Chief had found that they had not found, and what he had disregarded— after they had thought it important.

My main difficulty in teaching the Fellows was to convince them that in many cases a psychic factor was far more important than was the gallstone, or nodule on the womb, or inguinal hernia that they had found.

I had the same trouble with patients. Many a highly nervous woman so ached and hurt all over that she could not believe that "it was all nerves." Her only reaction to my diagnosis was to say I had not made enough tests. She was sure more examinations would reveal some terrible disease, and so she left to go and find a doctor who would make more tests.

In trying to convince people that a neurosis can oftentimes hurt even more than a cancer does, I used to tell the true story of a farmer's wife and her daughter. The nice old mother of 65 had a big cancer in her stomach, but because she was an "insensitive person," she had no pain or indigestion. She said, "Don't bother with me; I'm not sick; it is my daughter here who is very ill." What was wrong with the daughter? On coming home from the town where she was teaching school, and hearing what had been found wrong with her adored mother, she had begun to vomit every meal. By the time I saw her, she was so worn out and dried out that I had to send her into a hospital for the intravenous injection of some fluid.

So there before me were two women: one with the worst possible disease of the stomach—and no symptoms; and the other with no disease in her abdomen but with very distressing symptoms. Cicero once said so truly that, "The sufferings of the mind are more severe than the pains of the body."

In hundreds of cases, no matter what localized disease I might find and remove from the body of a person born frail and "inadequate," I could not work a "cure." In this connection I will never forget the thin, sickly little minister who came to consult me because of general discomforts affecting his whole body. Significant was the fact that his "miseries" always hit him hardest Sunday night after the evening service in his little church. He would then be "all in" until Wednesday.

He insisted that if I would only examine him carefully enough I could find a local cause for this illness. Because, from the start, I had told him that he was primarily a frail person with an overly sensitive nervous system, when I found a small cancer growing in his rectum, he crowed over me! He said, "You see; I was right."

I told him we would, of course, remove the little tumor, but, much as I would love to cure him, I could not hope to do this with the little operation needed to rid him of the growth. It was "silent"—in other words, not producing any of his symptoms. When he left Rochester, he vowed to return some day and show me how wrong I was. Four years later he came back and said, "It is lucky for you I am a minister of God with a compulsion to tell the truth. I have to admit you were right, and the removal from my body of *even a cancer* left me just as frail, and sickly, and sensitive to emotion as ever I was."

Often when I see a neurotic and fussy woman with her symptoms all pointing to a constitutional frailness—but anxious to have a big operation performed for a silent diaphragmatic hernia, a silent gallstone, or a small silent "fibroid" of the womb—I remind her of what the wise old Chinese say, that "One should never call in a tiger to chase away a dog!"

I see many an unhappy woman whose main trouble seems to be that she is married to a man who, while he shows signs of being loving, never learned to love a woman in an "acceptable way"; he never learned to do the many kind and thoughtful little acts, or he never learned that little gifts—if they show thoughtfulness and a remembrance of the loved one's liking for certain things—mean much more than a very expensive gift that was not well chosen.

In this connection I like the story of the beautiful princess who was wooed by great kings. One brought her a dozen generals whom he had taken in battle, and she was not pleased. An Eastern Rajah brought her a trunk full of diamonds, rubies, and pearls—and she would not have him. And then a poor poet brought her a rose and a sweet tender note, and she loved him!

I remember the wife of a banker who was full of aches and pains for which I could find no physical cause. Then, as I so often have to do, I asked, "Why are you so sad?" And she said she thought her husband loved her, but he did it in ways that gave her no pleasure, and sometimes even annoyed her. For instance, after their marriage he left with a florist an order to send her a dozen red roses every Friday. She said, "Perhaps I am wrong to feel as I do, but now, after two years, every time those roses come I feel like screaming and throwing them at him. The trouble is that they bring me no feeling of a thought-taking affection on his part."

Another woman I knew became much annoyed at her husband because he would never say that he liked or disliked the way she dressed—when actually she dressed only to please him.

One evening when they were going out to dinner she came downstairs in her nightgown. The husband said, "My God, go take that off and get dressed properly." And she said, "Now that you have at last noticed what I am wearing, I shall go and get ready for dinner!"

Other wives tell me of their lack of pleasure when, for their birthday, their husband brings something *for the house,* or worse yet, something for his hobby! To show what I mean by acceptable loving, I remember the great pleasure a patient of mine felt when her husband found a piece of rare Meissen porcelain for which she had long been searching to fill a gap in her collection. He showed real love for her, first, in knowing what she wanted, and then in spending much time searching for it.

After I became well acquainted with the clinical pictures of many syndromes which I came to call "minor equivalents" of psychoses and epilepsy, I found it easy to make many a diagnosis which in my early days would have been an unsolvable puzzle. For instance: one day, in from Paris came a Latin American diplomat who said that on sitting down to a meal, he would go into a "tizzy" in which he would feel as if he were going to die; his pulse would race, he would perspire freely, and he would become nauseated; areas of goose-flesh would appear on his skin; he would tremble all over, and he would hurry to the toilet, fearing that his bowels were about to move.

Because I knew this story, having heard it several times before, I just asked the man who in his family had been mentally odd, and he said he had two close relatives in a mental hospital, two uncles so violent that they were afraid some day they would kill someone, and several "goofy" nieces. When I told him I was satisfied that his nervous storm was his small share of the family curse of jittery nerves, he said he could easily accept this idea because for long he had suspected that he had inherited some of his family's neuroticism. Today, with a much larger experience to draw upon, I would look for an element of epilepsy in this man's type of hot-tempered family; I would get electroencephalograms made, and I would probably find the erratic wave forms of epilepsy.

Another case in which my idea of equivalents led immediately to a diagnosis was that of a stoutish, fine-looking married woman of 45 who said that she had always been well except for her tendency to wake each morning with a most distressing type of fatigue—a feeling of inertia so awful that it made her dread to try to get up and face the day. Often she had to go back to bed. Fortunately, the distress always wore off toward the end of the afternoon, and it was all gone after supper. She had suffered from this type of fatigue for most of her life, and it wasn't from overwork because she had good servants.

I just asked, "Who in the family had melancholia?" And she answered, "My mother went insane when I was born, and has been in and out of depressions ever since." I then told the woman's family doctor that I could not prove it—and I probably could not convince him I was right—but I was satisfied, from much experience with many people suffering from this type of *morning* fatigue, that the woman's distress was her equivalent of her mother's depression. The finding of one or a dozen such cases would, of course, not prove anything, but my finding of scores of them in which the person had depressed relatives seemed to me to be significant enough.

Early in my medical life I became interested in these odd families in which one member was psychotic or at times insane, and other members had milder nervous or psychic troubles—which looked to me like "equivalents." In 1958 I described 673 of these troubled families in a book called *Practical Leads to Puzzling Diagnoses: Neuroses That Run Through Families* (Lippincott). I wish it could have had some influence on the thinking of American psychiatrists but I fear my thousands of collected *facts* were not interesting enough; sexual theories, like those of the Freudians, are so much more fun.

During the years from 1932 to 1946, I was so swamped with

practice that often I could not do much research, and this distressed me. But somehow or other I managed to keep working on a few problems, nearly always by myself. Now I find a record showing that in my 25 years at Mayo's, I wrote 347 articles, several books, several chapters in *Systems of Medicine*, and goodness knows how many lectures.

Some of my colleagues wondered why I was always so anxious to keep doing research; and even some of my close friends asked me why I didn't call quits and take it easy. All I could say was that I was happiest when doing research and writing it up, and so I guessed I would have to carry on as I was doing.

For four years I spent most of my spare time studying the more puzzling types of abdominal pain, together with the world's literature on the mechanisms by which abdominal pains are produced, and I wrote a series of articles based on what I had learned.

In November, 1934, I began to write the editorials for *The American Journal of Digestive Diseases*, and in 1938 I became its Editor. In 1941 I started editing the new journal *Gastroenterology*. Between 1934 and 1950 I wrote 329 editorials for these two journals.

Although it means hard work, I like writing editorials; it gives me the chance to call to the attention of many thousands of physicians those advances in medicine which I think at the time have outstanding value and significance.

For a year or more I was on the Governing Board of the Macy Foundation in New York. I was on it long enough to learn how extremely difficult it is to allocate moneys for the purposes of research, with any probability of getting some return on the investment. After seeing most of our grants wasted on applicants who had not previously done much work of value, I decided that the most logical thing to do would be to help only those men who had already done some excellent research, and who seemed to have opened up a good "lead" into a problem.

But even with them, nearly all of our money went down

the drain, and brought no results. Even a man like Sir Frederick Banting, after his great success with insulin, confessed sadly to me that he could not get going again, although for years he tried hard to find "the secretion of the adrenal glands."

Incidentally, I was asked to resign from the Macy Board because I objected to our wasting money on those surveys which are so dear to the hearts of many heads of Foundations, but the reports of which, so far as I can learn, are seldom read or studied or used by legislators.

Friends often ask me how I manage to keep getting so much work done, and I say the secret is to keep using those many scraps of time which most of us waste. Always, and particularly when traveling, I have a briefcase with me, and if I have to wait anywhere—even for a few minutes—out comes my work. Naturally, I get much done evenings, and on Saturday afternoons, Sundays, and holidays. I work seven days a week.

Some may say, "But what a dull and stupid life that must be!" Actually, it is a most interesting and satisfying life, because it is the one I like to live. Every so often I take a few days off for a little vacation, perhaps combined with a lecture somewhere. I imagine I inherited my love of work from a very active father and mother. Like my father, I could never just sit and rest. I have always marvelled at people who thoroughly enjoy loafing. It must be a hereditary gift!

In 1928 I published a much enlarged second edition of the *Mechanics of the Digestive Tract*, and in subsequent years I brought out the third and fourth editions which were big quartos with a new title: *An Introduction to Gastroenterology*. In 1947 I finished writing the last edition, and since then I have not done much reading in physiology. My interests changed. In 1930, I published *Nervous Indigestion*, and the edition sold right out. Thirteen years later, in 1943, I much enlarged the book and called it *Nervousness, Indigestion and Pain*. This quickly sold over 35,000 copies, and now, rewritten in simpler English, it is going between paper covers to thousands of lay people.

Much of what I got done through the years was done with dogged persistence. If a committee refused me permission to go on with a certain bit of research, or if they refused permission to publish my work, I immediately went at something else.

Along the way I learned never to be dismayed or diverted from my work by the receipt of a highly critical or perhaps abusive letter. To illustrate: in the beautiful medical museum which I started in Rochester, the Director, Dr. Arthur Bulbulian, put in a fine exhibit showing the progressive development in the womb of the human embryo and fetus. When a sex-hating old maid complained, accusing us of showing obscenities and corrupting the children of the land, Dr. W. J. Mayo was so upset he called me and told me to take the exhibit right out.

I said, "Of course, Dr. Will, I will do what you wish, but why should we be influenced by this one stupid woman and not by the thousands of fine mothers and schoolteachers who each year bring crowds of children to learn from this exhibit something of the origins of human life? Actually, this exhibit is one of the most popular in the whole museum." "You're right," said Dr. Mayo, "Disregard the letter." The exhibit remained in place, and I never heard of another complaint about it.

I learned another valuable lesson about critical letters when I was helping Dr. Bulbulian to build the Mayo Clinic's exhibit at the World's Fair in Chicago. One day my merry friend, Professor Eben J. Carey, the physician in charge of building all of the medical exhibits, came to me much perturbed by a most unpleasant letter he had just received from an official of his school, scolding him for having permitted the showing of a collection of human fetuses—which actually was the most popular exhibit in the whole scientific division of the Fair. As Dr. Carey said to me, "I cannot understand why Bill wrote me that awful letter, because we are old and good friends."

The next time I saw Dr. Carey, he was happy, and said,

"Oh, that was all right; my friend had forgotten to tell me that he wrote that letter only so that he could give a copy to the bishop; and the bishop wanted it only to show devout church members that he had already protested against 'the outrage.'"

Many a time since then, when I have received a letter of bitter criticism from some pious woman objecting to perhaps a few words on sex in one of my newspaper columns, I have just chuckled and said to my secretary, "There's a letter that was written for the bishop!"

In the Mayo Clinic one of the things I used to try to teach my assistants was that on those rare occasions when one of them got embroiled with some testy or "difficult" or somewhat psychotic patient, it was because he had taken a dislike to the man or woman, and had shown it. Usually when I went in to calm down and appease the person, I found a good soul who was frightened, or felt he hadn't been treated nicely. All I had to do was to show that I liked him (her); to apologize, and then to see that the person got the best of care, and kindly treatment. Many of those supposedly "ornery" persons whom I saw a third of a century ago are still writing me a sweet note every Christmas; we have been good friends for all these many years.

I have always felt that to the three little Japanese monkeys who "see no evil, hear no evil and speak no evil" there should be added a fourth—the most important one—who will "*think no evil*." When I think no evil of a patient, and especially when I "take a shine to him" he usually likes me. Many a time I have gotten along beautifully, even with a psychotic patient, because I have talked to him much as I would have talked to a loved brother or an old friend. I have gotten along even with paranoiacs by never questioning the fact that they had noted something that had alarmed them; all I suggested was that I, who am not easily alarmed, would probably not have interpreted what they saw or heard as a threat to my safety.

Very satisfying was my experience with the many patients whose life-stories cheered me and warmed my heart—because they showed me what a strong love can make some people do. For instance: I have always admired the understanding and loving kindness of a certain ranch woman who, on discovering that her husband's "business trips" to the city were really dipsomanic debauches, or "lost week-ends," decided to go with him and take care of him. Because she saw so clearly that what he had was a form of mental disease, instead of blaming him and scolding him, she just went along and sat in his hotel room for several days, reading and knitting, while he lay on the bed, dead drunk. Later, when he would come out of his spell, they would quietly go back to the ranch and take up their usual way of life again.

Occasionally at Mayo's the behavior of a patient would give us a good laugh. One day I came into my room to find sitting there a bright, interesting, and sensitive young woman who was training to be an opera singer. What had impressed my tall handsome young assistant was the fact that whenever he took her pulse it jumped to 130 beats a minute. When I took it, I was amused to find that I could push it up only to 110 beats. When I told the singer what was happening, and remarked that obviously I was no longer the man I once had been, she rocked with laughter, and we were all much amused.

I regret that at Mayo's I never had a chance to bring up a group of disciples to carry on my work. My associates felt it was unwise to permit anyone in the place to build up a personal following. Especially at the end of World War II, I greatly regretted this policy when a dozen young ex-medical officers wrote saying they would like to come and spend a year or two studying with me, and I had to refuse them. There was no way in which I could put them to work.

In my last few years at the clinic I was fortunate in being excused—to a large extent—from seeing patients. Each morning I greeted all of the people who had come asking for me, and quickly referred each one to the specialist best prepared to take care of his problem. This left me with time to continue my research and writing.

My saddest day at the Mayo Clinic came in 1950 when I took off of a library shelf the volume of Osler's great lectures entitled *Aequanimitas*, which for a lifetime has had such a tremendous influence on my thinking, and my idealism, and my philosophy. Imagine my distress when I found that the pages *were not cut*; that in 46 years *no one* at Mayo's had looked into this book! And let us remember that the hundreds of graduate students who were constantly in residence were the "cream of the crop" of our best medical schools.

8

The Doctors Mayo

I ALWAYS ADMIRED Dr. Will Mayo. I had such respect for him that often when I met him on the street my hat was off before I realized what I was doing. He had a distinguished face with piercing eyes and the glance of a man with an iron will. As I looked at him I always had the feeling that he would have been a great leader in any business. There was goodness and honesty and often kindliness in his face; also great purpose and great dignity. There was so much dignity that not even eminent friends in the field of surgery thought of calling him by his first name or reaching out to touch him.

With one look he would seem to see into a man's soul, and to ascertain all he needed to know about him.

He was of medium height, but strongly built as became a man who in college had been a champion boxer. He always stood straight as a soldier, and until the end of his days he walked rapidly with a firm step. He always spoke well and convincingly.

I never ceased wondering how, when he first met me, he

knew instantly that he could tell me anything and I would keep it secret as long as he lived. In fact, some of the things he told me I do not feel I should reveal, even today, 24 years after his death. As early as the first week or two after I arrived in Rochester, he told me of his concern over the unwise behavior of three members of the Staff, and a little later he even asked my advice about possibly dismissing one or two of them. Imagine what a storm would have been kicked up in the Clinic if I had ever said a word about this! And I hadn't been around the place more than a few days before Dr. Will asked my advice in regard to a successor to a prominent member of the Staff who was retiring. When I suggested a certain man, Dr. Will said, "Send for him."

I marvelled at the quickness with which Dr. Will would make an important decision. One day, around 1932, when I suggested to him that we build a medical museum to house the many fine exhibits we constantly made for big meetings, he instantly said, "A good idea. Take the old school building across the way. Phone our architects in Minneapolis right now, and go to work tomorrow!"

And I did. It was typical of Dr. Will that that afternoon and the next morning he kept telephoning every two hours to make sure I had gotten the project started.

Dr. Will was the only man I ever stood in awe of, and yet he was easily approachable and very democratic. There were no secretaries sitting outside his office to keep people away. In the early days, when I was on an auto trip with him, and we had luncheon, his chauffeur would sit at the table with Dr. and Mrs. Mayo and their guests. In the Clinic anyone could come up to talk to Dr. Will, and often he would say to the assistant with him, "See that this person gets into the hands of 'so-and-so' "—the specialist that could best take care of the man's problem.

Dr. Will was always very kind to me, sometimes as kind as a father. He was always very appreciative whenever some little honor came to me. He would either send me a kind note, or he would come hurrying up to me in the hall to tell me how pleased he was. Often, to my great surprise, I found that he had read some paper I had written. I never could understand how he found the time to keep in such close touch with what those of us on the staff were doing.

Curiously, Dr. Will was once a bit apologetic to me, apparently fearing that I might think him lazy! When one day, on his big 100-foot Diesel cruiser on the Mississippi River, I came on deck and found him sitting, staring into the water, he said, "I think I am behaving wisely—sitting here, just thinking, because I am figuring how I can strengthen certain weak sections of the Clinic, and wondering how I can improve our public relations with the medical profession. I think I am of more use here, thinking and planning, than I would be at Rochester, operating." And I heartily agreed with him.

I always marvelled at the amount of reading he did. If he liked a book very much he marked it with an A, and it remained in his library. If he liked it but did not want to keep it, it was marked B, and given to one of his daughters. But if it was marked with a C, it went "out."

It was remarkable how closely he kept in touch with what was going on in the Clinic, and throughout the country. He could get by with only four hours of sleep a night. He said that the remainder of the night he just lay quietly and rested and thought. When out to a dinner, he always went home at 9 P.M., if only because next morning at eight he would be operating. He always took a brief nap after luncheon. He would lie back in a chair or on his bed and immediately get 20 minutes of sleep that would keep him going well all afternoon. In spite of all the terrible pressures on him, every day he kept his appointments—right to the minute. I never saw him drink hard liquor, and I never saw him smoke.

Occasionally he gave me a glimpse that showed that the strain of running the Clinic was heavy upon him. He admitted to me that he found it a very lonely job. He explained once how he could not have intimates among the Clinic men without making it seem possible, when a dispute arose, that his decision had been influenced by favoritism. I reminded him of the great Pharaoh Amenemhet, who, when turning over the government of Egypt to his son, Sesostris, warned him that a man in a position of power must live and work in loneliness. As the old King said,

> Fill not thy heart with a brother,
> Know not a friend,
> Nor make for thyself intimates.

This sort of reserve is good for a top executive, and it can be good also for the men working under him. I was surprised one day when one of my best friends among the older Clinic members said to me, "You be glad that Dr. Will does not show you any particular favor; if he ever were to start doing that you would surely get into trouble around here!" Then my friend went on to say that Dr. Will did not yet realize that unwittingly he was making it unpleasant for his sons-in-law and one of his nephews by constantly trying to push them forward into places of preferment. Later Dr. Will admitted to me that he was beginning to see that by this action he was embarrassing and hurting the men whom he had most wanted to help. But along with this he admitted that in the early days he had had some idea of founding a dynasty that would carry on the leadership of the Clinic.

He told me how hard it was on him, on rare occasions when he had to dismiss someone from the Clinic. He confessed that at such times he would leave town for a while until the storm had blown over. One of the oldest members of the staff told me that, in the early days, if a Clinic man was misbehaving, Dr. Will would call him in and give him a stiff talking-to. But in my day he used a special technique for admonishing a man without causing him to lose face or to have to remember a painful interview. Dr. Will would send the man's best friend to him to say something like, "I just saw the Old Man and I judged from what he said that he'd be much happier if you would do thus and so (or would stop doing something or other)." I know that when, in 1927, Dr. Will decided that I must spend my afternoons seeing patients instead of doing research, he did not say anything to me. He sent my best friend Dr. Leonard Rowntree, who said "Walter, I just saw Dr. Will, and you take my advice—you do right now what Dr. Will wants you to do." And I did it.

Only a few of the oldest members ever called him "Will." The rest of us called him "Dr. Will," much as in Spain a prominent man is called Don Luis or Don José. Once he remarked to an intimate that he would like to have more people call him Will, and another time when he saw an old friend put his arm around Dr. Charlie's shoulders, Dr. Will said, "No one ever did that to me." But then, he added, "If anybody did, I don't suppose I'd like it."

Dr. Will must have been one of the country's best executives, because he built the world's greatest Clinic so quickly. When choosing new staff members, he had an uncanny skill. Only rarely did he pick an unsuitable man and then usually it was due to bad advice with a touch of nepotism.

One of the many things I liked about Dr. Will was his fondness for giving a man a kindly pat on the back when he had done a fine piece of work. He was big enough to give a man credit and to do it generously, and while the man was still living! He would say, "An ounce of taffy is worth a pound of epitaphy."

No one of us is perfect, however, and sometimes I saw Dr. Will do things which seemed to me to be unwise. For instance, he told me he believed in "throwing a new man into a department" without first discussing the matter with the head of that department. I remember a day when he telephoned Dr. Hugh Cabot and invited him to join the kidney and bladder division of the Clinic. How strange it was that Dr. Braasch, who for years had been head of that section, was not consulted in the matter, and was not even told that the new man was coming!

Naturally, such behavior on Dr. Will's part was disturbing

to many of the men on the staff, and this made it extra rough on the new man coming in. Sometimes, when his welcome was not warm, the man would wish that Dr. Will would say a few words in his behalf. But Dr. Will told me he would never openly help a newcomer. He would say that if the new man succeeded in holding his own and perhaps fighting his way to the top, all well and good: he would have justified Dr. Will's faith in him. If he went under, that was just too bad, and he could leave.

I have known other top administrators who, like Dr. Will, would not say a word to help a man who was having serious troubles with his associates—men who had never desired his entrance into their department. Such behavior on the part of a top executive has always saddened me, especially when it has led to the expulsion from the group of one of their ablest men. I can see, however, that an administrator does not care to reprove a pack of small men who are trying to pull down a big man. The Chief knows that he has to keep the peace with the members of his group, and hence, often, he allows his ablest man to be harrassed, blocked, and perhaps driven out of the university, or company, or clinic. I have seen it done many times and in many places.

Dr. Will might not come openly to the rescue of a man in trouble, but he might call him to his office for a few words of cheer. Thus, when in 1927 it came to Dr. Will's attention that I had become fed up with some of the opposition that had arisen against me and my work, and I was thinking seriously of leaving, he sent for me and was kindness itself. He said, "Haven't you learned yet that if a man ever does anything unusual, or fine, or worthwhile, or if mentally or spiritually he raises his head up above the level of the crowd, a few men are surely going to take a crack at it? That is human nature. *It has always been that way in the past, and it will always be that way in the future.* Hence it is that, early in life, every hard-driving man like you should learn to take such attacks in his stride. Don't be bothered or upset. Just continue on your way, satisfied that what you are doing is right.

"Actually," he went on, "when I throw a new man into a section, hoping thereby to put a more vigorous life into it, to give it a better national standing, or to get more research out of it, if within a couple of months some of the men in that group do not come running to me to say, 'Stop him, it looks as if he is going to take over my job and add it to his,' I know I have made a mistake, and have put in the wrong man.

"The thing you must do now is to go out and grow a thick skin. God knows I had to do that once. When Charlie and I proposed to give $1,500,000 to the University of Minnesota for a Foundation, a number of the most prominent doctors in the State—men who we had always thought were our friends—went into the Legislature and fought us bitterly, try-ing to have the gift refused. No, this little ruckus you have run into just proves to me that you are 'stirring the pool,' and that is what I brought you here to do."

Dr. Will was wise enough to know that he could not hope to change human nature. Dr. Tom Dooley once said that if a man is going to be a good, able, and strong commander, he must expect to end up disliked by many of the men under him; that is a price he must pay for being a good leader. Benjamin Franklin, who knew well the jealousies that are stirred up against any man who accomplishes much, and then gets much praise for it, said wisely, "It is wonderful how much good a man can do in a community if he will only let someone else take all the credit for it!"

Only on a few rare occasions did I ever hear Dr. Will express contempt for any man, and then always it was because he had discovered that the man was not honest or loyal. Once when talking to me about the aged Sir Arbuthnot Lane, who was then saying many silly things about medicine, Dr. Will said, "Perhaps he is like some people who, having once basked in the limelight, when it moves away will do crazy things to get it back."

Some of the men in the Clinic thought that Dr. Will was sometimes too much of a dictator, but I greatly sympathized with him in his dislike of arguing at length about some inconsequential matter, or of waiting for one or two committees to pass upon it. He liked to get from someone the essential facts about a problem, and then to give a quick decision.

Twice Dr. Will remarked to me that as he grew older he had less and less stomach for fighting, and he got to craving peace, which did not always come easily. I marvelled that many of the doctors on the Staff would run to him and demand that someone be stopped from doing something or other. It never would have occurred to me to do such a thing. One day I remarked to one of my associates that I had invited my dear friend Professor Alfred Barclay of Cambridge University, one of the great research men of England, to come over for a visit and to use my X-ray movie machine for some researches he wanted to carry out. The next day my associate confessed to me that he had run to Dr. Will to protest strongly against Barclay's coming. He said he feared Barclay would overshadow him!

Dr. Will more than once told me how tired he was of being pulled this way and that by people. Perhaps because of this distaste for wrangling which developed as he grew older, he got into some difficulties. First, he would leave orders that some man's department be incorporated in another "section." Then, when the offended man ran to him to protest, Dr. Will would get kind-hearted, and would say, "All right, carry on as you were doing." But this was bad because it stirred up enmities in the place.

At times in his later years Dr. Will would vacillate in this way with me, or perhaps he would just forget what he had said. One day he would assure me in the most kindly tone that I could do any type of work I wanted. But a few weeks later he would say, "Stop your physiologic researches and your statistical work. Others can do that. You concentrate on getting the Fellows to do research." This sort of contradictory advice caused a number of the research-minded men in the place to feel very uneasy and insecure.

Dr. Will was one of the kindest men I knew. When one of the Clinic men lost his health so completely that he could never work again, Dr. Will saw to it that the mortgage on his house was paid. When another man died in his early fifties, leaving his finances in bad shape, Dr. Will ordered that his widow be cared for and his children's college education be provided for. One day as Dr. Will was going into the bank, he saw a young man coming out of the president's office looking very discouraged and sad. Dr. Will asked the president, "What's the matter with our friend who just went out?" And the banker said, "He wanted me to lend him a lot of money to buy a hotel, but he has no security."

Dr. Will said, "Look, I am constantly going in and out of that hotel, day and night, and always I find that man taking the kindest care of his guests. A man who works that hard and with that friendliness cannot lose. So, make out a note for what he needs, and I'll sign it." And Dr. Will was absolutely right. The man went ahead and succeeded eminently.

To show how quickly Dr. Will could make a decision: one night, when on his way to Australia, he stopped in Seattle long enough to attend a banquet given in his honor. When at this dinner he heard a man nearby talking about research in anesthesia, he pricked up his ears, because for some time he had much wanted to improve the practice of anesthesia in the Clinic. After the banquet, he chatted for 15 minutes with the young man who had been talking so intelligently, and wound up by inviting him to go to Rochester. And that is how John Lundy came to be one of the great anesthetists of the world.

Another instantaneous decision was made when Dr. Adson was chosen to be the first brain surgeon at the Clinic. "Ad" once told me how, one evening, after having had an unpleasant disagreement with the surgeon he had been assisting, and having been fired, Dr. Will asked him, "Is there any job around here that you would like to have?" And Adson said, "Yes, you much need a brain surgeon, and I would like to have the job." "All right," said Dr. Will, "here is a card to Dr. Charles H. Frazier" (then perhaps the country's greatest brain surgeon). "Also, here is a note to Mr. Harwick, telling him to supply you with whatever expense money you need until you are done with your period of training, and ready to come back here to go to work."

Another time, in London, Dr. Will heard of Dr. (now Sir) James Learmonth and his desire to be a brain surgeon. Dr. Will called Learmonth (in Scotland) and invited the doctor to come to the Clinic and get the training he wanted.

Once, when some of my friends were chiding me for writing about food allergy—a disease which they were sure was only "in people's heads"—Dr. Will came to my rescue. He came hurrying up to me in the hall to tell me that he had loved a recent article of mine on the subject. He said, "Keep writing about that disease because as yet the medical profession does not recognize it." Then he told me that he was so very sensitive to even a minute amount of cottonseed oil that he never dared eat out unless his own cook had prepared the meal.

But even with all the precautions that he took, at times he would get a violent gastrointestinal upset. Once Mrs. Mayo talked him into attending the annual (Congregational) church supper. As she said, she would be in the kitchen and would see to it that no cottonseed oil was used. But that night at ten o'clock, Dr. Will started to retch. Then Mrs. Mayo, much distressed, remembered that the ladies had bought Parker House rolls from a baker, and the bottom of the pan must have been greased with cottonseed oil!

Later, Dr. Will got "caught" while visiting in the winter apartment of one of his daughters. When he started to retch, the only articles of food that could conceivably be incriminated were some dates. But, as Dr. Will said, he had never had any trouble with dates. The next day he went to the market where he had bought the dates and asked the man if, in any way, they could have come in contact with cottonseed oil. "Why, yes," said the man. "People like them shiny, and so we go over them with an oily rag!"

An example of Dr. Will's thinking was revealed to me shortly after I started work at the Clinic. Perhaps three weeks after I had arrived he called me to his office.

"You still must have some strong impressions about this place. What things do you think are very wrong with the Clinic? Where are we weak?"

I said that my first surprise was that, with psychosis the commonest disease in the world, the Clinic had no department of psychiatry.

Dr. Will said, "Yes, that is a grave defect, but I have always been afraid of putting in such a department because it might get so big as to be unwieldy and perhaps too costly. Also, I am afraid that if I employ a number of psychiatrists, you internists may want to send all your 'neuros' to them. Obviously, you cannot do that. Every one of you in every specialty must take care of your own nervous patients." And I agreed that this would always have to be so.

I told Dr. Will that another department we could not much longer do without was one of statistics. All of our millions of data should be put onto punch cards—which could then be run rapidly through IBM machines. Dr. Will agreed that there was a need for this, but he warned me that most of the old-timers around the place, who were not research-minded, distrusted, disliked, and even hated statisticians. If we were to employ one, he would have to be only a "hired man" who would never be allowed to do more than get out figures for use by some Staff member who planned to write a paper.

Later, I got Dr. Henry Plummer interested in the project, and eventually he wangled the necessary appropriation for a fine statistical department.

But even Henry Plummer was hostile to the idea of turning a statistician loose in the place. My friends in the Clinic, from

Dr. Will down, warned me never to make any statistical studies myself. They assured me that any such work would get me into hot water. I didn't take their advice, so I got into hot water all right! I felt then like reminding Dr. Will that in 1900, the father of statistics, the great Karl Pearson of the Galton Laboratory of London, was warned by the Council of the Royal Society to keep his mathematical methods of analysis out of the field of Biology—or else! As a result, he had to found his own journal *Biometrika*, in which to publish the many papers that came out of his busy laboratory.

But I must emphasize the fact that I encountered this distrust of statistics some 36 years ago, when the science was new and when the old-timers around the place (now all gone to their reward) were men who in their college days had had no training in scientific research, and hence had little if any interest in it. Naturally, many of them had that dread of new things which most of us human beings always have. This sort of resistance was not limited to the Mayo Clinic. Almost everywhere I went—into many a great hospital or university Clinic —I found the older surgeons fearful of letting anyone check up to see what had been the actual results of their operations— particularly on the stomach. They seemed to dread what a statistician's "follow-up" studies might show.

I tried to show some of these surgeons—friends of mine working here and there throughout the country—that by holding back all information they were not fooling anyone. We internists knew approximately what their results were, and we did not like them. By keeping silent and by insisting that we clinicians keep silent, the surgeons were doing only one thing, and that was to destroy men's faith in them and their work. In those days about the only surgeon who would agree with me on this was my good friend Dr. Frank Lahey of the great Lahey Clinic in Boston.

In 1920, Dr. Will Mayo, having realized at last that the Clinic, which had started almost entirely as a surgical partnership, had grown so big that it had to have an adequate group of medical sections, brought in Dr. Leonard Rowntree, an able organizer, who had been professor of medicine in the University of Minnesota. By the time I arrived in Rochester, Dr. Rowntree had done a splendid job, and had brought into the Clinic many top-flight men. Rowntree soon built laboratories in a wing of St. Mary's Hospital, where he grouped about him a number of able young investigators. After a few years these men were heading departments in the Clinic—men like George Brown, E. V. Allen, and Philip Hench.

The coming of the new men into the place caused tensions to build up, particularly in the hearts of some of the old-timers who had never done much writing or lecturing. With some justification, a number of them felt that they had been so swamped with clinical work they had never had the time. It was easy for one of these older men to talk himself into believing that the newcomers were "taking his records and using them for the writing of such papers as eventually he would have written."

As might have been expected, when the new men came in, and with their researching and writing and lecturing, began to get much publicity, an old-timer might feel that the young men were constantly going to meetings, and leaving him to see the patients and make the money for the Clinic. As a result, he felt that the researchers were costly parasites who were taking money that should be staying in his pocket.

Naturally, this smouldering resentment of the old-timers against the new-comers flared up and became alarming when, after the crash of 1929, many people could not afford to travel to the Clinic or to pay their bill if they got there. With the drawing-in of our financial belts, the rumor spread through the place that there was to be no more research in Rochester. Worse yet, Dr. Will ordered the closing of the laboratories in St. Mary's Hospital.

Dr. Rowntree, who at that time was my closest friend, was outraged over this move, and he just could not accept Dr.

Will's idea that it was necessary. As Leonard told me, he was particularly angry because Dr. Will had made the big change without adequately discussing the subject with either him or with me, or with the other men who worked in those laboratories.

Dr. Rowntree was so distressed over the matter that his health failed, and he spent much of the next year in Arizona, trying to get rid of an acute arthritis. He felt so sure that his work at the Mayo Clinic had come to an end that he left and went to Philadelphia.

Several of the rest of us who had lost our laboratories at St. Mary's—and were unable to get any assurance that when the Depression was over our facilities for research would be returned to us—kept looking for some place to which we could go.

During much of this time Dr. Will added greatly to our mental distress by refusing to discuss our problems with us. My impression was strong that in the crisis he did not dare come out in favor of either the researchers or the old-timers. Though usually he did what he pleased around the place, this time he seemed to be afraid of the power of the men who openly said before me that research was a luxury which they no longer cared to pay for.

One day Dr. Will opened up and said to me that he was very tired of all the arguing and fighting. He said, "I am getting old. I want peace, and you researchers cannot expect me to do all your fighting for you." I doubted then if he was sure which group in the Clinic was going to win out.

Another day Dr. Will told me, frankly, that besides the need for cutting down on expenses, there was another great need he saw for closing the laboratories at St. Mary's. He said he had discovered that if men in an organization are to work happily together they must be under one roof, or on one campus. Put them under two roofs or on two campuses, and they will get to fighting one another. I knew he was right because I had observed the phenomenon in some medical schools.

What I greatly regretted was that Dr. Will had not told me this at the beginning. Then I would cheerfully have given up my laboratory and I would have helped him by trying to get all of my research-minded friends to accept the situation without so much bitterness and fear for the future. Dr. Will could have greatly helped the situation also by saying to us that in order for the Clinic to keep growing in usefulness to the country, and in order to keep its good reputation, the members would have to go on doing good research. As I said to Dr. Will, "We never could *afford* to stop doing research. If we did, we would become a purely commercial 'outfit.' "

But for some unknown reason Dr. Will remained silent, and I cannot remember when during this trying period he ever said an encouraging word to us researchers. Eventually, of course, as prosperity came back to the country and the Clinic, the researchers came back into favor, and later a huge research department became well housed.

Incidentally, this type of internal conflict, during the lean years of the "Depression" of 1929, was not limited to the Mayo Clinic. I heard of several clinics which were nearly pulled in two by conflicts like ours, and I remember one clinic in which the group fell apart so completely that they lost the fine building on which they had only a small mortgage left yet to pay.

When Dr. Will would ask me, as he occasionally did, to spend much of my time stirring up my associates to do research, I told him I would like to please him, but after years of watching many men failing to do worthwhile investigative work, I was convinced that good research is done only by the occasional man who was born with a gift for it—perhaps with a great curiosity, great powers of observation, great honesty, and a great ability to reason his way to a conclusion.

Hence I had no desire to talk *just anyone* into going through the motions of doing what looked like research. Many men, being unable to think of any important question to put to Nature, ask a stupid or a silly one. I heard once of a man who,

to get a Ph.D. degree, stood under the stairs of an elevated rail-
way and recorded the percentage of women who wore panties!

Many a man can never do even clinical research work, or
even make difficult diagnoses, because he has no curiosity—it
does not occur to him to follow up leads, and to ask questions.
To illustrate: one day an assistant told me that all that was
wrong with the handsome unmarried woman of 50 who was
sitting in my office was that she had some gallstones. With a
few questions, I learned that these stones had never bothered
her; they had never produced any indigestion or abdominal
soreness or even one single colic. Obviously, they were not the
cause of her troubles.

On looking over her written history, I saw my Fellow's note:
"When she was 18 she had a nervous breakdown." That was
all. Evidently, the Fellow had had no interest to go on and find
out *why* she had had the breakdown, or what it was like. After
I had suggested to him that he kindly leave us alone a few
minutes, I asked the sad-looking woman what had caused that
early breakdown. She said it was the discovery that she was so
decidedly homosexual that she could never hope to have a
beau, a husband, a home, or a child. The shock of this had
almost unseated her reason. This information immediately led
me to get her admission that it was the recent break-up of her
long-lasting Lesbian attachment to a woman that had produced the depression which was then causing all of her distressing symptoms.

On a few occasions, Dr. Will discussed with me the des-
perate efforts he was having to make to keep journalists and
science-writers from writing up the Clinic. He knew so well
that if such an article were published, hundreds of doctors
throughout the country would jump to the conclusion that we
had paid for the "advertisement." Dr. Will would try to get
the editor of the journal to see how much bitterness any
article he might publish would stir up against us. To show how
much conditions have changed in the last 30 years, I need
only remark that recently when Victor Cohn wrote a series

of excellent articles on the Clinic, I heard no growls from anyone.

I regarded Dr. Will with such respect and even reverence that I rarely felt I had a right to disagree with him. One point on which I did disagree was his failure ever to discuss the grave shortcomings of the several operations for peptic ulcer. My hunch was that Dr. Will had done so much to perfect and popularize the operation of gastroenterostomy (in which a new opening is made between the stomach and the bowel), that in a way, it was a favorite child. As we all know, many a parent just cannot see that from the point of view of the neighbors, his little darling is a brat. Now that I think of it, it seems remarkable to me that, as close as Dr. Will and I often were— I, revering him, and he being very kind to me—we just never did say a word about the subject of the surgical treatment of ulcers. I guess we each sensed how the other felt, and we each knew that we could never agree, and so we never discussed the problem.

I was surprised and pleased when one day Dr. Will told me how enthusiastic he was about an article I had written on a simple and economical nonsurgical treatment for duodenal ulcer—with the patient up and about and doing his work. For years, every medical man was supposed to do as Dr. Bertram Sippy for so long had taught: to put every ulcer patient in the hospital for a month. So far as I can remember, I was the first man to come out and say frankly that since more than half of the patients so treated would soon have a flare-up of their old ulcer symptoms, why should we put them to such great expense? Why not let them stay on their job, taking the extra food between meals that would keep most of them comfortable?

After Dr. Will read my paper, he said to me, "Many men in medicine fail for lack of a social sense. They do not think of trying to save the patient heavy expense. I see from this article of yours that you have plenty of social sense, and I like that."

One highly significant fact that shows how the physicians

and surgeons in Rochester really felt about the operations for duodenal ulcer was that in all my 25 years at the Mayo Clinic I can remember only one of the many members of the Staff with an ulcer who was operated on, and he was driven to it late in life by a complication.

One of the things which made the Mayo Clinic possible was Dr. Will's good sense in never interfering in the personal lives of his men. He had some few on the Staff who were very "good" and very religious, and he had others who never went to church. He had men who were excellent husbands, and he had a few who were involved in scandals. He had some who were teetotalers, and some who spent every evening drinking. I admired him much because he did not expect all of us, when off duty, to be angels instead of men.

Sometimes, also, when he probably disagreed with what one of us was saying in public, and even when doctors were writing in to demand that the speaker against the party line be muzzled, or squelched, or fired, Dr. Will would not interfere with the man's freedom of speech. But I strongly suspect he would have been much happier if the man had first asked if he might take a certain stand, or make a certain statement that would cause the Clinic to be attacked by physicians.

We all know the old saw that no man is a hero to his valet. But Dr. Will was so fine that Louie West, his old chauffeur, once told me that in all his years of traveling around the country with his Chief, he never had had from him an impatient word. Also, Dr. Will's able secretary of many years, Mrs. Nora Guthrie, recently told me that the longer she worked for Dr. Will the more she admired him. She and Mrs. Mellish, our chief Editor for several years, were two people around the place who had the strength of character sometimes to say to Dr. Will, "You should not do that."

Dr. Will was a great man and I am the better for having known him. Like all great men, he had a few failings and he made a few mistakes. What was very remarkable was that he could confess to some of these.

That Dr. Will was the "Boss" around the place was evident when occasionally he would reverse a decision of the Board of Governors without bothering even to notify them that he had changed his mind. A few times during the years when a man on the Staff kept rocking the boat, Dr. Will would go ahead, apparently on his own, to dismiss the fellow. He would call the man in and say, "I have an idea that you would be happier working alone by yourself," and that would be that.

These difficult decisions he would make apparently without worrying about what the Board of Governors, or the men on the Staff, would think or say. But when it came to certain matters on which the old-timers felt strongly, Dr. Will seemed to spend much time feeling his way. Even an autocrat knows that he had better keep the peace with that faction in his organization that contains the greatest number of politically-minded men who will vote together.

That the Chief realized the limitations of even his great power around the place became evident to me when once I said, "Dr. Will, can anyone today justify the putting of carbolic acid on the stump of the amputated appendix, and then alcohol? Isn't that a sheer waste of time?" "Yes," said Dr. Will, "it is a silly relic of our ignorance of 40 years ago." I asked, "Why, then, don't you tell the surgeons here to stop doing it?" "No," he replied, "I would not even try. I couldn't stop the practice."

Another time I asked Dr. Will, "Why, when we give a hypodermic injection, do we dab the skin with alcohol? We all know that in a moment it cannot kill any germs: all it does is to waste a gauze sponge and some alcohol." "You are perfectly right," said Dr. Will; "But you try to stop the practice"; and I had to admit that it will probably never be stopped.

On another occasion I said to Dr. Will, "Isn't it awful that the nurses wake a terribly tired postoperative patient at five A.M. to wash her face, at six to take her temperature, and at seven to give her her breakfast. How much better if the poor soul were allowed to get some much-needed sleep." "Yes," said Dr. Will; "This early waking of people is a barbarous, heartless, and senseless practice, but, again, you just try to stop it!" Apparently, someone did stop it because when in 1960 I was operated on in the Methodist Hospital, the nurses let me sleep until seven or eight when I woke.

Once I was talking to Dr. Will about the demand that most people make that *something* be done for a loved relative with scattered cancer. They keep saying, "*Well, do something.*" Dr. Will said, "Yes; it reminds me of a day in the St. Lawrence River when a little French steamer broke away from a tug and started to swirl around and to bear down on some rocks. The captain yelled at the mate, 'Throw overboard the anchor'; and the mate answered, 'It's no good. It's come loose from the chain.' 'Well,' said the captain in his desperation, 'Throw it overboard anyway—*maybe it will help some.*'"

I remember standing on the sidewalk outside the Clinic chatting with Dr. Will, when a "gabby" chap limped up and greeted my Chief with great effusiveness. As the man left, Dr. Will said, "Thirty years ago, when I was young and eager to tackle problems, that man wanted me to try to re-make his undeveloped hip-joint. At first I intended to tackle the job, but then, as I came to know the man and his loquacity, I said to myself, 'If, as is quite possible, I fail to get a good result, that fellow will spend the rest of his days saying to everyone in Southern Minnesota, "See that bum hip; Dr. Mayo done that."' So I let some other surgeons have the job, and you can see how well they succeeded."

Dr. Will went on to say that sometimes, after years of work in the Clinic operating rooms, a young surgeon has left Rochester well trained technically, but because in his first location he started operating on persons whom the wise local surgeons had had sense enough to leave alone, he soon acquired such a bad reputation for failures and deaths that he almost had to leave town. In one case he *did* leave town. I used to wish, as

did Dr. Will, that we could hammer into the heads of all our
students the fact that there is much more to surgery than a
brilliant operative technique. A fine surgeon will know when
not to operate, and then, if he has great honesty and devotion
to the best interests of his patients, he will not operate. He
won't operate even when he knows that his "knife-happy"
competitor next door will soon take on the job.

Dr. Will could be a clever internist if he wanted to be. He
told me how once when he was on a vacation in Miami, a
millionaire there kept insisting that he come and treat him for
an attack of painful palpitation that woke him every night at
3 A.M. and scared the life out of him. No one had been able
to help the fellow. Dr. Will kept refusing to prescribe, saying
he was a surgeon and on vacation. But finally, to get rid of
the man's importunities, he gave him a powerful barbiturate
and said, "Set your alarm for 2 A.M.; take this medicine, and
then go back to sleep." The man did as he was told; by 3 A.M.
he was sleeping so soundly he did not wake, and that was the
end of his "heart disease"!

Typical of Dr. Will's ability was the way in which he once
saved the life of a bullfighter who had been gored in the ring
and was rapidly bleeding to death. The bull's horn had entered
the front of the man's thigh and had gone up under his skin
to the groin, where it had torn a hole in the big artery which
supplies the limb. When the doctor on duty in the operating
room under the bull ring could not find the artery to clamp it,
he begged Dr. Will (who had been taken to the bullfight by
friends) to come down and help him. Dr. Will told me that
when he came into the room and saw that the doctor was
trying to clamp the artery by blindly poking a long "hemostat"
up through the tunnel in the thigh, he picked up a scissors,
slit open the top of the tunnel, and in a few seconds had
clamped shut the hole in the blood vessel!

Dr. Will always urged me never to utter a word of criticism
of the medical profession. But much as I respected his wisdom

in most matters, on this point I could not agree. I have always been much impressed with the fact that 140 years ago, when a "scrappy" English physician named Thomas Wakley founded one of the world's greatest medical journals—the *London Lancet*—every week he lashed out at the bad, selfish, unfair, and stupid practices in British Medicine. Naturally, the London specialists struck back at him as hard as they could, but the rank and file of the profession gradually came to see the value to them of what he was doing, and in the end he won out.

My personal experience has led me to believe that when able and idealistic doctors hear a fellow physician speaking out against some bad practice in medicine they admire him for his courage. They know that he is telling the truth. They know he is doing an unpleasant job that has to be done sooner or later by someone, and they are glad he is doing it.

I have always said to my friends, "We all know there are some bad practices in medicine, and there are some 'bad actors' with an M.D. degree. Wouldn't it be better, then, for us to try to clean up the mess in medicine ourselves—rather than to wait for a senatorial committee to do the work?"

I have always known that it would be "healthiest" *for me* to keep my mouth shut about the shameless, or stupid, or venal practices in medicine, but as I have said before, if I hadn't spoken out, I would have been a coward, and today I would be ashamed to think that I had remained silent.

As early as 1699, Sir Samuel Garth, an able physician, complained as some of us do today:

> Now sickening Physick hangs her pensive head.
> And what was once a Science, now's a Trade.

Always I have preferred not to be a worldly-wise man who, on all occasions, knows what is best for his own skin and then does just that. I have had to pay some price for my often quixotic behavior, but today I have no regrets. Actually, I regret that I have not always been as courageous as I would like to have been, or perhaps should have been. What often has held me back has been my knowledge that a man who tries hard to help the cause of medicine will often seem to many of his colleagues to be only a traitor—and that is what hurts.

A few physicians have written me to say that we should wash our "dirty linen" in private. First of all, some of the dirty linen has too long been out on the line—in plain sight. Second, nothing makes lay people feel more kindly toward us physicians than our occasional admission that we are not always all-wise, perfect, kind, thoughtful, generous, disinterested, idealistic, honest, or highly-skilled. I have received scores of letters from lay readers of my newspaper column to prove this. Such laymen saw clearly that there will be no improvement in our behavior until, like the Prodigal Son, we say, "I have sinned." Such laymen have written me to say, "So long as every one of you doctors thinks he is 'a tin Jesus on wheels' we will dislike and even hate you. We will keep looking forward to the day when, as in Great Britain, you will all be employed by the State, and then we can order you around or have you kicked off your panel."

One of the kindest and most reassuring letters I ever received came from Dr. John C. Brougher, who wrote that to him constructive criticism of doctors is an indication of the critic's high respect for medicine as a profession. He realized that when a doctor criticizes a bad medical practice it is only because he so loves medicine that he wants to see the practice of it grow better.

Dr. Osler, who was one of the kindest and most generous of physicians, could not close his eyes to "the lapses and mistakes which are inevitable in our work." He sometimes spoke unhappily of the physicians who labor only for money, or who, throughout a lifetime, fail to keep up-to-date. He used to speak sadly of those many young doctors who, after graduation, die a "mental death, and come away, stillborn from college."

In spite of all my criticism of certain practices in medicine,

I still feel much as did the great Dr. Langdon-Browne, when he wrote, "Despite some disagreeable eddies and unsavory backwaters, medicine's main stream runs clear, and sweeps onward with a gathering impetus."

In 1939, cells from a malignant ulcer in Dr. Will's stomach had grown up into the glands of his neck. He got his old associate and friend Dr. George Eusterman to examine them and asked, "What do you think?"

George's eyes filled with tears, and he said, "I guess they must be metastases (daughter growths)." Dr. Will said, "Don't take it so hard, George. I've lived long enough, and I am perfectly ready to go."

Dr. Will used to say that he wanted very much to go before he became a forgotten "has-been." That he could not face.

When he saw that death was approaching he sent for the few persons with whom he had had conflicts of opinion and perhaps harsh words, and asked for their forgiveness and the return of their old friendship. I chatted with Dr. Will the day before he died. He was badly jaundiced, but his mind was as clear as ever it was. I guess he felt the need to talk to many people because, in those last days, he sat under a tree in his front yard, where many passers-by stopped to visit with him.

He went suddenly, with his mind clear, still making wise plans for the future of the Clinic. The day before he died he told the Board of Governors never to put a son of a Clinic doctor on the Staff until first he had gone out into the world and shown that he could build a good practice—which was a very wise idea.

As many people know, Dr. Charles H. Mayo was very different from his brother. They were different in appearance, in temperament and in interests. Dr. Charlie was less awe-inspiring than Dr. Will, but this had its advantages; one could come closer—mentally and spiritually—to Dr. Charlie, and one could feel an affection for him such as one could not easily feel for Dr. Will.

I had much affection for Dr. Charlie, and I think he sensed it. He knew also that I always loved it when he came up to me to tell me one of his funny stories. Dr. Charlie always seemed to me to be much like Will Rogers, with much of Rogers' combination of wisdom and fun.

So far as I know, Dr. Will had no hobby besides the Clinic and his cruiser on the Mississippi River; but Dr. Charlie loved farms, of which he had several—all stocked with good cattle and horses.

Although Dr. Charlie was shrewd, with much good "horse sense," so far as I could learn he never had any desire to carry the heavy administrative burdens of the Clinic, and I much doubt if his talents ran in that direction. Many people, because of their affection for Dr. Charlie, tried to foster the idea that he was just as much a builder of the Clinic as was Dr. Will. I imagine that in the early years he worked as hard as Dr. Will did—seeing patients, operating on them, and building up the practice. But in the later years, or certainly after I joined the Staff, it was obvious that Dr. Will was carrying most of the burden of administration.

Friends of Dr. Charlie told me that he liked to live for the day—enjoying life with his loved ones about him. It was Dr. Will who spent most of his time planning far ahead for the Clinic. I never thought of blaming Dr. Charlie for not caring to do this sort of thing, if only because I could not have done it myself. I hate planning. With all my strong affection for Dr. Charlie, his son Dr. "Chuck," and his daughter Louise, I never could see any sense in stirring up an argument as to who had had most to do with building and running the Clinic.

Fortunately, in many a situation like this, two very different partners can get along comfortably, as Dr. Will and Dr. Charlie did—accepting the fact that their interests and their abilities are different. What is sad sometimes is that their women-folk and close friends will get into an argument as to who is the better man. I greatly honored Dr. Charlie for cheerfully having lived a life which, I suspected, was not the one he would have chosen if he had been left to himself. Actually, one day Dr. Will, in one of his moments of great frankness, said to me that he knew that with all the many demands that he had made on his younger brother, he had caused him often to live a life that was not quite congenial to him; and for this he was sorry.

Dr. Will was probably enough of a psychiatrist to realize that it is not easy for a home-loving and farm-loving man to live and work alongside a dynamic, hard-driving, very successful, and very famous older brother. Fortunately, Dr. Charlie seemed never to feel any jealousy. He always seemed full of good nature, good sense, and good humor. I never saw in his behavior or heard in his speech any sign of resentment against his brother, even when Dr. Will made an important decision without consulting him. Two of the oldest secretaries in the Clinic and one of Dr. Charlie's oldest and closest friends all told me that if there was any big difference of opinion between the brothers, Dr. Charlie was always perfectly willing to let Dr. Will have his way.

On one occasion I personally discovered how unwilling Dr. Charlie was to get into a fight for what he wanted to do. He had become so keen to have me go on a good-will speaking tour to the medical centers of South America that, when I got back from a trip, I found he had my tickets all bought and ready for me. Then, one of my friends who thought *he* should be the one to go—although he could not lecture in Spanish as I could—raised such a fuss that, although it must have been embarrassing to Dr. Charlie to let me down, he gave in. He said not a word to me; I said nothing, and the matter was just dropped. No one went.

Fortunately, Dr. Charlie always stood resolutely by his brother, even when one day Dr. Will had to dismiss one of Dr. Charlie's sons-in-law. One of the finest things that Dr. Charlie ever did was to tell the Staff right then that whatever happened, he would always stand with his brother. When Dr.

Will came home from a trip and heard this, the tears came to his eyes, and he turned and walked away.

Right after these events, Dr. Will got Dr. Charlie to go with him to the annual meeting of the American Medical Association, supposedly so that everyone would see how close they were.

Dr. Will must often have consulted his brother about problems that came up in the Clinic. Many a time, as I passed by the two men, I heard them talking earnestly together. But also, as I stated elsewhere, occasionally I saw Dr. Will make a decision without discussing the matter with anyone—not even Dr. Charlie or the Board of Governors. On several occasions, even after the Board had repeatedly taken a stand against some action, Dr. Will—on his own—would reverse the Board's action.

In Dr. Will's later years, in order to be as fair as he could be to his brother, he never got up to speak before an audience without beginning with the statement that Dr. Charlie was equally responsible for everything that had ever been done and that then was being done in the Clinic.

I remember once when, just before a lecture, a close friend of Dr. Will's said to him, "Oh, please, can't you for once spare us that old preamble?"

And Dr. Will said, "No, I just have to say it, it has become so much a part of me and my thinking, and my great desire to be fair to Charlie and to make some amends to him."

I loved Dr. Charlie's kindliness and humanness, and his delightful sense of humor. It was much like the droll and very wise humor that his son "Chuck" has. Dr. Charlie never impressed me as being as much of a student or a reader as his brother was, but I suspect he knew better how to live a happy life, surrounded by his devoted wife and his children and good friends. I have often heard that he was a wonderful father to his children, and that at 10 P.M. each evening his sons would walk over to the big home and bid their parents good night.

On the lecture platform Dr. Charlie generally put aside his

manuscript, and started telling delightful stories. One that I loved was about the voluntary fire company which, in the old days, used to run to fires pulling a hose cart. When the captain became old and rheumatic, the company elected a new Chief, and decided to have a big celebration in the Armory, at which time they would present the retiring Chief with a gold-headed cane. For six weeks the old captain and the new one met every night to practice their "extemporaneous" speeches of delivery and acceptance. Finally the great night came and the Armory was full of people. The young captain got up and started on his speech, but at the end of two sentences he got stuck. After an agonizing period of looking at the floor and the ceiling, he began again at the beginning. Again he got stuck, so again he started. This time, when he got stuck, he just said, "Here, take your goddamned old cane!"

I remember a time at a huge medical meeting when there had been much acrimonious debate about something or other. Then Dr. Charlie got up, and with a short funny story he showed the doctors what they should agree on. They roared with laughter, and that was the end of the argument.

Dr. Charlie once told me about a farm boy who had brought up a calf. Eventually the animal got so big it dragged the boy around, and he was glad when he could steer it a bit. Dr. Charlie said that that was the way he and Dr. Will felt about the Clinic. He and Dr. Will once told me that in the early days they thought of the organization as just a partnership, but soon everyone began to call it a clinic.

I often saw Dr. Charlie show much wisdom with patients. One day when a half-crazy man became insulting, Dr. Charlie just walked out of the room. When the colleague with him said, "Why didn't you give that fellow the dressing-down he deserved?" Dr. Charlie said, "One damn fool in a room is enough."

Another time, when someone urged Dr. Charlie to bawl out some very unpleasant person, Dr. Charlie said, "If you get into a fight with a skunk you'll soon smell like a skunk!"

Typical of Dr. Charlie was the story he told me once of a decidedly hypochondriac, but otherwise normal, man who insisted that his perfectly good kidneys weren't working well. Dr. Charlie told him to go and eat a watermelon and that would cure him. Later, when the fellow returned to say he was no better, Dr. Charlie asked, "Where did you buy the melon?" "From Jones' grocery." "Oh," said Dr. Charlie, "there's where you went wrong. You should have gotten it from Smith's, across the street." Dr. Charlie loved fun like that, and often his patients joined in the laugh and felt much better for it.

One day when another hypochondriac patient asked if he should sell his business and move to the Southwest, Dr. Charlie said, "That might be a good thing to do. I'm trying to remember its name . . . there is a town down there so salubrious that they had to shoot two men in order to start the cemetery! You ought to go there."

Dr. Charlie taught me a very helpful trick in diagnosis which, many a time since, has gotten me out of a tight spot. He said, "Whenever you cannot guess what is wrong with a man, just ask his wife and she'll tell you what it is." It is remarkable how often I have found this to be true. When a stout jolly farmer came complaining of spells of violent nausea and I couldn't find anything wrong with him and was stumped, I remembered what Dr. Charlie had said. Turning to the wife, I asked her what was bothering the man. She said angrily, "I don't know why he comes here to waste our money. He knows darn well what's wrong with him. He gets nauseated when he goes on a binge of chewing tobacco and swallowing the juice!" When I asked the man if his wife was right, he grinned sheepishly and said, "Yes, but I hoped you'd find something else, so I could go on chewing!"

Another time, Dr. Charlie used this technique to make a most remarkable diagnosis. For 10 days I had studied the illness of a farmer's wife who was suffering from a severe and constant diarrhea. When I had to admit that I had no idea what the disease was, the farmer said, "I'd like to see Dr.

Charlie." So I went to Dr. Charlie's office with the couple, and quickly told him that all of the tests had failed to give any hint as to the diagnosis. He simply turned to the farmer and asked, "What do you think has caused the diarrhea?" And the man said, "It's them chickens. They got the diarrhie. She nursed them, and then she got it." Dr. Charlie said, "Bring in a few of the sick chickens and we will examine them." They were found to be full of tuberculosis, and when the woman's discharges were examined for tubercle bacilli, there they were —by the million!

One day Dr. Charlie advised a neurotic woman with a lot of hysterical complaints to go to a faith healer. The woman said angrily, "That's a foolish bit of advice." "True," said Dr. Charlie, "but you have a foolish disease!"

Typical of Dr. Charlie's love of fun was his telling me one day that he had just seen a man with a "seven year itch" who was six months behind on his scratching!

One day when he was a boy Dr. Charlie got caught in some mischief and was sent to the principal for a whipping. As the principal got out his rattan, he asked Charlie if he had anything to say, and Charlie said, "Yes," he'd like to go home and put on a thicker pair of pants. The principal was so amused he let Charlie go free!

I feel I must say here a few words about Dr. Henry Plummer who was one of the original partners of the Doctors Mayo, and the most unusual character around the Clinic. He was one of the oddest and most absent-minded of men. Many a time— talking to himself—he passed me on the sidewalk, three feet away, without seeing me. At other times he would grab me like the Ancient Mariner, and start talking to me in a monologue for four hours—or as long as I would stay. The difficult feature of these interviews was that I generally came away from one of them with but a vague idea as to what Henry had been trying to tell me. His mind seemed to run on ahead and leave his lips behind to talk by themselves!

One day Henry opened his heart to me and talked more

lucidly than he had ever done. He said that none of the original partners, besides Dr. Will, had ever shown any love of planning ahead, directing, managing and building the Clinic. Each day they did their work with patients, and that was that. He it was who had to build laboratories, an X-ray department, and most of the machinery needed for the handling of patients and their histories and X-ray films, etc. Henry said he had always felt that he was largely a "hired man" who kept taking over Dr. Will's plans and quietly implementing them, and working out their details. Often, however, if he saw that something like a new building was much needed, he would keep talking to Dr. Will about it until eventually he wore him down and got his permission to go ahead. As Henry said, he marvelled at Dr. Will's lack of any interest in erecting buildings to house the Clinic. In the early years, Dr. Will seemed content to *rent* space, and to get along with terribly crowded quarters. When I first went to work in the Clinic, it was like a rabbit warren, with burrows leading out into the second floors of many of the buildings on the block.

One day, I was much surprised when Henry told me that he had always felt, just as I did, the loneliness of a man who "did not belong." As Henry said, we both had had to suffer for much the same reason: neither of us had ever settled down into any well-known "groove in the machine." He had to do much building, while I did research and lecturing and writing. As he said, this sort of non-conformity upsets people, most of whom love a well-ordered, well-known, and unvarying routine.

Obviously, Henry's extremely useful and constructive activities had been very different from those of any other man in the Clinic, and hence he "did not belong to the gang." Also, as often happens with a man who has a touch of genius, he had none of the play-habits or petty vices of the crowd; he had no cronies, and all of this must have made for great loneliness.

I could tell a dozen remarkable and amusing stories about Henry and his extreme absent-mindedness, but instead I will tell a story which will astound his old friends. One day I said to him, "In three weeks Dr. Walter B. Cannon, my dear old professor from Harvard days, will be here, and I am inviting a group of research-minded men to have luncheon with him at my house; will you honor us by coming?" Henry said, "I will be glad to." On the morning of the luncheon I called Henry's secretary to ask her to remind him.

"Oh, no," she said, "he so wants to meet Dr. Cannon, that all by himself, he remembered." And exactly at twelve he walked in!

Once he told me that it can be a great help to a busy man to have a reputation for extreme forgetfulness: it can get him easily out of all sorts of time-consuming commitments!

9

Chicago Days

BECAUSE OF THE "age limit" I was retired from the Mayo Clinic in September, 1950. It so happened that shortly before that time the just-appointed editor of the new journal, "GP" (General Practitioner) died. To help an organization I admired, I jumped into the breach and, very busy as I was, I took over the job of getting the journal out. Later, I was made official editor. What with this work, the problems of pulling out of our old home, selling most of my big library, cleaning out my files at the office, and wolking on my big book, *The Neuroses*, I was swamped.

When I arrived in Chicago I thought I would have some months in which to take life easy, and to visit my friends at the several medical schools, but immediately my days became filled with work. Shortly after I arrived, my old friend, Dr. Herman Bundesen—head of the Chicago Health Department —insisted that I come and help him build up the free Clinic he had started. For over a year, this work took part of each of my days.

When I opened my office, patients flocked in until soon I

had to call a halt. I could not do all my editing, writing, and answering of mail, and also see patients all afternoon. And so I begged my good friend, Dr. Samuel Hyman, to help me out, and this he has done ever since with a kindly devotion.

In June, 1951, as I had dinner in Atlantic City with my good friend of many years, Mr. Jack Cohen, I told him I had decided to give up work on *GP*. Next morning he telephoned to say that the editor of *Modern Medicine* had fallen seriously ill, and if he did not recover, would I be interested in taking the job.

Two weeks later I accepted the position, because I have always been particularly interested in graduate medical education, and it seemed to me that a good abstract journal could be the best medium for such education, and for the bringing of new knowledge quickly to the attention of physicians all over the country. In 1952, I became editor, also, of *Geriatrics*. Ever since I joined the staffs of *Modern Medicine* and *Geriatrics*, my relations with my Chiefs and my associates in Minneapolis have been particularly happy.

As I was preparing to leave Rochester, my old patient and good friend Mr. C. W. Follett did something that changed the course of my life. He, who, with his sons, had built a huge publishing plant in Chicago, asked me for something from my pen that he could print. When I showed him the manuscript of a lecture I had given before a big crowd in Cleveland on *How to live with your Nerves*, "C.W." was so enthusiastic that he said he would sell a million copies. Actually, he promptly sold 120,000 copies, and then sold the right to publish the article to *Cosmopolitan* and to the *Reader's Digest*, who later translated it into 10 languages.

Early in 1951 Mr. Follett persuaded me to write some 15 booklets designed to help laymen understand their diseases, and he began to syndicate these booklets in many newspapers. The material was so well accepted that by the end of a year *The Register* and *Tribune Syndicate* signed me up to write four columns a week for them. On December 19, 1952, C. W. Follett died, and I lost a dear and very helpful friend.

Before long my column was in more than 80 papers in the United States and Canada, and in 20 more papers scattered all over the world. Soon I was receiving over 100,000 letters a year from people who were asking me for help and advice.

I sensed at first that some physicians doubted if my writing for the lay public was quite "ethical," but soon most of them seemed to understand what I was trying to do and began to see that I could help not only the public, but also the whole cause of medicine. If I had confined my work to the practice of medicine in my office, I could have helped perhaps a dozen people a day; through my column I could help millions. One opthalmologist in a city of 100,000 told me that a column of mine on eyes had caused over 100 people to come to him to see why their vision was failing, and several had come just in time to be saved from blindness. Mothers wrote that they had been warned by a column of mine just in time to save a child from death due to a severe form of diabetes.

An able businessman once wrote to tell me that one of my columns had just brought him great peace of mind because at last, after many months of fruitless consultations and examinations, he knew what one day had hit him, and in a moment had left him miserable and unable to work. He said, "It is now obvious that a year ago I had a typical 'little stroke' such as you describe—a stroke that did not injure the nerves going to an arm or a leg, but which severely damaged much of the thinking part of my brain. I should be sad because I know now that I am not likely to get well, but curiously, I am very happy because at last I know the worst. I know what went wrong, and I know what I have to face."

My book *Live at Peace with Your Nerves* was published in 1958 by Prentice-Hall, and appeared for a while on the best-seller list. By now it has been translated into 10 foreign languages, and is well known throughout Europe.

My most recent book, *Minds That Came Back,** contains
condensations of 65 very interesting autobiographies of persons
who were either mentally disturbed, alcoholic, or very nervous. In the last 50 years I have collected some 500 of these
autobiographies—several written by men and women of note.
When I want to know about Tibet, I do not read the books
of men who have remained at home in an armchair. I read the
accounts of those few brave travellers who once explored "the
top of the world" or lived for years in Lhasa. Similarly, when
I wanted to find out how it feels to go insane, and why people
go insane, I did not read only the literature of the psychoanalysts; I read the scores of books written by men and women
who once were psychotic, and perhaps for months or years
had to live in a mental hospital. Interestingly, none of these
people mentioned penis envy, or castration fear, or an Oedipus
situation—the all-important foundation-stones of psychoanalysis.

The great Dr. Alfred Kinsey died in 1958, and again I lost a
good friend. Even before I had gone to Mayo's, I was distressed because I did not know enough to help the many
people who came to me worrying themselves sick over sexual
problems. Dozens of women came to ask if they should divorce
their husbands because they kept asking for some variant of
the sexual act. Other women came asking what to do with a
son who was sexually attracted more to boys than to girls. In
college I had never heard a single lecture on such subjects and,
later, much of what reading I had done had left me dissatisfied because so much of the writing was evidently based, not
on research, but on armchair theories.

Unable to learn of any university where sex was being
studied, I went to my good friend Dr. Raymond Pearl, and
told him he ought to tackle the job. He agreed that it was a
disgrace that so few scientists in America were studying the
sexual behavior of men, women, and children, but he said he
had so many irons in the fire he could not put in another.

* Lippincott, 1961.

Later, when I heard that Dr. Kinsey had gone to work on the problem, I went to Bloomington, Indiana, and found a fine, dedicated scientist—a man for whom I soon felt a warm friendship. He had seen the need for studies of sex when in his seminars his students kept asking questions which he could not answer. All his days he had been a student of gall-wasps, and he told me that to study them he had walked, knapsacking it, all through the West—going wherever there were oaks with galls on them.

He was a tireless man who never took a day off from work.

Dr. Alan Gregg of the Rockefeller Foundation told me that because for so long he had felt the great need for someone to study sexual behavior in man, it had seemed like an answer to prayer when Dr. Kinsey had come in to ask for a grant for the founding of an Institute for sexual studies.

Dr. Kinsey told me he had had his troubles with some professors, and even with prissy physicians who had disliked what he was doing. But eventually he had made friends with most of his opponents. Shortly before Dr. Gregg died, he told me that along the way he had had his troubles with some people on the Rockefeller Board who disliked any study of sex. He said he had taken many a "shellacking" because he stood up for Kinsey.

Dr. Kinsey, although often sneered at as "a publicity seeker," was not that at all. He suffered much at the hands of reporters, correspondents, and science-writers. Once when in New York I tried to telephone him at his hotel, I learned that no one could call him or even find out what room he had. Fortunately, I ran into my good friend Dr. Wardell Pomeroy of the Kinsey Laboratory, and he took me up to Dr. Kinsey's room where we had a good visit.

My impression is that Kinsey's life was shortened by the terrible strain of being forced into the public eye. I know how shocked I was one day when I met him at the Chicago Airport and flew with him to California. He had aged so, and he was obviously exhausted. He slept for most of the four hours of our trip. He explained that he had just had a most tiring session with a lot of correspondents who kept insisting that he give them a story about what he was planning to do next.

He told me that when the first great wave of publicity broke after the publication of his first book, he was soon so sadly in need of rest that he fled to California, and while reporters searched for him in every hotel in San Francisco, he hid out for three weeks in—of all places—San Quentin Prison! There, his friend the Warden saw to it that he got some much-needed peace and sleep.

What distressed me when Dr. Kinsey's books appeared was that so many people, even eminent people, attacked him either for not having written in a sweet kindly vein, or for not having been outraged at what he had learned from the thousands of men and women he had questioned. Few people seemed to be able to see that Dr. Kinsey had not written a book to shock, titillate, amuse, or elevate. He was a scientist who had done little more than publish the figures that had come out of his *IBM* machines. He had just reported *what people had said they had done*. He had not felt any need for going on to express strong disapproval of their confessions. It was saddening to me when even some scientific men, who should have known better, could not see that Kinsey had written a book on statistics and not a diatribe on supposed immorality. His book was about what most people do, not what is supposedly *wrong* with what they do.

I often wondered what it was about Kinsey that enabled thousands of people to tell him about the most intimate details of their lives. I think they must have sensed what a fine, dedicated man he was—a man who would not "turn a hair" no matter what they told him. Also, he noted down what they told him in a code that was memorized and never put on paper. Hence, if in the future his records should ever get into the wrong hands, no one will ever be able to understand a word of them. Even today, the few men who know that code are careful never to travel on a plane *together*. If they were all to die in an accident, there would be no one left to decipher the thousands of records that are in the files in Indiana.

As Art Linkletter says, "People are funny." He sees many funny ones, and we physicians see many more. One day in Chicago a good friend of mine—an able, very likeable, and good-natured architect—came in to ask me to see if I could put some sense into his wife, who was threatening to divorce him. When I asked her what he was doing that annoyed her so much, she was vague, and about all she could say was that he "was just impossible." I said, "Well, let's start with what bothers you most—what is that?"

After thinking a while she said, "Look, he won't use a washrag, as a sensible and proper man should!"

Another woman of this type, when threatening a divorce, told me she could not stand living with a man who put on his pants before his shoes! A physician friend told me of another fussy woman, a terrible hypochondriac, who was always "crying wolf" about some disease she was sure she had, but which her doctor could never find. Eventually, when she did start to die, she ordered that on her tombstone there be carved the words, "Doctor; I always told you I was sick!" They say a woman likes to have the last word!

Often when a man tells me that his wife is terribly bossy— so much so that he has learned always to give in to her and to let her have her own way, I tell him that in my father's country, Spain, they say to a young bridegroom that if his wife ever gets it into her head that he must jump off a roof, he had better pray to God it isn't a very high one!

One day a girl of 17 was brought to me because she was still wetting the bed. What amused me much was her mother's remark that just then she was all right because she always gave up her bed-wetting for Lent!

So often we doctors are expected to be marriage counselors. An unforgettable couple once came to me—he, a tall, austere young New England minister and she, a sweet and loving young thing. When I quickly sensed a tension between them, and saw that this could be the cause of the wife's insomnia, indigestion, and headache, I asked them to tell me what had gone wrong. She said that her husband had the idea that sex was so sinful that it should be tolerated only rarely, and then only for purposes of procreation. She was too affectionate for an unloving marriage of that type. I gave the man a talking-to, and got him to admit that if the good Lord had given us— His children—this strong impulse to be loving, He probably wanted us to use it. The next day I was much pleased to note that when the couple came into my office, they were happy and were holding hands like newlyweds.

Another patient who taught me much about the vagaries of sex was a sweet-faced, lovely, and decidedly feminine Cuban woman of 32, who had never menstruated and had no breasts. For years she had been the well-loved mistress of the man for whom she worked. A careful study, including a surgical exploration of her abdominal cavity, showed that she was as much a male as a female, with tiny glands of both sexes. Because she wanted to go on living as a woman, her very small male organs were removed.

What her case showed me so clearly was that feminine charm and the ability to show warm affection depend more on something in the brain than on something in the sex glands. I cannot remember ever having learned in books the lesson this woman taught me, and taught me so well I will never forget it. Along the way, I gave her great pleasure by sending my secretary out with her to buy a pair of falsies to put in her bra. With these, she was as pleased as punch.

All my days I have been impressed with what Plato once said, to the effect that in order to be understanding and efficient, a physician should have had the disease he is attempting to treat. I thought of this several times in April, 1960, when X-rays taken at the Mayo Clinic showed a good-sized cancer in my large intestine, and I had to be operated on. The thought then came to me that all my life I had been "dishing out" the diagnosis of cancer, and now here I was "on the receiving end." I was glad when I found I could "take it" without any sense of fear.

I went back to my office in Chicago for a couple of days, to put my financial house in order, and to warn my business associates that if I should fail to come through the operation alive, or if the tumor should be found to be inoperable, they would soon have to start searching for someone to take my place writing my columns and editorials. Then I returned to Rochester and entered the hospital.

Fortunately, the operation—expertly performed in 45 minutes—was very easy on me. My dear old friend Dr. Chuck Mayo and his first assistant Dr. Kent Cullen could not have been kinder, and in three days I was up and walking around. Three weeks later I was back in my office and comfortably at work. Today, three years have passed and I feel so well that it looks as if I am going to "beat the rap." I hope so, because there is so much work I still want to do.

At 79, I am busier than I ever was in my life. I still see a few patients—mainly old friends. They help me to "keep my hand in." There are still several books, for the making of which I have gathered hundreds of facts, and now I hope I can live long enough to write them.

When friends ask me, "Why do you go on working as hard as you ever did?" my answer is that I feel driven to go ahead and get many things done. I am like Dr. Selman Waksman, who, after discovering streptomycin, said that a driving force caused him right away to start on a new study.

I hope when I am gone that I can, to some extent, merit the epitaph of a hero of mine who, around 1849, in the "Gold-fields" of California, died, after an up-and-down life. As I remember the story, his friends put on his tombstone, "He done his damndest; angels couldn't do no more!" I love a man who, in this world, does his damndest. If he does that I think we should all be willing to excuse him for a few mistakes he may have made.

I am happy to say that in my late seventies I am still full of enthusiasms. I would hate to be without them—they make life so much more worth living. I love the Greek meaning of the word enthusiasm—"a god within." How unfortunate the man or woman who has no god within!

To show how a man can keep learning even in his seventies I will say that in my now small practice I have of late been greatly interested in the many patients I have seen with seizure-less epilepsy—people with serious temperamental difficulties. These troubles have come to fascinate me, and I now have here in my study a pile of notes on their troubles which I hope soon to write up.

I have also been fascinated, watching the rapid progress that of late has been made in the field of human genetics. I hope I live to see the present-day taboo against speaking or writing about heredity broken down.

The following story has always amused me, and it has supported my strong belief in the importance of heredity. Once, when, in a certain city, I spoke about families in which there is much degeneracy, a nice old doctor came up and said, "I know of a queer family down on the mud-flats by the river. One day a patient of mine, a census-taker, told me of a day when he came to a shack there and knocked on the door. When a slattern, stupid-looking girl appeared, my friend asked if her father was home. 'Naw, he's in the penitentiary.' 'Well, is your mother home?' 'Naw, she's at the State Hospital.' 'Have you an older brother?' 'Yes, he is in the Reform School.' 'Have you perhaps an older sister?' 'Yes, she works in the red-light district.' 'Well, have you a younger brother?' 'Yes, he's in the medical school at Harvard!' 'Goodness gracious,' said the census man, 'You don't mean to tell me you have a brother who is professor at Harvard?' 'Naw, he's no professor; he has two heads; he's in a bottle of alcohol!' "

Often I tease my friends, the psychiatrists, but then again, I will show some of the "old-timers" the admiration and even affection I have for them. I like the following story because a merry psychiatrist once told it to me on himself. He said that one Monday a well-dressed man had come in to ask for a thorough mental examination. The man said that people kept following him; he would go to the police and demand protection, but the Chief, thinking him crazy, would never do anything. "Now," said he, "I want you to examine me and give me a certificate that I am sane." The psychiatrist, though satisfied that the man was psychotic, turned him over to his assistants for the examination he wanted.

On Friday, he called the man in and said, "I have an apology to make to you. Last Monday, when you came, I thought as did the police that you had delusions of persecution, but my secretary promptly noticed that, when you came in, a couple of men were following you. Each day they waited behind the tree in the parkway, and when you went out, they followed you." "Oh, no," said the patient. "Don't pay any attention to them; they are the detectives I hire to keep the other fellows farther back."

Some persons who know something of my very busy life, ask, "But haven't you some hobbies? Don't you sometimes get a rest and a bit of relaxation?" Most surely, yes; I still find joy in travel, and particularly in travel into my beloved mountains, where I enjoy taking color pictures of the scenery. Twice in the last year I have been to the great Yosemite Valley of California. A year ago my good friend Professor Chauncey Leake and I explored the several high passes in the Sierra Nevada, beginning at Lake Tahoe and working down toward the great Tioga pass that leads into the Yosemite country.

In recent years I have been to Cuba, Mexico, Hawaii, and the glorious mountains of Western Canada; also my beloved Teton country and Glacier Park. I hope in the next few years I can keep going up into the hills that I have always so greatly loved.

I love also meeting old friends and having grand chats with them. I have been most fortunate in that two beloved sisters —Florence Spaulding and Mabel Alvarez—and one beloved brother, Dr. Harold Alvarez, are still well and strong and active. I have been very fortunate also in that my four children and ten grandchildren have all been a joy to me. In order of birth, my children are Gladys, Mrs. Raymond Archibald; Luis, an eminent professor of physics at the University of California; Robert, a Ph.D. in Library Administration, and Bernice, married to Dr. Bradley Brownson.

I am happy to say that we are one of those loving families in which the children love their grandparents and uncles and aunts, and we all love even our in-laws.

In the old days when my children were small, I liked to do my reading and writing out in the living-room, rather than in my den; I wanted the contact I had with them as they sat and played or read or did their homework.

10

Doubts, Dissatisfactions and Loneliness

I HAVE OFTEN been troubled by a sense of loneliness. This has been due in large measure to my bookishness and my lifelong inability or unwillingness to enjoy life with those of my fellows whose main love is to hunt and fish, and to play golf, bridge, and poker. In *Figures of Earth,* James Branch Cabell spoke of the loneliness of some men: "There is no hour in my life but I go around in reserve ... and in my armor I am lonely. Freydis, there is no way in which two persons may meet in this world of men: but we can exchange, from afar, despairing friendly signals. My distrust of all living creatures— even of you, dear Freydis, when I draw you closest—must always be as a wall between us—a low, lasting, firmly-set wall which we can never pull down."

Most of us have built this wall of reticence around ourselves. With some it is very high and impenetrable, while with others it is not so well built as to keep everyone out. Seldom does a man love anyone enough to let that person come wholly within the wall.

183

Most of us must live two lives—one which all can see, and one which perhaps only a very few people know about. In his book *Minority Report*, H. L. Mencken once remarked, "I know a great many more people than most men, and in wider and more diverse circles, yet my life is essentially one of isolation, and so is that of every other man. We not only have to die alone; we also, save for a few close associates, have to live alone."

At the Mayo Clinic I was often amazed at how freely a patient would talk of the problem that was tearing at his heart to the stranger sitting beside him in the big waiting-room— when he would not talk of his sorrow or shame to me, his physician, or even perhaps to his mother or his wife.

And I have long puzzled over the fact that a person who is unusually reserved when talking to friends or relatives may write an autobiography in which he lays bare his soul to all who care to read of it.

In the cases of many men, the ordinary feelings of loneliness which most of us feel are heightened and made more distressing by the fact that the man is unable to mix comfortably with the crowd about him. Also, in the office or business in which he works, the unusually gifted man may never be allowed to feel at home—like "one of the gang." Especially if he joined the group after he was 30 or 40, he may never have come to feel that he "belonged," and this can be a sorrow to him. In railroading they say that a top executive is a rank outsider unless he "came up through the roundhouse"—as an oiler or a mechanic. I had a similar experience at the Mayo Clinic where—partly because I joined the group when I was over 40 and partly because I never settled down to be a quiet "cog in the machine"—I never really felt an accepted member of the group. I seemed always an interloper who somehow got in—perhaps uninvited.

At a party many a lonely man will do as I often have done —he may sit by silently as an onlooker. Often at a dinner where I have tended to withdraw into myself, I have suddenly realized that I had a duty to my hosts, and so I pulled myself together and joined in the conversation.

Luckily for me, my loneliness was lessened by the fact that I followed the advice of my great mentor Sir William Osler, who used to say to his students, "Mix as much as you can with the outside world, and learn its ways." This "will enable you to conquer the diffidence so apt to go with bookishness, and which may prove a serious drawback in after-life."

Loneliness is bad enough for the sane and well-adjusted man; it must be ten times worse for the shy, reserved, mildly schizoid person. Many of these mentally troubled people have told me they craved affection, but when it was offered them, they could not accept it. They pulled away icily and went on the defensive. One of the best descriptions of this sort of schizoid behavior is to be found in *Wuthering Heights,* in which Mr. Lockwood—who closely resembled the highly gifted but very odd Bramwell Brontë (brother of the Brontë sisters) —tells of having met a "goddess" whom he continued to see much during a month's vacation. He fell deeply in love, but could not bring himself to say a word of his feelings to the girl. "She understood me at last and looked a return.—And what did I do? I confess it with shame—shrunk icily into my-self like a snail; at every glance retired colder and farther; till finally the poor innocent was led to doubt her own senses and fled in shame."

A good description of a lonely man who "never succeeded in becoming one of the boys" is to be found in William Swanberg's life of William Randolph Hearst. Swanberg says "there was . . . built in a failure of communication, an aloofness, an air of secrecy and loneliness, an inability to unbend, a lack of easy spontaneity. . . . Now and then he would be close to breaking through, only to recede again like a turtle withdrawing into its shell." *

One day in my intern year I suddenly learned that some

* W. A. Swanberg, *Citizen Hearst* (New York: Charles Scribner's Sons, 1961).

schizoids cannot stand being touched even by a friendly and affectionate person. One of my surgical teachers was an alcoholic who hid a kind nature behind a gruff exterior. Because, youngster as I was, I had penetrated his disguise and had come to like him, he had become friendly with me. One day, while engaged in eager conversation with him, I unconsciously, but in all kindness, touched his arm. I was shocked when he pulled away from me as if I had seared him with a hot iron.

After that experience I used to warn my students to avoid touching schizoids. I got to calling them "touch-me-nots." Many such a person has told me that even in his childhood days he resented any effort by his mother or a sister to reach out and touch him or put an arm around him. Some "untouchable" people have told me that they were very lonely and much in need of affection, but when it was offered it had to be rejected with coldness and disdain, as was the case with young Bramwell Brontë.

The man who pioneers in a new field of science is likely to feel lonely if only because so few of his contemporaries understand what he is saying or doing, or trying to do. Even the few friends who praise what a pioneer is doing will often say something which will show him that they do not really understand either him or his work. And this saddens him a bit and makes him lonely.

Sometimes I have felt particularly lonely when a close friend of mine showed by some word or act that he did not really know me. One day I was saddened when one of my best friends—an able physician—advised me to get rid of all of the hostility that had been distressing me—by giving up my research work, my writing, and my lecturing. He said, "See patients all day and keep your mouth shut, and then no one will fear you. No one will envy you. No one will notice you, and hence no one will make trouble for you." He might just as well have suggested that I get rid of my annoyers by committing suicide, or having someone bury me alive!

Another friend knew me so little that, after he had had a

heart attack, he asked me to leave the Mayo Clinic and to come to his city where he would turn over to me his huge and highly profitable practice.

Another friend wanted me to come to his university to be Dean of the medical school—a position which would have left me with no chance to do any of the things I wanted most to do.

These old and good friends evidently did not know what interested and motivated me, and this made me sad and lonely.

One would think that when an innovator publishes the results of his very valuable discovery he should soon wake up to find himself famous. But rarely does this happen. Many a great discoverer has had to watch his contribution to civilization being either reviled or, more often, just ignored. One thinks of that genius, Michael Faraday, making his first working model of an electric dynamo in 1831, and then seeing this tremendously valuable invention entirely ignored. It was not utilized until 50 years later.

Or let us think of Johann Kepler's book on the laws governing the movements of the planets—one of the great works of all time. It lay unappreciated and unused for many years until another genius—Isaac Newton—came to carry on from where Kepler left off. How lonely Kepler and Newton must have been!

I imagine that if a man is to be really close mentally and spiritually to some man or woman he should be able to share at least some of the interests and ideals that motivate his friend. Olive Schreiner once wrote, "For so many years I have longed to meet a mind that should understand me, that would take away from the loneliness of my life." Then she met Havelock Ellis, and wrote, "Now I have found it." They could talk freely—without fear of misunderstanding and criticism—of the many thoughts about sex and life that interested them both, but which at that time were not mentioned by "nice people."

It often occurs to me that many a gifted man lives happily

for years with a woman who has little understanding of his work and his problems. When questioned about this, he may say that on arriving home at the end of the day he wants peace and quiet, and affection—not more medicine, or more architecture, or engineering. When a gifted friend of mine, a widower of 40, married a young woman of little education, friends said, "That marriage will last at most six months." It lasted happily for years. My friend explained: "When I go home all I want is much affection, and that she gives me."

Sometimes a man can overcome some of his loneliness by mentally sharing beautiful sights and experiences with a loved woman—even when she is far away. I have always delighted in the words that an ancient Egyptian wrote (in the Beatty Papyrus) to the woman he loved—when he was on a long journey— "I am with thee in every pleasant place!"

As one would expect, the man with a high IQ or a bit of genius in him is often lonely if only because there are so few men who can speak his highly technical language or share his thoughts. I have read that because of his genius and great interest in higher mathematics, an eminent nuclear physicist felt so lonely in his youth among his nonmathematical fellows that he thought seriously of suicide. Norbert Wiener has shown in his autobiography * that many a youth who is abnormally bright has to suffer because of his isolation. He cannot be one of the crowd. Too many of the people he meets bore him.

I sometimes wonder if, to be most nearly happy in this life, a man should be a Babbitt. When he feels at home among the crowd this should be a great comfort to him. And yet students of psychology tell us that the *average* man is always anxious for fear that he will differ in some slight way from his fellow Babbitts. Even an important executive may fear that he will not look and dress and act exactly as other executives do.

I have always derived great pleasure from meeting and talking to those rare characters who think well, and think independently. One reason why I love to travel is that I then keep

* *Ex-Prodigy*, Simon and Schuster, 1953.

coming in contact with unusual persons scattered about the country. If I had spent all my days in one city I would have missed coming to know many of them. So often when I meet a brilliant man whose conversation is a joy to me, I wish he were living nearby, so that often we could have luncheon together. I console myself with Goethe's words—just "to know there are people with whom we are in accord, and who are living along with us, even in silence, makes this lonely planet a peopled garden."

An important point about which I feel strongly is that when I find a man whose personality, intelligence and learning delight me, I do well to keep corresponding with him, perhaps for many years. One must *cultivate* friendships if one is to hold friends and enjoy them.

A hundred times I have mused over the fact that rarely will a man open his secret heart before other men, and admit that he has a fine, gentle, idealistic and perhaps poetic side to his nature. He may admit it before a sensitive, spiritually-minded woman, yet rarely before a man. But why? Why should a man be ashamed of having a philosophic and poetic soul? Why should an artistic and perhaps music-loving young man always pretend before his fellows that he is a "tough guy," whose main interests are baseball, golf, hunting, fishing, and wenching? I imagine he does this because of his desire to appear like a "hundred per cent American," and a man of business and substance.

That fine play, *Tea and Sympathy*, gives a touching portrayal of a sensitive young man almost destroyed by the cruelty of those around him. Because of his artistic and gentle nature they suspected him of being a homosexual. I knew such a man who admitted that he had taken up mountain climbing and big game hunting just to show everyone how manly he was. But it was rough on him, and eventually he gave up and stopped pretending.

Many a man will fear also that if he does not espouse the sports and many of the habits of his fellows they will suspect he is criticizing them and setting himself up as holier than they. I remember once chatting with my dear old friend, Dr. Ezra Rich of Ogden, Utah—who was telling me about his father, a former close associate of Brigham Young. Although in his early days Charles Rich married six women, Dr. Ezra doubted if he had ever been much interested in women. Charles could cheerfully have remained a bachelor or the husband of one wife, but he knew that if he did not take several wives it would look as if he did not approve of the behavior of the men with whom he was closely associated, and this would not have been wise.

Albert Schweitzer once wrote, "None of us can assert that he really knows someone else, even if he has lived with him for years. Of that which constitutes our inner life we can impart, even to those most intimate with us, only fragments. . . . We wander through life together in a semi-darkness in which none of us can distinguish exactly the features of his neighbor."

I like Schweitzer's idea that no one should try to force his way into the personality of another . . . "for there is a modesty of the soul which we must recognize . . . the better we get to know each other, the more mystery we see in each other."

Many a marriage would be much happier if neither one of the two partners ever *demanded* confidences of the other. No matter how much a man may love a woman, he will do well to be interested only in whatever intimate details of her life and thoughts she cares to share with him. He will probably have a much more comfortable and happy time with her if he never asks her about her love life before he met her.

My old neighbor and good friend Dr. Francis J. Braceland, the eminent psychiatrist, recently wrote of the great loneliness of many aged people—the loneliness that comes when they realize that their useful life has ended, and they are no longer needed. Often an aged man "disengages himself emotionally from his surroundings, and withdraws with an increasing preoccupation with self."

Dr. Braceland feels that in order to conquer loneliness a

man must get rid of his inordinate self-love and feelings of hostility. These qualities make it impossible for him to communicate well with his fellows. Also, great loneliness often comes to us when we have lost something—perhaps a loved one, or our money, or our old status in the community. Perhaps we have "lost face." When that happens we must keep fighting to stay social.

I suspect that John Oxenham was right when, long ago, he wrote,

> Art thou lonely, O my brother?
> Share thy little with another!
> Stretch a hand to one unfriended
> And thy loneliness is ended.

I know that on those occasional days when I suffer from a depression with distressing feelings of loneliness and sadness, only one thing quickly relieves my great suffering, and that is to try to help a patient. As I help him I soon recover my usual good spirits and my happy outlook on life.

I I

The Faith of
a Physician

RELIGION IS SUCH an important part of a man's
life and thinking that I must say something now of my puzzle-
ments about it. I should emphasize here that I am not at all
militant about my agnostic state (lack of knowledge). I have
no convictions that I want to force on anyone, and I certainly
would hate to distress the many good people who, if they were
to read this, would certainly differ strongly with me. The last
thing I want to do is to hurt them and their faith.

I do wish that all devout persons, and persons who do not
want to be outraged or to have their faith disturbed, would
skip this chapter in its entirety. It was not written for them.

I write here for those scientific workers who, like me, cannot keep their minds divided into two separate compartments:
one for comforting, reassuring, and soothing statements of
faith, and the other for the bitter facts of life, such as can be
noted every day on the front page of any newspaper.

I would not say that I am an atheist, because, as I say in the
chapter on Evolution, it is very hard for me to believe that the
millions of complicated living things on this earth could have

developed without some guiding wisdom. In some of my thinking I am a bit like kindly old Sir Thomas Browne who, in his quaint classic—*Religio Medici* (the "Religion of a Physician")—written about 1540, said, "For my Religion, though there be several circumstances that might persuade the World I have none at all (as the general scandal of my Profession, the natural course of my Studies, the indifferency of my Behaviour and Discourse in Matters of Religion, neither violently Defending one, nor with that common ardour and contention Opposing another;) yet in despite thereof I dare without usurpation assume the honorable stile of a Christian." Like Sir Thomas, I am basically a Christian, but, like him, I never care to argue about my religion or my lack of an orthodox one.

I should emphasize the fact that I am not against religion, and am not fighting it. I hope only to show how it might well be changed a bit—that is, if it is to be made acceptable to scientifically trained people, or people with an inquiring and reasoning type of mind. I have only admiration for the men who, each Sunday, try to show their parishioners a better way of life. I wish them well.

I wish that in their pulpits they could answer frankly—as many would gladly do—the questions that bother me and my scientific friends. What is sad is that they cannot do this and remain in the ministry. I happen to know how hostile wealthy old head deacons can be to anything even slightly different from the old type of religion. "What was good enough for their fathers is good enough for them." My dear friend Professor Frederick Badé (once a Professor of Hebrew in a fine seminary) used to tell me that in his classes the students liked to discuss with their teachers the problems I puzzle over here, but later, when they got a church, they soon saw that they had better stick to the old-fashioned type of sermon.

When I was young, I was more-than-usually religious for a lad, and I tried to be as religious as my mother wanted me to be. Later I taught a Bible class in the YMCA, and years later, partly to please my wife, I became a deacon in a big Congregational church. But soon, as I watched the bitter fight which sprang up and then raged between the old conservatives and the young liberals in the congregation, I lost all desire ever to go to church again. As usually happens, the people who wanted an old-fashioned and nonintellectual type of religion won; and so we lost the finest minister I ever knew.

I have always been impressed with what Dostoevsky once said, that as a youth grows into manhood he has to outgrow some of his boyish ideas. They "get shattered into fragments" by the impact on them of the many hard facts of life which soon assail him.

My good friend Granger Westberg, that very able hospital chaplain, described in his book *Minister and Doctor Meet* (Harper & Bros.), the old man who grieves over the loss of his religious faith—*"faith which had been adequate in his child-hood, but not in the world he now faces."* These words sum up perfectly the main religious problem of an old physician and scientist like me.

Like the people described by Professor Westberg, by the time I was thirty, I had grown out of the religion of my boy-hood. I found it inadequate to meet my adult knowledge and my adult needs. Much of it seemed to me to be childish, silly, even offensive, and not at all suited to the ways of thinking and the intelligence of our present generation. Constant adula-tion, praise, and flattery of God, expressed in many of the hymns sung in church, began to offend and revolt me. I could not imagine even a bad or a stupid *man* so vain that he would want to listen all day and every day to hymns praising him for omnipotence and omniscience, which incidentally, as I show in the chapter on Evolution, He appears never to have had. No sensible *man* could tolerate such slavish adulation for two hours, and yet our God is supposed to expect it all day and every day, and to love it. According to our weird and incon-ceivably stupid ideas of heaven, it is a place in which for all eternity we will take joy in spending all our time in church, singing hymns and praising God, and thereby giving Him and ourselves infinite pleasure!

Charles Darwin used to be accused of wilfully turning against religion, but he said so honestly: "I was very unwilling to give up my belief. Disbelief crept over me at a very slow rate, but was at last complete. . . . I can indeed hardly see how anyone ought to wish Christianity to be true; for if so, the plain language of the text seems to show that the men who do not believe, and this would include my father, brother, and almost all my best friends, will be everlastingly punished. And this is a damnable doctrine." Amen, say I.

When on one occasion I was chided by a minister for, as he thought, *wilfully refusing* to accept a faith, I told him that that was not my difficulty. Like my father, I had wanted a religion, but most of what faith I once had had been driven out of me when in church I listened to stupid or antiquated sermons and what I felt were offensive hymns.

I have often been impressed by the fact that many people who were deeply and narrowly religious in their youth, later, as they grew older, became more liberal and open-minded. Some became disillusioned and perhaps disgusted with the behavior of some of the religious people whom they had met and worked with along the way. My ministerial father-in-law— a fine, devoted, and brilliant man, a scholar and a splendid preacher—by middle life was so greatly disillusioned over the petty church politics and angling for a bishopric, that he did not want either of his sons to follow him into the ministry. Furthermore, he was swindled out of every dollar of his life's savings by two of the head deacons in his church! They did not go to jail, only because his widow and children were too kind to prosecute them.

Incidentally, one of the worst things a man ever said about himself was what Bryan said at the Scopes "Monkey Trial" in Tennessee. He was reported as having said, "What I thought 50 years ago I think now." No man after 50 years of education and mental and spiritual growth should be able to say such a shameful thing.

When I was young I was far more prone to condemn a man for some failure to abide by the commonly-accepted mores and sexual code than I am today. Today I am immensely more tolerant; I am much more willing to make allowances, or to suspect that there probably were extenuating circumstances that would explain an erring friend's behavior. If today I hear that a man hasn't been faithful to his marriage vows, I refuse to criticize bitterly because I have learned in my consulting room that in many such cases a pathologically frigid woman drove the man out of her bed and then out of his house. In hundreds of cases, when I have learned that a mildly psychotic and sickly woman for many years was no wife to her husband, I have marvelled that he accepted the situation as long as he did—that he remained kind to her, and that he never kicked over the traces.

Many of the readers of this book may well wonder what a mere physician like me is doing, meddling into matters of religion which are not his province; but I am following a good precedent. The first man to study the text of the Bible with a scientific and open mind was a distinguished European physician, one Jean Astruc. Because he had no desire to be burned at the stake, he published his book (in 1753) anonymously.

He pointed out an obvious fact, ignored by Fundamentalists, which is that in Genesis there are two different accounts of the Creation. In one of these accounts God is called Elohim, or "gods," and in the other He is called Jahveh (formerly spelled Jehovah, by mistake). Of special interest is the fact that in the first mythical account no mention is made of Adam's sin, which later was so much talked about by Paul, and today is used as a basis for thousands of sermons designed to explain why God had Jesus so cruelly sacrificed for us on the cross. Actually, as experts have pointed out, the sin of Adam was not such a terrible one. To an anthropologist who knows the mental processes of primitive peoples, it is clear that all Adam did was to break a food taboo. Such taboos still rule the lives of millions of "Stone-Age" men and women in Asia and Africa. They were quickly outgrown in Hawaii when the missionaries came, and Jahveh, too, should have outgrown them long years ago.

Adam sinned, also, in reaching out for more knowledge than Jahveh wanted him to have. The Greeks had this same idea in regard to Prometheus, who, as most of us know, was punished for his sin by being bound to a rock for all eternity. Stories of the Creation and the Flood are versions of ancient myths which were current in Mesopotamia and Egypt some 2,000 years before the Old Testament was written. Curiously, in several of the oldest stories the gods are said to have made man out of clay—turned and moulded on a potter's wheel. All educated people will immediately say, "But that is an idea in Omar Khayyám's poetry," which is right; it is there.

Sometimes the relation between a very ancient myth and the accounts of Creation in the Bible is apparent in a sort of pun, obvious only to an archaeologist who can read both Sumerian and Hebrew. He will tell us that in Sumerian, the word *Ninti* means both "Lady of the rib" and "Lady of Life," and in Hebrew, *Hawwah* (Eve) means "Life." I could go on and fill pages to show that the Creation stories are modifications of very ancient legends which had spread all over the then-known world long before the Old Testament was written. It seems so silly, then, for us to be worrying about Adam's sin, and how it made us all "born sinful," and hence in great need of redemption. Most remarkable are the several ancient Sumerian and Babylonian stories of the Flood which the writers of the Old Testament—hundreds of years later—incorporated into the Bible almost *word for word.*

To me, it has always been a puzzle how civilized people, who, a few hundred years ago, gave up most of the very cruel practices of primitive man—and even of the men of the Middle Ages, who loved to burn at the stake persons who differed with them about some little article of faith—can still accept without question the old idea that even a child who fails to be baptized, or "baptized properly," must be burned in fire *everlasting*. Just imagine: if today a man were to pour kerosene on his dog and set the animal on fire, the people in his city would be so angry and outraged at him they might suggest lynching him. But on Sunday the minister can speak with satisfaction and apparent pleasure about all the people who must keep burning for all eternity, in a lake of boiling brimstone, because of their failure to believe in some dogma, or creed—and no one in the congregation seems to see anything unseemly or cruel about it.

When I have complained about this to good church people, they have said, "Oh, we don't believe in that sort of thing any more: we just don't notice what the minister is saying, and he does not notice either." But I am sure they are wrong. I have had in my office, as patients, priests of God who were ill and utterly miserable because they feared that once, when mumbling the Latin ritual for extreme unction or for baptism, they had used the wrong words, and hence the man or child before them had been condemned to spend eternity in flames. When I have said to these men, "But surely, Father, you don't believe that the God you worship could be so unjust and cruel as to condemn an innocent person to eternal torture simply because *you* made a harmless slip of the tongue," most have answered, "No; we live by the Book; that is the Law; and no one can change a word of it."

Incidentally, as a physician, I can comfort millions of frightened people by saying there can be no such thing as endless torture in a "lake of fire" or "flames everlasting." *No constitution could stand it.* In a few seconds a man would go into shock and become unconscious.

Friends have said to me, "Oh, quit tilting at windmills; ministers no longer believe in the cruel old God and the cruel old religion of 1500 B.C."; but again I must maintain that they are wrong. Recently, one Sunday morning, turning on my radio, I heard on "The Church of the Air" program, the leader of a great Christian denomination preaching a horrible old "fire and brimstone" sermon, saying that the only way that God could provide for the salvation of our congenitally wicked souls (derived from Adam's sin) was through the old Bronze-Age practice of appeasing His wrath by murdering His son and then bathing us in the son's blood.

In those days, if the people in a besieged city saw that things were going against them, the King was likely to try to get back into his god's good graces by murdering his own son and offering him up as a sacrifice. He might do the same thing in an effort to stop a severe epidemic.

Let us all remember that among primitive peoples their god is not expected to have any morality or decency. For instance, Enlil, the great god of the Sumerians, when he fell in love with the goddess Ninlil, raped her. Others of the great Sumerian gods used to get drunk. As we all know, Kronos, the great god of the Greeks, killed and ate his own children; and Jove was anything but a faithful husband or admirable character.

Another thought has kept coming to me: Why did God have to have Jesus killed in order to save all of us from His wrath? Why didn't He just forgive us, and let it go at that? That would have been so simple. Besides, why should God have nursed His anger against us for thousands of years, and all because of an ancient myth about Adam and his breaking of a taboo? Most of us men and women could not stay angry, vindictive and murderous for a month.

That a Christian minister can still believe in a murderous god was shown me one day when I attended the funeral service of a fine young man, the son of the leading layman in the church. I felt so sorry for that minister as he tried to explain why God, "in His infinite wisdom and loving kindness" had killed the young man in an auto accident. I felt like standing up and saying to that minister, "Why not quit accusing God of ordering that death? Why not just say that, so far as you really know, 'He had nothing to do with it?'"

But I knew that that minister was caught in a dilemma. All his life he had been telling his parishioners to thank God for every good thing they received, and so now he had to say that God was responsible also for the very bad thing they had just been handed.

Some 36 years ago I was surprised to find that even my dear, fine mother-in-law—a minister's daughter, a minister's wife, and an able college graduate—had the idea of a cruel god who could strike her down for some childish whim. All her days, from when she was 19 until she was 58, she had devoted her life to the service of God, and especially to foreign missions. She had done magnificent work in China; and when she came back to this country, she often wrote letters until 2 A.M., raising money for God's work.

And then one morning she woke partially paralyzed and unable to say a word. Later, when much of her speech had come back, she kept asking me again and again why God had struck her down so cruelly. What could she have done *inadvertently* to have so greatly offended Him? What mistake had she made? Neither she nor I could think of any.

I marvelled that such an intelligent woman could believe that her God could have struck at her without any conceivable cause. All I could say to my dear mother-in-law was that I was sure God had had nothing to do with her "stroke." All that had happened was that her high blood pressure had caused an artery to break on the surface of her brain.

Many people cannot seem to see that a man of science who, for all his life, has demanded proof for every fact, cannot so change his ways on Sunday morning that he can then accept a very improbable or obviously wrong creed. Also, the scientist who is curious about everything cannot accept a religion without being curious about that, too. He just has to examine it carefully and to ask questions about it. And he is shocked when he finds that he is not supposed to do this. He is shocked when he finds that, in church, blind faith is more highly appreciated than is anything else. As Hilaire Belloc once said,

> Oh! let us never, never doubt
> What nobody is sure about.

Some of the old church fathers were even proud of the fact that they believed a thing *because it was absurd*, or even because it was impossible ("Certum est quia impossible est"). Even Christ is reported as having said, "He that believeth not shall be damned" (Mark 16, 16). I doubt if He ever said this, because it does not sound like Him. That statement was almost certainly stuck in around 300 A.D. by some dour old theologian who could thoroughly enjoy burning a man to death because of his "lack of faith."

In the Middle Ages one of the deadliest sins a man could commit was not to believe in some theological quibble; and for not believing, hundreds of thousands of people were imprisoned or put to death!

The scientist differs from the theologian in many ways. For instance: when he hears his minister say something, he immediately thinks of all of the logical sequences to the statement. When the minister keeps saying every Sunday how all-powerful God is, the scientist immediately thinks, "Well, then, why has He permitted the world to be so full always of brutality, war, famine, and horrible disease? Why, also, does He (supposedly) permit a Devil to tempt us and to run a hell? Why was a bot-fly made, with its thousands of maggots designed to eat alive and torture to death hundreds of thousands of cattle and deer?"

One of the great temptations that comes to an occasional scientist as he grows older and somewhat philosophical is to try to reconcile science and religion. Any book the man may write on this subject is likely to sell very well, because most good people love to hear that their faith is supported by the discoveries of science. But these attempts do not satisfy anyone. The scientists are disgusted with such subterfuges as the well-known one that each of the "days" of the pre-Biblical myth of Creation represents a billion years. Also, the Fundamentalists will have none of this sort of thing. They have to stick to the idea that the universe is only 4,004 years old, which, of course, is preposterous.

I probably could not disturb the faith of a Fundamentalist even by showing him the *National Geographic* magazine for June, 1962, with photographs of the bones of a long-extinct mammoth that was killed by prehistoric men living in Wyoming some 11,000 years ago. They cracked open the animal's ribs in order to eat the marrow, and they left on the site some of their stone knives. The scientist is sure of the year, because of his "carbon dating," but the Fundamentalist would probably not be impressed either by this remarkably accurate chemical test, or by the well-known fact that mammoths died out in North America before 5,000 years ago.

Our Fundamentalist would probably not be impressed with another type of atomic dating that tells us that a certain primitive ape-man, or "missing-link" sort of creature, some of whose bones were recently found by Dr. and Mrs. Leakey in Africa, lived about 1,700,000 years ago. If a Fundamentalist is to cling to his faith, he must feel sure that hundreds of the world's great geologists, paleontologists, astronomers, physicists, and others are either fools or liars who have wasted their lives in universities, "teaching impious ideas" which, as many people in Tennessee still feel today, should be prohibited by law. As I write this, I read that two teachers in Tennessee have just had the courage to get up and defy their superiors who told them not to mention evolution in their classroom work. No open-minded man can walk through a large natural history museum without being convinced of "the obvious fact of evolution."

Any intelligent minister knows that the King James translation of the Bible was not dictated by God. What I marvel at is that a Fundamentalist does not notice that in the middle of each page of many a Bible there is a column of "variant readings." What does he think these mean if not that in trying to translate thousands of verses, the experts could not be sure which of the old Hebrew or Greek texts was most nearly correct. In thousands of places the text was so garbled no one could be sure what it originally said.

Usually, if I speak to a religiously inclined friend about my doubts and puzzlings, he just says, "Go read your Bible, and have faith." But I have read so much about the most ancient manuscripts of the Bible, and the ways in which the texts have become changed by manual copying through the ages, that I cannot settle my doubts by reading a passage or two. Many a time, as I wrote this chapter, I read a verse in the Authorized Version; then in the American Revised Version; then in the fine Moffatt and Goodspeed translations, and then I did not know which translation to use.

In trying to find out what the New Testament writers most probably said, I have found most helpful the big book about Jesus written by Professor Guignebert, one of the two greatest of the world's experts on the Biblical text.* He has spent his life reading the oldest Biblical manuscripts in Greek and Hebrew, and searching through the Apocrypha (the several "Books" which some people think are worthy of being included in the Bible, but which most reject), and through the writings of the old "Church Fathers" and Saints—for every scrap of information he could find on what Christ probably said and did.

What impressed me greatly as I read Guignebert is his statement at the end of chapter after chapter that the text of the early manuscripts, versions, and translations has been so badly garbled during the many centuries of copying by hand, that today, in several places on each page, no one can do more than guess what the words originally were and meant.

Worse yet, as Guignebert and all experts keep saying, many theologians, hoping to strengthen their argument in favor of the dogmas of their particular sect, for two or three hundred years kept adding here and there a sentence or two. Many of these additions are easily recognizable and certainly spurious, and many more are probably so. In one place the added phrase sticks out like a sore thumb because the man who put

* Charles A. H. Guignebert, *Jesus* (New Hyde Park, N.Y.: University Books, 1956).

it into the Greek text wrote in Aramaic (the language of Jesus)!

Furthermore, as Guignebert says, the New Testament is made of at least two parts: one containing what are probably the sayings of Jesus, and the other devised to put a foundation of dogma under the religion that, in the course of the first three or four centuries after Christ, was developing, by accretions (ideas derived from other religions), into what is modern credal Christianity.

Guignebert pointed out that Jesus could hardly have spent any thought, energy or time on the planning of a religion—because He was so sure that in a few months or years, with the coming of the end of the earth, His "Kingdom" would be there to solve all of the religious problems of the Jews. Day after day, as He walked through Galilee, His main teaching was that His hearers should repent and prepare for the Kingdom "that was soon to come." He is reported to have prophesied that it would come during the lifetime of some of His disciples. But it never did come, and Guignebert thinks that as the months and years went by, Jesus must have felt ever more puzzled, embarrassed, and disappointed about this. Obviously, He was mistaken in His main idea, and this unpleasant fact must be faced by all of us. Curiously, I cannot remember ever having heard this fact discussed by a minister.

Another important fact I never heard a minister mention is that the sayings of Jesus, every word of which my religious friends urge me to believe, were not taken down by a court reporter; they were heard by men and women—for the most part, simple country folk—without any ability to write and to make notes of what they had heard. Worse yet, *the sayings had to be transmitted by word of mouth* for from 40 to 80 years before Mark, Matthew, and Luke used them in the writing of their Gospels.

Unfortunately, the three Synoptic writers had not had the privilege of listening to Jesus as He preached, and so they had to accept what old people told them of what they or other people could remember having heard long years before. Anyone who ever read the Bible with care must know that the four accounts of Christ's life vary in many details. Experts agree that Mark, who wrote the earliest Gospel, put the book together some 40 years after the death of Christ; Matthew wrote later, and Luke did not write until 70 or 80 years after Christ's death. John's Gospel is so decidedly different from the first three that it is in a class by itself—with many details doubtful.

Extremely important is Guignebert's statement that it is obvious that by the time of Luke, each of the several groups of church Fathers were far more interested in building up a strong argument in favor of their particular brand of Christianity than they were in giving us the best possible account of what Jesus had actually said and done.

Even when I was a boy it seemed obvious to me that two different groups of men, with two incompatible ideas about Jesus, must have written the New Testament. One group had insisted that His mother was a virgin and His father was God, while another group, who wanted to win the support of the Jews, had, in the first chapter of Matthew, put in a long line of "begats" to prove that Jesus' father was Joseph, and Joseph was a direct descendant of Abraham and David! How remarkable that thousands of men and women can accept without comment or question or wondering two such markedly different and irreconcilable ideas about the origin of Jesus!

As I said above, Professor Guignebert keeps saying sadly that today no one can be sure of what Christ said or did. "The original statements are too vague, and often too greatly in conflict to be reconciled in any way." Unless more "Dead Sea Scrolls" turn up in some very ancient tomb, we probably will never be able to learn the truth.

The first reaction of many devout people to Guignebert's writings may be to assume that he was hostile to Christ and Christianity, and trying to undermine our faith. But, no; the impression I gain is that the professor, like most of us, had only admiration for the greatest religious teacher who ever lived; and much of his lifetime of research into musty old tomes was done with the hope of finding out what Jesus actually said, and separating His real utterances from the words that were later ascribed to Him by people with creeds which they much wanted to strengthen.

We must now accept the fact that Christianity, as we know it today, with a Trinity, a Heaven and a Hell, angels, devils, cherubim, the Beasts of Revelation, the worship of Mary and of the many saints, was put together long after Jesus' death; and parts of it were picked up from many people, such as the Greeks, the Egyptians, the expatriated Jews, the Persians and others. As many wise divines have pointed out, if Jesus were to come back to earth tomorrow, He would be greatly puzzled over much of our Christian dogma—which in His day He never heard of. How surprised He would be to learn that His little barefoot and probably illiterate mother has been made "The Queen of Heaven," with a crown of rare jewels on her head!

Much as the writers of the Old Testament kept railing at the Jews for their tendency to add foreign religious ideas to their Judaism, so Paul in his epistles kept scolding the early Christians for their tendency to keep picking up and adopting religious ideas from their neighbors. Obviously, Paul strongly disapproved of these ideas, and fought them as hard as he could. But he could not stop the process; often concessions had to be made to satisfy groups of new converts.

For instance, people such as the Egyptians, who for hundreds of years had worshipped their goddess (Isis) with a child on her lap (the infant Horus), could easily change over and worship Mary, holding *her* Child. Also, people who for ages had been polytheistic could enjoy praying to dozens or hundreds of Saints. As I write this, some of the more liberal Cardinals and Bishops meeting with the Pope in Rome are suggesting that some day the Church purge itself of its large

amount of legendary material for which there never was any
valid or written evidence.

The idea of a Trinity was almost certainly unknown to Jesus.
We know that the addition of a third element, or Holy Ghost,
came partly from Philo's idea of a *Logos* (a rational principle
supposed to govern and develop the Universe), and partly
from St. John's vague statement that "In the beginning was
the Word, and the Word was with God, and the Word was
God."

For a few hundred years theologians kept attacking and
even excommunicating one another because of their differing
theories as to the exact nature of Jesus and God. (See Dr.
Homer Smith's great book *Man and His Gods.*) * Finally, in
380 A.D., the Emperor Theodosius officially put an end to the
fighting by declaring that the Father, the Son, and the Holy
Ghost "were of equal majesty in the Holy Trinity."

From my boyhood days onward, one of the things about
religion that bothered many of my scientifically trained friends
and me was the fact, so plainly apparent in the earlier-written
books of the Old Testament (and already commented on in
this chapter), that the original Jahveh was anything but an
admirable person. Obviously, the primitive people of perhaps
1,500 B.C. who had developed a mental picture of Him had
patterned it after the vicious and immoral kings of that day—
men with cruel and murderous impulses—who constantly kept
demanding flattery and propitiatory gifts, and who perhaps
had to be approached on hands and knees. My fellow scientists
and I could never reconcile the Biblical descriptions of the
earlier Jahveh with the "Kind Father" of Christ.

Then a dear old friend of my mountain-climbing days, Professor Frederick Badé, helped me much by telling me that, in
his opinion, one of the best things that ministers could do
would be to keep pointing out to their parishioners that the
Jahveh of 1,500 B.C. was not the Jahveh of 30 A.D., or the God

* Homer Smith, *Man and His Gods* (New York: Grosset & Dunlap, Inc.,
1956).

of 1910 A.D. Jahveh had changed; he had improved with the times and with the better education and refinement of the people; and along the way had become a much kinder and nicer person.

Eventually, in 1915, Badé published his splendid book, *The Old Testament in the Light of Today* (Houghton Mifflin). I so prize this book that I still keep it on the stand by the side of my bed. The idea I got from Badé is that the only detail the several Jahvehs have in common is the name.

Like the rest of the gods of His day, the first Jahveh had no concern with morals. Sometimes Abraham or Moses had to scold Him, and talk Him out of doing some unfair or disgraceful thing (Gen. 18:25). As Abraham once said to Him, "Shall not the Judge of all the earth do right?" As all ethnologists know, the god of a primitive tribe is concerned with perhaps four things: one, insuring good hunting or fishing; two, insuring good multiplication of the tribe's herds and flocks; three, helping his people to rob their neighbors and win battles; and four, maintaining a detailed ritual in his temple worship.

An important point that all of us should keep remembering is that a primitive god is concerned with the welfare of *only* "*his people.*" Like a god of desert dwellers even today, he is concerned only with the behavior of one of his tribesmen toward another. He has not the slightest interest in the welfare of the neighboring tribe on the other side of the mountain; and he thinks it permissible for his people to rob and murder any *stranger* who happens to pass by! Mohammed had the same idea when he said that Allah advised his worshippers to be good *to one another*, but always murderous and merciless to the infidel. As I have said, in several places in the Bible we read that Jahveh was dishonest, and not ashamed of it.

Another interesting point is that the god of a primitive group presides over only a small area, perhaps a few hundred square miles. Jahveh was not supposed to go down even from the hills of Judea to the nearby coastal plain inhabited by the

Philistines. Once, when the Jews signed a treaty with the "Peoples of the plain," the Bible writer tells us that the commissioners could not swear by their god "because Jahveh wasn't down there!" Similarly, when the Jews once attacked a city in Moab, they had to give up the siege and go home, because in Moab the local god, Chemosh, was more powerful than was Jahveh. Jahveh did not have any jurisdiction there!

As many people know, about the time of Amos and Hosea, the Jews, with their advancing civilization and improving culture, began to see that there should be more to religion than just a set of taboos and regulations in regard to temple worship and the sacrifice of animals. They began to get the idea that a religious man should be a better-than-average person who would not despoil the "widow and the fatherless." After this, Jahveh became a more likeable character than He had ever been before. As Samuel Butler once said so truly, *"a fine god is one of the finest works of man!"* Interestingly, in his splendid book, *The Dawn of Conscience*, the eminent Dr. Breasted shows us that the Egyptians had the idea that religion should mean goodness 2,000 years before the Jews got it.

Anyone who is conversant with the myths about the ancient Greek gods on Mt. Olympus knows what a childish, peevish, immoral, and adulterous lot they were. Lucretius, the great poet of Roman times, said that surely the destinies of this world should not be left in the hands of such a despicable crew!

We must face the fact that a scientist, when he tries to conceive of a God, does not think of an old man who, in the evenings "walks in the cool of his garden," and if he goes out for a drive, goes in an ancient two-wheeled chariot. The scientist does not think of a god such as was depicted so interestingly in that wonderful play *Green Pastures*—an old Negro sitting at a roll-top desk, giving a cigar to the angel Gabriel.

No; the scientist thinks perhaps of *a mind* filled with such infinite wisdom as would be needed for the conception, planning, designing, and working-out of this vast universe. He thinks of an intellect enormously greater than that of even a great genius. He is not likely to think of a man-like (anthropomorphic) body to go with the mind.

A big question that I never heard a minister discuss is: Is the God who presumably built this universe still running it and supervising it, and modifying its behavior for the benefit of a few of the people on it who happen to worship Him, and who do this in a way acceptable to Him; or did He leave it eons ago to run by itself with the help of immutable laws? Dr. Homer Smith tells us (in *Man and His Gods*) that in 1678 the Rev. Cudworth, an English divine, wrote a book in which he asked these questions. Cudworth preferred the view that Divine Providence left the universe to itself, and is not now constantly watching over every detail. As a result of the publication of his book, the Rev. Mr. Cudworth was, of course, promptly thrown out of his church as a heretic.

For many reasons, some theists eventually sided with Cudworth and chose the non-immanent view of God, even though, in doing this, they had to abandon their much-loved belief in the efficacy of prayer. Obviously, if the Deity cannot interfere in the operations of this universe, prayer—for intervention—is useless. I am not saying it is, because I do not know; but as I shall soon show, an answer might be obtained through a scientific study, if anyone cared or dared to make it.

It would be particularly interesting to study several thousand "faith healers" and to find out if, on the average, they live longer and have any less morbidity (tendency to illness) than most of us have. Hard-headed statisticians would fear one possibility, however, and this is that many faith healers may be people who started out in life with unusually rugged health. I am thinking of the woman who once asked me to examine her carefully to see if she was healthy enough to join a faith-healing group, and never again to see a doctor!

More than 80 years ago, that kindly, and absolutely honest and scientific Quaker, Sir Francis Galton, tried to get an answer to the question, "Are there any statistics to show that prayer is efficacious?" He thought that if prayer often has an influence on the course of disease, this should have been noticed by physicians. But after talking to many doctors, he found that none of them had been impressed with the value of prayer. Disease in a devout minister seemed to run the same course as it did in an unbeliever. Galton found a study reported in the *Journal of the Statistical Society* for 1882—a study which gave no proof that prayer helps.

Galton then searched for evidence to indicate that people such as kings and queens *who, every day are prayed for in all of the churches of their land,* live longer than commoners do. Dr. Guy made a study of this, and found that among a number of groups of people, the average age at death was *lowest* among members of the Royal Family! * Many royal persons suffered, also, from psychoses; and the more pious and godly kings and queens were not particularly fortunate in their health. A study of the average ages at death of many distinguished divines, lawyers, and doctors showed that the pious divines did no better than the often godless doctors!

Then Galton made a study of the health and longevity of much-prayed-for missionaries, and found that upon arriving on the foreign field, many of the men and their wives quickly caught some tropical disease and died. Often the missionary suffered so much from ill health he had to be "invalided" home.

Once when a much-loved child of mine lay at death's door, I tried to pray but I could not do it very well. I was not sure enough that there existed the sort of man-like God who would take pity on me and help me, and I was far from sure that if He wanted to help me He *could* change the laws of the Universe enough to help my child. Certainly, if the child had fallen out of an upper story window, the Good Lord could not have turned off the force of gravity for even a moment. If He had, in a single second everything on the surface of this

* *Journal of the Statistical Society, 22:* 355.

earth would have flown out into space. There, all of us would quickly have been destroyed.

Many wise men have concluded that since all of the laws of this universe are intimately related, God cannot abrogate anyone of them without wrecking everything. If this be true, there is not much use in our praying for relief from disaster. As the poet Francis Thompson expressed this so well (in "Mistress of Vision"),

> All things by immortal power,
>> Near or far,
>> Hiddenly
> To each other linked are,
> That thou canst not stir a flower
> Without troubling a star.

Once, I got to wondering how God can find the time to listen to all of the millions of prayers that go up to Him every day. Each year I get requests for help and advice from a mere 100,000 people, and I cannot find enough time to *read* all of their letters—let alone to answer them. And so I wonder what God does with all the millions of prayers that must go out to Him. Sometimes I marvel at the egotism of people who will pray to God for an hour or two—perhaps about some trivial matter.

Everyone who likes to pray long prayers should read Edmund Gosse's remarkable book *Father and Son.** There (p. 268) Gosse, the son, tells how one day when he was eleven or twelve and wanted to go to a children's party, his overly pious father, suspecting that such a party would in some way be very sinful, got down on his knees and "wrestled" with God for some time—trying to find out what His wishes were in the matter! If I had been God, I would quickly have told the man to quit bothering me about so utterly stupid and picayune a matter. Who ever told him that he and his small problems

* Charles Scribner's Sons, 1907.

were so tremendously important to the Director of the Universe?

I have heard ministers say that no one can be good without the help and guidance of religion, together with the great fear of hell that goes with a religious faith; but I have always doubted this. I could point to many an old friend of mine—in medicine and science—who led an exemplary life in spite of the fact that he had no religion.

I was interested once in what my old friend Professor Raymond Pearl said to me as we were discussing the question of why many churchless men live good lives. Pearl was a vivid character and a man who spoke his mind frankly and forcibly. He said that a godless man, such as he, often had many virtues just because he was more comfortable and better satisfied with them than without them.

"For instance," he said, "as is the case with many a man, I sometimes meet a charming woman who attracts me, and who, I can soon sense, would not be too greatly averse to having an affair with me. Why, then, don't I go ahead and have the adventure? If I don't, it is not because I am impotent, or lacking in the spirit of adventure; or lacking in the love of making a conquest; it is not because I have any religious scruples to deter me; and not because I would be distressed with the idea of sinning.

"No; I leave the woman alone for several reasons: one, that my wife and I are such good friends and chums that I would not feel it was cricket for me to cheat on her; two, I so hate lying I couldn't be bothered to be constantly carrying out deceptions; and three, I am too busy—I would not want to spend the time that would be needed to pay court to the woman!"

I can imagine that many ministers of the Gospel would be disgusted with this type of godless goodness, but the world is full of it, and it works well enough. Actually, sometimes it works much better than does the morality of some deeply religious people who are not averse to fleecing a trusting friend.

I do not have to labor here to prove that there are godless men who are kind and honest, while there are some very pious men who can be very unkind and very dishonest.

In this connection I am much interested in what Samuel Butler once wrote. He, the agnostic son of a minister, said that he had taken pains to correct impatience, irritability, and other like faults in his character—"not because I care two straws about my character, but because I find the correction of such faults . . . makes life easier, and saves me from getting into scrapes."

A fact which, curiously, none of the devout people of this world seem ever to worry about is that since the people in thousands of religions and sects are sure that *only they* have the key to heaven, *all the others obviously must be wrong in their beliefs, and hence must be locked out and damned.* But the proverbial man from Mars would say, since there are scores of religions and hundreds of sects, the chances that any one of them has the key must be very small. If I were a devoted adherent to any sect, I would feel very uneasy about all those many chances that my group might belong among the thousand or more that are mistaken, and might be made up of people for whom there is no hope of salvation, and no future in heaven.

Incidentally, I wish it would occur to millions of people that they are silly in being so sure that only their sect has the secret of worshipping God acceptably. They forget that they were born into their religion, just as thousands of us Americans were born to be Republicans or Democrats. They argue as if, in their youth, they had studied and compared hundreds of religions and sects, and then, with great wisdom, had chosen "the only correct one out of the lot—the only one that leads to heaven."

Actually, if in my childhood, I, who was born a Catholic, had been adopted into a Methodist family, I would, of course, have grown up as a good Methodist. If my father and mother had kept their original faith and had not, in 1896, become

Unitarians, I might have remained, at least nominally, a Catholic! When a devout Methodist tells me he would rather see his daughter dead than married to a Lutheran or a Presbyterian, I say, "Why feel so bitter about this? Remember that your being a Methodist is only an accident of birth." Occasionally my friend has the honesty to say, "That's right; I hadn't thought of that."

As I said above, in my studies of the beginnings of religion, I have been influenced by my lifelong reading in archaeology, anthropology, ethnology, and the thinking of primitive man.

Another thing that much study of archaeology has done to me has been to make it impossible for me to believe in the resurrection *of the body*, a belief in which is demanded by some churches. In the first place, I know as a physician that within a few minutes after a man is dead, his brain is so changed chemically that if he were to be resuscitated, he would be an imbecile—a sort of "human vegetable." Certainly after he is embalmed his brain is almost as badly destroyed as if he had been cremated.

According to one translation made of a difficult, garbled passage, Job says (Job 19, 25-27)

> And after my skin, even this body, is destroyed,
> Then without my flesh shall I see God.

A point I have never seen discussed is a highly significant one, and this is that if we were to go with a group of archaeologists out into the bone-dry deserts of Egypt, and there dig into hundreds of graves, dating back perhaps some 5,000 years, what would we find? We would find the harder parts of the skeletons of the people who died and were then supposed to start right off for "the other world." Their relatives were so sure their loved ones would leave *immediately* that, in the bowls in the tombs we find the dried remnants of the bread and other foods they were to eat on the journey.

But here is the important fact which I have never seen or heard mentioned anywhere: those persons never got up to go.

And if they haven't yet started after 5,000 years, is it likely that they will ever go? Also, are *our* bodies, when dead, likely to do any better, in getting away quickly for our supposed immediate journey "up" to heaven? (Incidentally, where today can we possibly locate Heaven? Certainly not "up," because in 12 hours, as the earth rotates, "up" will be "down.")

Also, what good would it do for a terribly emaciated or badly crippled person, or a person with most of his bodily organs riddled with cancer or tuberculosis, to wake in heaven—with his wreck of a body? What pleasure would that give him? To be happy, he would have to get a new and better body; but when and where and how would he get it?

People who take refuge in the idea that only their soul will go to heaven or hell are not quite rational in trying to solve the problem. They expect to feel the bliss of heaven or the torture of hell; but will a disembodied soul (whatever that is) be able to feel bliss or terrible punishment in the next world? I wonder.

As a life-long reader of archaeologic literature I have always mused over the fact that hundreds of the great gods who for three or four thousand years were worshipped in great temples all over the Middle East are now gone, and so forgotten that their names are known only to archaeologists. And I muse over the fact that all that saved Jahveh from this fate were such facts as that the Jews held together as a religious group; they kept easily available their ancient books; and the Christians incorporated the Old Testament with their New Testament to make the Bible.

Whatever good has been effected in this world by Christianity has been largely counteracted by the centuries-old demand of good church people that men stop thinking, stop getting educated, and stop using their powers of reason. I imagine this insistence of the church and the "Holy Inquisition" that men not study and not think had much to do with producing the Dark Ages.

I read now that the Amish (a very conservative religious sect) are thinking of emigrating to Canada to save their children from having to go to a public school. The impression of the newspaper editor, whose column I read, was that the Amish do not want their children to get an education: they probably see that an educated man would not feel as they do that a man's religious salvation depends on such a minor detail as his remaining too old-fashioned ever to get into an automobile!

About 1915 I became particularly disgusted with organized religion in America when a gentle, kindly, very intelligent and able minister came to me, sick and broken-hearted because he had just been forced out of his church and out of California. A fine speaker, and a fine, friendly, consecrated "man's man," preaching in a college town, Dr. L. had been filling his church every Sunday evening with students from the nearby university, but hardly a one would join, and this puzzled him.

Finally, when he learned that their only objection to joining was their fear that fellow students would come to jeer at them when they went up into the tank for total immersion, Dr. L. asked his Board if he might baptize the students in his study with a little sprinkling. The Board gave its approval, but then two retired ministers in the church led a bitter and vicious fight to have the Rev. L. thrown out. The conservatives won—as they usually do—and the church membership was split into two hostile camps. Then, with cruel vindictiveness, the two old ministers not only got my friend debarred from every church of their denomination in California, but tried, also, to run out of their State Seminary all those teachers who, during the controversy, had kept silent and had failed to join in the attack on Dr. L.

Incidentally, one question about religion that has kept puzzling me all my days is this: when a minister has spent his life preaching Christ and His great kindliness, how, when a church row starts up, can he behave like those two old ministers did—in the most vicious and un-Christian way? How, in perhaps 40 years of preaching Christ, could he have failed to absorb even a trace of His gentle spirit? How could he have failed to note that He particularly despised people like him, whose main concern with religion was with some small unimportant item of ritual? I have no doubt that if those two ministers had lived in the Middle Ages, they would have thoroughly enjoyed having Dr. L. burned at the stake as a heretic!

One thing that has always disturbed me is the tendency of many parents to cram religion down the throats of their small children. As a physician, many a time I have seen this do much harm to an easily worried and frightened youngster. Edmund Gosse's remarkable story of his life with his overly pious father (*Father and Son*) shows vividly how much damage can be done if religion is forced upon a child. As the younger Gosse wrote (p. 348), "What a charming companion . . . my father would have been . . . if it had not been for this stringent piety which ruined it all." The constant efforts of his father to make of him a priggish saint forced the lad to leave home as soon as he was old enough to get away.

It has interested me to read that in ancient Rome, Seneca remarked on the fact that some of his country's leaders, who had lost all of their faith in the ancient gods, kept insisting that the *forms* of the old religion be observed by the priests and the people. The authorities were convinced, as many people are today, that religion is *good* for children, and hence it must be drilled into them.

I agree with that famed professor of English, William Ellery Leonard, who wrote that "Sometime the race of man will be wise enough and courageous enough not to speak of God to little children." In *Redbook* magazine for December, 1961, there was an excellent article by Ardis Whitman on "What you should *not* tell a child about God." I was so glad to find this highly intelligent daughter of a minister feeling exactly as I do about the inadvisability of filling children with a lot of very questionable ideas about God. I have seen many cases in which such religious instruction definitely intensified a child's inherited tendency to mental disease.

I myself remember my terror as a child when, in Hawaii, we would have a torrential tropical downpour that would quickly make a pond out of our yard; and I would fear that another Flood was coming in which we all would be drowned. One never knows what a nervous child is going to make out of the ancient religious ideas that are drilled into him. How much happier I would have been if my parents had known, and could have told me, that the Story of the Flood was only an ancient Sumerian myth, probably based on a faint memory of some tremendous Mesopotamian flood that drowned thousands of people, perhaps around 4000 B.C.

When our children were small I used to say to my wife, "Let us never fill their minds with religious ideas which can disturb them, or which later they will see are either groundless or definitely wrong."

If an occasional reader has stayed with me this long, he is now likely to be asking, "But if you haven't a definite religious faith, *what do you have* to live by? Don't you believe in anything? How can you go on with life if you see no purpose in it? Why do you bother to live decently and honestly if you are not sure there is a Supreme Being who cares what you do? Why do you keep working hard all your days doing good, if in the end you will have no reward? Haven't you a conscience? Haven't you a soul? Can you imagine a fine, kindly, idealistic, devoted, and unselfish human being—without a soul? Don't you believe that most people would prefer to be good, and that the great goodness of many men and women proves that there is a kindly God somewhere? How do you explain the behavior of those innumerable persons like the early Christian martyrs who willingly died for an idea? What is your feeling in regard to Christ? Don't you try to follow His teachings?"

I find the answering of some of these questions difficult, perhaps because I seldom spend any time puzzling over them.

Like the centipede in the jingle that I quoted earlier in this book, I like to live each day, just walking along, without trying to figure out which leg "comes after which." Similarly, whatever goodness there is in me seems to have been there from birth. I suppose some of it was taught me, but my impression is that my "education" in Sunday School and church had no influence on me.

If I always have had a natural tendency to be honest with my patients; to save them from needless expense, and to go out of my way to be kind to them—which behavior, incidentally, is most of my religion—I cannot take credit for it; it is the way I am made. I think it is my inheritance from my good parents.

Not many people realize that medicine can be practiced either as a sort of kindly religion—a "calling," as the great Dr. Osler said it should be—or as a rapacious business in which a man, by "making work" or by performing operations of very doubtful value, can get from each patient who comes in every cent he or she can spare. I was happy during my 25 years of medical practice in the Mayo Clinic if only because there I had nothing to do with the business of medicine; all I had to do with a patient was to try to help him. In a clinic where the physicians are all on a fixed salary, no one has any temptation to "make work" or to order an unnecessary operation.

During the years in which I practiced alone, and had to earn my living by my profession, my kind-hearted secretary often did the charging; and we had agreed that little should be asked of those many people whose income was small and whose responsibilities were great.

I think that in this book I have said enough to show that I live happily by the satisfactions I find in my work, which I trust has for long been helpful to my fellow men. If I were not driven by a desire to be useful to my country and to the cause of medicine, I could retire into an immensely less laborious life than the one which I now lead.

I think life has a purpose when a man keeps trying all his

days to leave the world a little better than he found it. Also, he is happy if he can be doing each day something creative— making something that is of value.

I imagine many people want to feel that a Divine Being is constantly observing what they are doing, and is approving of it. I know that I am made happy when, as occasionally happens, a physician tells me he has found a book of mine so useful and helpful that he has kept rereading it until it has gone to pieces in his hands; or I am glad when an old student comes up to me to tell of his great indebtedness to me for some training I once gave him, not only in medicine, but in living worthily. For me, an occasional reward like this is heart-warming; but it is not at all necessary. I could work cheerfully for years without a pat on the back from anyone. My joy in "getting things done" is a sufficient reward.

Yes; I have a conscience; but it is not of the type that can be a nuisance to a man. When I make a mistake I regret it; I am sorry, and I hope I will not make that particular mistake again, but I never brood over it.

I know I could not be happy unless I were dealing in an honorable, kindly, and generous way with my patients. I wonder if perhaps I am like a Lee of Virginia or a Cabot of Boston, who will not do anything that is shameful or dishonest because such a thing "just isn't done in his family."

I do not have any opinion about the souls of men, because I cannot see one or get hold of it in any way so as to study it. Hence, why should I argue about it or try to understand it?

I would prefer to believe that there is a kindly God somewhere, but because I have found no way of becoming sure of this, I do not spend time arguing about it. I have great respect for the teachings of Jesus. But in all honesty, I have to admit that there are a few of them I will not follow. It would probably be unwise of me to give all I have to the poor; and I will not try to be meek, or "poor in spirit." Neither will I give up all that I am doing and spend my time preparing for the end of the world. I feel no need for a life in heaven or in hell, partly because I think most of us make our heaven or hell right here and now—on earth. I am satisfied that the mythical heaven and hell were devised by priests who felt the need for scaring men who had thumbed their nose at religion. In a way, the priests said, "You may have escaped us in this life, but we'll get you in the next one."

In trying to find words with which the better to express my ideas about beliefs, I have been greatly helped by two autobiographies of great men: one written by the eminent physicist, Professor Millikan (1951), and the other written by a former high prelate of the Catholic church—Father Ildefonso—a man whose business and joy it was, until he was over 40, to keep splitting hairs in arguments relating to the philosophy, laws, creeds, and dogmas of his religion.

Strange to say, both of these men—approaching the problems of religion from two very different points of view and with very different types of basic training and reasoning— reached the same conclusion, which is that there are two parts to the Christian religion: one, a faith in the simple and kindly teachings of Jesus, and the other, a faith in the innumerable, weird and unprovable theories about the exact nature of Christ, God the Father, the Holy Ghost, the Virgin Mary, and others; theories which for ages have been argued about and fought over bitterly with no profit to anyone. Since no one can know anything definite about these subjects, men can argue as violently and for as long as they like—and get nowhere.

Professor Millikan stated his faith in this way: one type of religion is based on that altruistic idealism and unselfishness which is the message of Jesus, and the other is based on a collection of "superstitions, silly theologies, bigotry, intolerance and other excrescences." I agree with Dr. Millikan that the determination to subordinate one's own immediate desires and "short-range interests" to the good of one's fellow men (as we see it) is "the essence of religion."

I agree further with Dr. Millikan when he says that it is

hard to divorce goodness, with an altruistically moral conduct and a sense of duty, from the idea that in the universe there is something which gives significance and meaning and value to existence—something that we can call God. The main difficulty that faces both the scientist and the theologian is to *define* this God. In the most thought-compelling book of all, the Old Testament, we find Zophar asking the question which we scientists are still asking today, "Can'st thou by searching find out God?" (Job 11:7).

As I said early in this chapter, the unlearned man, who knows nothing of the inconceivably great vastness of the universe and the inconceivably great complexity of even a snail or a cricket, can be satisfied with the mental picture of a God who dresses in a robe and sandals, and has a long white beard. Great scientists feel the need for a God so full of knowledge of chemistry, physics, and mathematics that they just cannot form any concept of Him.

As a great physicist once said to me, if, in the days before the discovery of X-rays and radioactivity, a group of the world's ablest scientists could have asked God to tell them about the make-up of the atom, when He started talking about such things as the many tiny particles, or about quantum mechanics, or radioactive isotopes, no one would have understood what He was saying. Similarly, today, if God were to tell a group of atomic physicists what they still want to know about the atom, again, His listeners would probably not understand a word of what He was saying—the mathematical vocabulary He would have to use would be "Greek to them." How strange that over 2,000 years ago Job would seem to have understood some of this when he said:

> What I did not understand, I uttered,
> Things far beyond me of which I had no knowledge
> (Job 42:3).

Just as I received great help from Dr. Millikan, so also I got great help from the life story of a professional theologian—

Father Ildefonso (later called John Tettemer)—once a learned prelate and advisor on church law to a group in the Vatican.* How wonderful that after great mental travail this very lovable man wound up with practically the same religious ideas that Dr. Millikan had—and I have.

During a long stay in a TB sanatorium, Father Ildefonso had time in which to do much thinking, and as a result, like Job, he lost his faith "in the power of the human mind to know Truth and the Ultimate." The important point is that while he lost his faith in the orthodox and dogmatic details of his religion, he retained his faith in the simple teachings of Jesus, and he retained his desire to follow Him.

To me, the most important paragraph in Tettemer's great book is the one in which I sense his regret over the fact that always theologians have kept arguing and fighting over all sorts of details of dogma about which they could never really know anything anyway.

What is cheering is that with Tettemer's renunciation of that large part of the religion that he had once held so dear, he felt a release and an uplifting joy. He felt he was coming out into a new world, away from the old small one formerly pictured in his mind. He tells of the pleasure he got when he began to study science. Instead of feeling that he had lost much, he felt he had gained a new life. Although this involved the unlearning of most of what he had ever learned, he felt strangely happy and closer than ever to God.

Tettemer said that in writing his book he did not want to take from anyone his faith; all he wanted to do was to urge men to try to distinguish well between the two elements of the Christian religion: the faith in Jesus; and the belief in many creeds and dogmas. As he said, "The tragedy of men's lives is that this true faith of Jesus is nearly always confused with faith in a creed."

As Tettemer went on to say, "Conformity, orthodoxy, is the idol of small men, and we are all small. . . . Love, friendship,

* *I Was a Monk* (Alfred A. Knopf, 1951), p. 255.

beauty, altruism, pure faith, true religion, sacrifice, mother love, life itself, all are begot of God, and are beyond the explaining and the leveling influence of our intellects."

What strikes me as remarkable is that I, whose life-training has all been in science, find myself now so closely in agreement with this great and kindly student of theology. We both wound up agreeing that when we men and women strip religion of all its creeds and dogmas, its weird and unprovable and unnecessary theories, and get back to the simple religion of Christ—then we have something that we can accept and can live by.

12

Thoughts on Evolution

PEOPLE ASK ME, "How did you, a physician, happen to get interested in evolution?"

The answer is that any person, so constituted that he must spend time puzzling over religion and God, is likely to become —like me—a life-long student of geology, paleontology, and evolution. These are sciences which show us when and how the myriads of living things that once existed and still exist on this earth came into being, and how they evolved and developed.

The record is there in the fossil-bearing rocks, waiting for anyone who cares to read it. One can begin near the floor of the Grand Canyon of the Colorado—that 4,000-foot-deep gash in the side of the earth. Reading from bottom to top, one can see how through millions of years little sea animals evolved and gradually became more complicated.

When I was eleven or twelve and wanted to understand better the origins of the mountain ranges and tufa cones of the island of Oahu on which I lived, I started reading many books on geology. Somewhere along the way, I heard of the tablet

226

which the great architect Sir Christopher Wren placed in St. Paul's Cathedral in London after he had finished his work. In it he suggested that anyone who wanted to know something about the man who had built that huge edifice should *look about him*. This suggestion struck me forcibly, and confirmed me in my belief that the surest way in which I might learn something about the Great Architect of the Universe would be to "look about me," to see just how He had done His work. Such a study should certainly tell me much about Him and His "mental processes."

And this is why, ever since, I have devoted some of my spare time to reading the works of the great men who have spent their lives studying the many living things that have appeared on this earth, and I have noted the ways in which, in the vastness of time, one form has replaced another. I have puzzled over the inferences which it seems to me must be derived from the study of the series of fossils that now runs back for two billion years.

I think I was in my thirties when I bought most of the books written by Charles Darwin, Thomas H. Huxley, and Alfred R. Wallace, and in what little spare time I had, I read them with great interest. Also, I have read everything I could find on primitive Stone-Age man.

As I read, I soon began to see that the Great Builder—if there was one—did not begin like a man who is omniscient and knows exactly what he is going to do. He began more as a man would do who at first knew little, and only gradually learns—by constant experimenting. Like a man, He learned at times from successes, and often He learned from failures.

Scientists can now be fairly certain that some two and a half billion years ago the Designer started making such creatures as the ultra-microscopic viruses, the microscopic bacteria, and the microscopic single-celled amebas and yeasts and algae. We cannot expect to find fossil records of such creatures because they were too soft and too tiny to leave a recognizable imprint in the ancient rocks.

The first fossils of simple marine animals so far discovered are in rocks (in Australia and Canada) which can be shown with modern chemical methods to be two billion years old. To me, the important point is that the earliest living things were primitive and simple in their construction. They lived in water. Only gradually, over the course of many millions of years, did plants and animals become more complicated and better designed. Only after millions of years did a few animals (the lung-fish and amphibians, like frogs) crawl out of the water to live on the land. Later, some mammalian land animals, like the otters, the seals, sea lions, sea cows, and the ancestors of the dolphins and whales, went back into the sea— they had their bodies changed in shape, and they learned to live much like fish.

The Designer worked like an inventor of today; He threw out some of the botches He had made, and He often kept the good part of a mechanism and redesigned the bad part that had been giving trouble. Some very ancient animals, like the horseshoe crab or the opossum. He left as they were. He kept them as "living fossils," and curiously, they still survive today, teaching us much.

A believer in an anthropomorphic, or man-like, god might say that when He saw He had made a mistake and had poorly designed many millions of animals, He threw them out and started again like an automobile-maker—with a new and better model. But it would doubtless be unwise to ascribe to the Designer the appearance of a man and the thoughts, motives, and acts of a man.

The early animals were "cold-blooded"—they had to accept the temperature of the water or air about them, and this was a handicap. Often the cold must have made them sluggish. Later, many animals, like man, were equipped with mechanisms which kept the body temperature constant, and warmer than that of the surrounding winter air.

Many of the earliest little animals had to live for almost all of their lives stuck to one place on an underwater rock. Later most animals were built so that they could move about and search for their food.

Interestingly, one of the first things the Designer did when He wanted a more complicated animal was to make something like a centipede, with a number of segments much alike, and a head at one end and a tail at the other. To some extent, this design is still in our bodies, where we have a backbone made up of some 24 segments—bones called vertebrae.

The big question that I still puzzle over is: Did all of the marvelous mechanisms like the eye and the ear develop haphazardly, or were they built according to design by a Supreme Architect who saw the need for a special organ and then built it with great knowledge and wisdom? It is very hard to see how some organs could have developed accidentally, as Darwin envisaged it, with a series of little improvements which could give an animal a better chance to survive in the presence of its enemies. How could a complicated organ with many essential parts give an animal any advantage until it was all finished and ready to work? Let us consider the protective mechanism of a skunk. The little bag that contains the vile-smelling chemical was transformed out of a smelly anal gland that can be found in a number of animals. But it had to be modified so that it could make one of the foulest chemicals known to man. Then, probably, a special muscle had to be devised to do the squirting; also, special nerves coming from the brain had to be made—to cause the muscle to contract. Until all of these devices were finished and ready to work, the skunk would not be an animal to be feared.

Another example is that of the halteres—the two little rods which, by vibrating rapidly on each side of certain flies, serve to keep them on an even keel, much as a rapidly spinning gyroscope keeps many a humanly devised machine flying well. First, there would seem to have been a Designer who saw that the fly could profit from having such a mechanism, and hence started building it. Then there would have to be several parts of the mechanism designed in detail for a special purpose.

Finally, all of these parts would have to be properly fitted and made to function together.

Because I worked for years as a physiologist, I know the necessity for the Designer's having devised a very special kind of muscle which could keep contracting and relaxing at a tremendous speed, without quickly becoming fatigued. Ordinary voluntary muscles, such as the ones that move my pen as I write this, could not possibly serve. The specially devised muscle would have to have an unusually rich blood supply designed for it. Also, special nerves would have to connect the insect's central nervous system, and perhaps particularly its "head ganglion," with the halteres and the wings. Finally, there would have to be an inconceivably complicated chemical mechanism put into the chromosomes and genes of the insect —a mechanism which would enable the whole apparatus to be inherited and built into each one of the innumerable subsequent generations of the fly. I just cannot imagine all these complicated parts of the mechanism arising by accident.

I marvel, also, how a carnivorous plant which catches and digests bugs could have developed. First, where would the idea have come from? Why, also, if there was only one Designer, was the idea of a bug-consuming plant worked out in *different ways* in a number of plants? Some plants have a pitcher-like cavity full of fluid, into which the bugs fall, are drowned, and, later digested. Perhaps at the top of the pitcher there are glands which produce some sweet substance to attract the bugs; then perhaps there will be some hairs out onto which they will venture and from which they will fall into the water. There must be a device to keep the pitcher full of liquid, and probably, also, some glands to produce a pepsin-like ferment to digest the bugs. Also, a mechanism for the absorption and use by the plant cells of the chemicals derived from the bugs is needed. How were all these separate mechanisms designed and fitted together to make a well-functioning apparatus? It is hard for me to believe that the separate and needed parts were all formed by accident.

The Designer, if there was one, went at the problem in another way in making the "Venus-flytrap." In this plant, two "leaves" come together to grab an insect and then hold it until it is digested. Again, the mechanism must be a complicated one, and can hardly work unless all of the several parts have been well designed and built, and put together, each for a special purpose. There would be no use in the plant's grabbing a bug unless it could hold it for a while and digest it, and then absorb and use the resultant juice.

Another thing that puzzles me is how we came by our color vision. I can see how, gradually, by little improvements, the complicated eye of a color-blind animal might have begun as a light-sensitive spot on the head of a primitive aquatic animal, and then developed by thousands of small additions to form the complicated camera-like eye of a man, or the remarkable compound-eye of an insect. But I cannot see how, *accidentally*, we human beings could have become supplied with color vision!

Because this is a faculty which we did not absolutely need, I have the feeling that a Designer with some esthetic and ambitious feelings must have gotten the idea and then worked out the exceedingly difficult chemical details—with color-sensitive pigments and special centers in the brain.

Another puzzle: While during perhaps 300 million years the hind paws of some ape-like animal were being changed into feet, such as today enable human beings to walk erect, how did it happen that several of the animal's already well-designed organs (such as the eyes and ears) escaped serious change and injury by mutations? Perhaps the answer is that these organs did occasionally change—much as they often change today in men and women who are born blind or deaf. But what happened millions of years ago was that any animal born too defective to gather his food, or too weak to keep away from carnivores, or too weak to steal a female away from an old male was soon gone. He did not survive and he did not reproduce. Try to imagine a nearsighted buzzard finding some food, or a lame deer keeping away from a pack of wolves. We can probably say, then, that any animal with a hurtful mutation promptly dropped out of the running and hence had no influence on the development of a new variety of animal—such as the ape, who was learning to walk upright on his hind legs. Perhaps only helpful—or at least not too harmful—mutations were retained.

There is a curious idea about evolution which someone, sometime, must have pondered over but which, so far as I know, has never been written up. This is the thought that if there ever was a Designer, He must have had *several assistants* or Deputies—each of whom, for millions of years, must have remained out of contact with his fellows. Why was this? And why did each one of these local Assistant Designers remain so ignorant of the great changes that were going on elsewhere in the world in the designs of thousands of plants, insects, and animals?

The fact that several Designers—if there were such—were separated and out of contact with one another can easily be demonstrated by studying the animals of Australia, a land which was cut off from the rest of the world in the Cretaceous period some 130,000,000 years ago. At that time, most of the animals on this globe were marsupials. As we all know, their young were born in an early stage of fetal development, and were left to finish their growth in a pouch on the mother's abdomen. There they licked off a sort of milk which was formed in primitive glands—forerunners of the breasts of our present-day mammals.

Now, what puzzles me is this: If, when Australia became an isolated continent, a Deputy Designer was left there—cut off from the rest of the world—the evidence shows that he never learned anything of what was happening on a huge scale elsewhere on the globe. He never seemed to have learned that in Europe, Asia, Africa, and the Americas the marsupials had practically all been killed off and replaced by the more efficient and quick-witted mammals.

How did it come about that the Deputy Designer in Australia never heard of mammals, or never had enough originality to think up and design one, or never noticed in the bayous the mammalian dugong (sea-cow), or never noticed the many mammalian seals or dolphins or whales which must often have come up on a beach to die? Through millions of years the Deputy Designer in Australia kept building dozens and dozens of new animals, but *all of them were marsupials.* Curiously, many of these look like mammals. One of them looks like a little bear, another like a wolf, and others look like meadow voles or rats.

More evidence suggesting the isolation of Deputy Designers is to be found in the large island of Madagascar, where so many of the animals are lemurs or lemur-like creatures, left behind from an early pre-monkey stage of evolution. Also, one must note the tendency of animals to be different in the several continents. This was commented on years ago by Darwin, when he was studying the fossils and the living animals of South America. If there had been a Deputy Designer in South America, he showed a remarkable fondness for South American animals and some lack of knowledge about, or interest in, animals of other continents.

A peculiarity of the Great Designer is His prodigality. Some experts say that a healthy man, during one orgasm, can eject as many as 100,000,000 spermatozoa—most of them designed so marvellously that if it were to enter a woman's ovum it could help to produce a human being. Why should so many spermatozoa be formed? I can see some sense in some little sea animal's putting out in a year millions of tiny swimming forms, because all but a few of them will promptly be eaten by larger animals.

A good example of the prodigality of Nature is to be found in the occasional reddening of the sea for many miles off the coast of Florida. This coloration is due to the presence in the water of a tiny flagellate, a microscopic bit of protoplasm. There are some 60,000,000 of these in a pint of water, so try to imagine how many there are in many cubic miles of sea!

And they make such an extremely powerful poison that millions of fish are killed by it. And why is that?

I have always been impressed by the fact that whenever the Designer has made a herbivorous animal, He has usually designed a carnivorous one with perhaps a special skill in catching and killing the herbivore. One could hardly expect to find a carnivore fleet enough to catch a gazelle, and yet a member of the cat family, the cheetah, was made so fast on its feet that when it gets hungry it can run down a gazelle and kill it.

Especially curious to me is the fact that the Designer seems never to have had any great fondness for the innumerable creatures He has built. He has always been ready to design viruses, bacteria, malarial organisms, and many other deadly parasites made to kill animals and men—often by the millions. In Africa He designed a Tse-Tse fly which—with its associated tiny blood-invading parasite (the trypanosome)—can quickly kill every animal of a certain species that it can reach. In man it produces the horrible "African sleeping-sickness" (encephalitis), which partially destroys the brain of thousands of natives.

Often the Designer has shown great ingenuity in developing particularly complicated and vicious parasites. In Egypt there is the Bilharzia, a fluke—a sort of worm which, with its thorny eggs, causes an inflammation of the inner lining of the lower bowel of man. If the egg of the parasite goes out in a man's feces into the water of a canal, it hatches and out comes a little swimming animal which soon enters the body of a certain snail. Later, from the snail, there emerges another swimming form of the animal which can work its way through the skin of the feet of a man, and then up into his liver and certain of his abdominal veins where it forms a new fluke. This soon lays eggs and starts the cycle all over again. In my youth, when I was a student of tropical medicine, I used to marvel at the complicated cycle some parasites go through as they keep going from a "reservoir" in some wild animal, perhaps through some insect, and then into a man.

I was brought up in the tropics and hence know full well that mosquitoes are hard enough to live with—just because of their constant biting which at night makes sleep so hard to get. This should have been bad enough, but for some curious reason the Designer went out of His way to build into the blood-sucking mechanism of certain mosquitoes a small syringe which enables them, after they have bitten an animal or bird or man and have sucked blood, to add insult to injury by injecting into their victim some of the tiny parasites which live in their salivary glands. On coming into the body of a man, these malaria-producing "plasmodia" enter his red blood cells and destroy millions of them, thus causing an anemia, chills, and fever. Sometimes these parasites will badly injure the man's brain or kidneys, and often they will kill him. Another type of mosquito, when it bites a man to get some blood, will also do a "dirty trick"—it will inject the virus of yellow fever. Few people realize that years ago in our Southern and Eastern seaports terrible epidemics of yellow fever used to kill thousands of Americans.

But enough of the unpleasant aspects of biology and evolution. There are many good features. Let us for a minute marvel at the great knowledge of a chemical engineer so able that perhaps a billion years ago He could design that remarkable substance chlorophyll, which, with its "chloroplasts" (extremely minute organs), enables plants to convert sunlight into the energy needed to produce vegetable tissues, starches, and sugars. Let us marvel, also, at the complicated chemical hemoglobin, which in our blood does a magnificent job of carrying oxygen from our lungs to our tissues, and then carries carbon dioxide back from our tissues to our lungs.

But still, with all the Chief Chemist's great skill, why did it take Him millions of years to solve certain problems? To be sure, they were immensely more difficult problems than are those being solved by our biochemists today. Yet I have the feeling that an "all-wise" Chemist *could have obtained the solution of many a problem much more quickly than He did.* A million years is a very long time—so long that we can have no conception of it. Man has a written history for only some 5,000 years. Nowadays, our chemists, who, after all, are only men, will set out to synthesize an antibiotic or an antidiabetic, a brain-calming or a cortisone-like drug, and in a few months or a few years they will finish the job. Also, nowadays, our chemists will work out the structure of a very complicated molecule, such as that of insulin, in a matter of a few years.

I have always marvelled at the many signs of the remarkable conservatism of the Designer. For instance, when I look at my hands—with their five fingers and their several small bones in the wrist, in the palm of the hand and in the fingers—I marvel that a little lizard, which is a survivor of reptiles that lived hundreds of millions of years ago, has tiny hands almost exactly like mine.

The Great Designer for eons has been using many "basic patents" like this one of the hand. Often when He wanted to make a new structure, He built it not "from scratch" but out of an old and perhaps no longer needed part. Thus, when He made for us human beings an ear-lobe, He made it out of bits of tissue which, in our fishy ancestors, served as gills. To this day these bits of tissue remain in our neck, where sometimes they form little tumors called branchial cysts.

One of the very curious facts about the Designer is that He will occasionally place in an animal a colony of bacteria or of single-celled amebas to serve as organs. Termites are able to eat wood only because they keep amebas, like servants, in their digestive tract. My old Chief, Dr. K. F. Meyer, found that in certain snails, colonies of nitrogen-handling bacteria serve as kidneys!

Naturally, to thousands of people the most interesting theories of evolution are those that deal with the origin of man. For many years after 1859, when Charles Darwin published his great book, people refused to face the thought that man developed by slow evolution from some ape-like creature who got up on his hind legs, developed feet like ours, useful hands, a bigger and more intelligent brain than an ape has, and finally learned to talk.

Today we have much more knowledge about all this than Darwin had, because "missing links" have been found in many parts of the world. For a while, most scientists probably thought of the evolution of man as having taken place during perhaps 15,000 years, but now we know it started much earlier than this.

Recently, Dr. and Mrs. Leakey found in Africa skeletal remains of an ape-like man who lived some 170,000,000 years ago. This date was arrived at with exact chemical measurements in two great American laboratories.

Of course there is an enormous amount of information which students of primitive man still lack, and must dig out of the rocks. Again there comes the great question posed by theologians: Just when did an ape become a man, and if man has a soul, when and how did he get it?

In bringing to a close this brief discussion of a small part of an enormous subject, I can only say that I find it very hard to see how the many marvellously designed organs like the human brain and eye and ear could have been built without the help of an inconceivably able Architect. But I am forced to conclude from abundant evidence that: 1) He learned as He went along; 2) He never designed a new large animal on any island far out in the ocean; 3) He made many mistakes, which He often destroyed wholesale; 4) He showed no fondness for any creature He ever made—not even man; 5) He kept destroying millions of men, women, and children with needlessly cruel mechanisms; 6) obviously, He has been immensely more concerned for the health and the comfort of uncountable billions of malarial parasites than He has been for hundreds of millions of men. If there ever was a Designer, there is little evidence I can see in the record that He was kindly or considerate, or ever concerned with what happened to the innumerable creatures He made. For almost every creature He ever made He designed a cruel killer; for our children He designed a polio virus, a diphtheria bacillus, cancers of the brain, and cruel diseases by the dozen.

13

On Decerebrate Medicine

For most of my life—in fact, since I was an intern—I have been constantly fighting what I call the practice of decerebrate (unthinking) or push-button medicine. A decerebrate animal, of course, is one from which a surgeon has removed the important upper part of the brain—the part which has to do with thinking and deciding. Hence, by a decerebrate type of practice I mean one in which the doctor follows routines, or uses rubber stamps, and fails to worry about his lack of much thought as to what he is doing.

Let us say that Mrs. Brown telephones her doctor that Junior has the sniffles. Immediately the doctor is almost certain to prescribe penicillin. If he were to think for a minute, he would remember that penicillin has no effect on the virus of a cold. If Mr. Brown gets a flare-up of his old fibrositis—a mild arthritis-like disease which generally quiets down by itself in a few days—the doctor may automatically prescribe cortisone. If he were to think for a moment he would remember that cortisone is not likely to have any effect on a fibrositis; also, that if taken in large doses for too long a while, the drug

239

could wreck the health of Mr. Brown in any one of several ways.

If Mrs. Brown has a curetment—a minor operation with practically no loss of blood—her physician is likely to order a transfusion of a pint of blood. As experts on blood diseases keep reminding us, if the doctor were to think a minute, he would realize that the woman does not need the blood; also, that if she *did* need some, the transfusion of only a *pint* would not be enough to do her any good. All that such a transfusion can do is to make the woman liable to get an attack of serum hepatitis—a severe inflammation of the liver—which, in one case in 30, produces a long spell of invalidism, and even death.

Some 150 years ago, a prominent man nearly bled to death from his tubercular lungs. Obviously, the worst thing that a doctor could possibly have done for him would have been to bleed him, but because, in that day, practically all patients were bled decerebrately for whatever ailed them, the doctor came and "bled him from both his right and his left arm." As was to be expected, the man promptly died. It is sad to think that even today, after all these many years, some of our treatments are just as thoughtless—just as decerebrate.

We physicians have always followed fads and for periods of time have treated most of our patients in one and the same thoughtless way. I have read that over a century ago an Englishman called on a consultant whose office, very properly was in London's Harley Street. The footman refused him admittance, because the waiting-room was full. Late that afternoon the man returned to say that he was so ill he would just *have* to see the doctor. Again, the footman said there was no chance of his getting in, but then he whispered, "It might help you, sir, to know that so far today Sir William has sent *all* of his patients to Harrowgate to take the waters!" The inference was obvious!

In the office of an allergist I knew, every patient who came in got 300 skin tests, ordered decerebrately—whether he needed them or not. In the office of some other physicians, almost every patient who came in was treated for six months for the then-fashionable diagnosis of brucellosis (undulant fever)—a rare disease of ranchers, meat handlers, and veterinarians—which the many patients who were city dwellers, almost certainly did not have. A teacher of medicine came to be kidded by his students because he thought he was finding amebas in the bowels of most of the patients who came into his office.

One can hardly blame a young physician for choosing to practice this type of unthinking medicine because it needs no mental effort; the problem of diagnosis does not have to be struggled over. Most of the work in the office is done by nurses or technicians; and the faddish type of practice brings in a large clientele, and with it, a large income.

Why is this decerebrate medicine so popular with many sick people? I think because it delights those many persons who feel that in all their going about from doctor to doctor they have never gotten a definite diagnosis. Often their physician has outraged them by diagnosing "just nerves," and hence how delightful it is at last to find a man who instantly makes a positive diagnosis, which, as he says, "everyone else missed. The other doctors never found the brucellosis, or amebiasis, or low blood sugar, or cystic ovary that they should have found." Hence many a nervous woman is delighted—she loves her new doctor, and everywhere she goes, she brags about him and "his outstanding scientific knowledge and skill."

Another type of person who adores the practitioner of decerebrate medicine is the mother of an epileptic son. She is so delighted when the doctor says, "This isn't epilepsy; this is a disease called 'low blood sugar'; and in the next 6 months we can cure it with daily 'shots.'" Naturally, the woman loves that man. It does not bother him at all that at the Mayo Clinic, a while ago, the neurologists studied some 2,500 epileptics, trying to find one whose seizures could be ascribed to a low blood sugar, and found none!

Sir William Osler knew well the dangers to a physician's mind and soul that can come with the practice of decerebrate medicine. Once he said, "The peril is that when he [the physician] ceases to think . . . he becomes a mere automaton, doing a penny-in-the-slot business which places him on a level with the chemist's clerk who can hand out specifics for every ill, from the pip to the pox."

I am not here accusing my friends in medicine and surgery of dishonesty; I am sure they think they are doing good work. Their fault is that they have fooled themselves. They have become enthusiasts, and they have espoused some diagnosis that is popular and fashionable at the time.

Always we doctors have had an unfortunate (decerebrate) tendency to pick up a drug, such as quinine, which we long ago found very helpful in cases of *malaria,* and to give it to all patients we see with any kind of fever—in spite of the fact that it probably has no effect except on *malarial* fever. Worse yet, for a century or more, we doctors gave quinine to almost everyone as a "bitter tonic," although it probably has no tonic effect. Actually, today, I am not sure that there is such a thing as a tonic!

One reason for much of the peculiar behavior of physicians is that patients are so anxious to try out every new "wonder drug" that comes along. Many people *demand* of me that I give them some of the new medicine, even when I say I cannot see any need for it. To illustrate: around 1943, the wife of the vice-president of a neighboring republic was brought to me suffering from a simple melancholia. She needed a few electro-shock treatments. At that time penicillin had just been produced commercially, but the U.S. Army was taking all that was available. My patient felt so sure that the new "wonder drug" would cure her that she fussed and fussed until her husband brought enough pressure to bear on our government to cause some of the precious drug to be released to him. The woman took it, but, of course, it had no effect on her depression.

Thousands of physicians cannot be blamed at all for the practice of decerebrate medicine because the poor men are so terribly overworked for seven days a week. No wonder they are too tired to think. One of my classmates, who had a huge practice, used to tell me that most of the time, for lack of sleep and rest, he was so weary he could work only as a robot. He had a set of prescriptions which he and his nurses handed out for the several common symptoms. One day he was so tired he dozed at the wheel—and drove his car into the side of a train! Fortunately, he was not badly injured.

As I say elsewhere in this book, one of the worst decerebrate mistakes we physicians are constantly making is to assume that whenever a silent gallstone is found in a woman's abdomen, or a small silent nubbin of muscle (called a fibroid) is found on her womb, this must explain all of her symptoms; and all we need to do is operate. In thousands of cases today we doctors fail to talk to the woman long enough to learn that all of her symptoms are those of a depression, or those of worry about an alcoholic husband, or of worry about a child with attacks of epilepsy or asthma. Years ago, whenever my graduate students received an X-ray report of a silent and harmless gallstone, I found it hard to convince them that it was not causing the woman's severe headaches, or her dizziness, or her ear noises.

Here is what can happen when a physician does not bother to think. One day an able internist friend of mine sent me a patient with an "incurable" diarrhea, supposedly due to a tiny intestinal parasite—an ameba, which a laboratory worker had found in the man's bowel. If my friend hadn't been so perfectly satisfied with this diagnosis that had been handed him, he might have noted that the man's skin was feverishly warm to the touch, showing that he had a highly toxic goiter. A few days after this was removed by a surgeon the man was well, and his diarrhea was gone! In such a case any good senior medical student, if he had been thoughtful and observant, could easily have made the correct diagnosis.

A curious feature about decerebrate medicine is that my medical students used to look on laboratory reports as if they were Holy Writ—never to be questioned. Actually, a laboratory worker can occasionally make a mistake, just as I can make a mistake, or any other human being can make a mistake.

Another miserable feature of decerebrate medicine is that some physicians, and even some eminent ones, will refuse to see and talk to a patient who has just come in with perhaps an obvious toxic goiter, or a duodenal ulcer, or a terminal, scattered, and hopeless cancer. They feel that the only scientific way in which to practice is never to see anyone until he has had perhaps $300 worth of laboratory and X-ray studies made. This often is not only silly, as when all of the desired tests have recently been made by some very able people, but often it is cruel to the patient and his family, as when they are hard put to it to pay the huge bill that is needlessly "run up on them."

During the Second World War, when I wrote a paper to show how physicians—by asking a few simple questions or by making a few simple observations in regard to a patient—could easily avoid ordering many tests, and thereby could take great pressure off our then short-handed and over-worked laboratories, some of my able medical friends were much distressed, because they feared I was trying to throw medical practice back into the Middle Ages.

Millions of dollars are being wasted today because many interns and assistant physicians, without any thinking, are ordering hundreds of unnecessary tests and X-ray studies. To illustrate how this can be done: one morning I just happened to see an unemployed laborer—a man of 50 and a chain-smoker —whose bill was to be paid by his little unmarried daughter. The man had a constant cough and some symptoms suggesting that he was losing his mind.

When I saw the fellow, my new assistant had already written out orders for almost every test he could think of, not only to check the man's lungs and brain, but his digestive tract, his prostate gland, and some painful joints. I said, "Let's first make a guess what this trouble is likely to be," but my young friend was reluctant to do this; as he said, his old Chief in medical school had taught him never to attempt a diagnosis until all the lab and X-ray reports were in.

I said, "Yes; but that is often decerebrate medicine; let's think a moment, even if this is not the scientific, or proper, or fashionable thing to do; let's think what this man *might* well have." My assistant thought a bit and admitted that such a heavy smoker could have a cancer of his lung, with a big "daughter growth in his brain." I said, "Good; that is the logical diagnosis; order an X-ray film made of his chest, and this afternoon, when it comes, let me see it." When the film came, and showed an inoperable cancer extending into both lungs, I think even my test-addicted assistant saw that there was no sense in going ahead to order a few hundred dollars' worth of laboratory and X-ray work.

I have known a number of men with very little knowledge of medicine who made a fortune practicing decerebrate medicine. All they needed was a good "bedside manner" and the ability to prescribe aspirin, penicillin, cortisone, barbiturates, antihistaminics, and tranquilizers. Every so often, both here in America and abroad in Europe, the police will discover that some man who has built a big practice is really an escaped lunatic or an ex-army-orderly who has had practically no training in medicine!

To show how profitable decerebrate medicine can be, I need only note here that a surgeon I knew had *one* idea in his head, which he publicized so much, and became so famous for, that he was knighted. All his life he preached from the text that most diseases are due to "intestinal stasis" (constipation). He operated on many nervous persons, removing their large bowel. This is a big, dangerous operation which often leaves the patient utterly miserable, with the irritating contents of his small bowel coming out every so often onto his abdominal wall. Fortunately, in this country only a few surgeons tried the operation, and they soon lost their enthusiasm for it.

A very distinguished doctor friend of mine once went to the famous surgeon's clinic, and watched him present to the audience a number of colon-less patients who, he said, he had cured of this and that. My friend managed to get into the room where these supposedly "cured" patients were awaiting their turn to be demonstrated. In answer to his questions, they said they were utterly miserable and unable to work, but the surgeon gave them a little money each week to come and be demonstrated, and "they much needed this help."

I have always regretted that my professors in medical school never taught me to disregard findings that cannot possibly be producing the symptoms complained of. I wish that in college I had been taught that fibroids (nodules of muscle on the womb) can never produce sick headaches, and gallstones can never produce symptoms such as are typical of a little stroke.

I hope that some day Deans of colleges will agree with me that soon we should have, in every medical school, a good course on the symptoms or illnesses certain diseased organs cannot produce.

A while ago I saw a sweet old lady with a pain *in her left hip*. Five years before, an able internist had tried to cure this by having the woman's gallbladder removed. I marvelled that my friend had never been taught that disease in the gallbladder can never produce pain in a hip joint. Actually, I soon learned that the old lady had been unusually well until a day when a typical little stroke had hit her, as she was crossing an avenue, and had left her standing there much confused. Fortunately, a man standing on the sidewalk noticed she was in trouble, and running out, he took her arm and helped her into a nearby drugstore. Typical of a little stroke was the fact that after this episode she never felt well again in either her head or her whole left side.

I cannot help being worried nowadays when I see the trend toward the taking of a scant and inadequate history, and then expecting to have the diagnosis made in the laboratories and X-ray department of a hospital.

If I have learned anything in the last 50 years it is that in many cases a good, well-taken and well-interpreted history is the most important single factor in the making of a difficult diagnosis. Today, in spite of all our wonderful laboratory aids, there are many diseases, like the psychoses and neuroses, that can be diagnosed *only from a history*—and sometimes a long one, taken a half-hour at a time over the course of several days.

Surely, if ever there was a profession in which the practitioners should constantly be thinking, observing, puzzling, and reasoning, it should be medicine.

14

My Dislike of
Psychoanalysis

MANY PEOPLE MAY wonder, why this big chapter
on "extraneous material"? Ever since 1909 when I studied
Freud's American lectures, I have been much interested in
psychoanalysis and its weird fantasies. With my life-long curiosity about cults in medicine, and the way in which their
theories become accepted widely and rapidly—no matter how
unfounded or preposterous they may be—I had to study the
new "religion" of Freud; and I had to try to understand how a
lot of proved and unprovable ideas came to infiltrate from
top to bottom the thinking, writing and speech of most of our
people.

As I shall point out, it seems clear to me that psychoanalysis,
with its sometimes almost unintelligible gibberish, is a mani-
festation of the present-day worship of the unintelligible—in
painting, in sculpture, in philosophy, and in psychiatry. Also,
analysis seems to me to belong in "decerebrate medicine," and
my fight against that form of medicine represents a considerable part of my life.

Moreover, it can help the reader who would like to know

how I work, to see an example of the way in which I study a phenomenon that interests me. Already I have discussed religion and evolution, and now I will give some of my thoughts on analysis.

Good friends assure me that any biography of me must contain something about my long-lasting disagreement with analysis—so here goes.

In order to refresh my memory, I have just re-read the several biographies of Freud, and some of his writings.*

Freud, of course, had to be an unusual man or he could never have had such a tremendous influence on the thought of the world. Even the average man in the street, if the acquaintance with him cannot instantly remember a friend's name, is likely to say, "Aha! Unconsciously you hate the fellow," or if the acquaintance makes a slip of the tongue, its significance is promptly analyzed for him. If the two men look at a tower, they may remark that it is a phallic symbol. Everywhere I go I hear people giving psychoanalytic explanations for the quirks of character of their relatives and friends. As Mr. Philip Rieff said in his recent book,† in America Freud's intellectual influence is greater than that of any other modern thinker.

As one would have expected, Freud worked very hard for

---

* Most helpful for a quick appraisal of psychoanalytic theories and practices is the splendid book by Andrew Salter, The Case Against Psychoanalysis (New York: Holt, Rinehart and Winston); also, the scholarly 66-page review by that eminent neurologist and psychoanalyst Dr. Percival Bailey (Perspectives in Biology and Medicine, 1961, p. 199). For an understanding of Freud, his character, his thinking, and his work one must read and re-read the splendid three-volume Life by his devoted and clear-thinking disciple, Dr. Ernest Jones (Basic Books, 1953). See also, Doctor Freud, Emil Ludwig (New York: Hellman Williams, 1947); Freud, His Life and His Mind, Helen W. Puner (New York: Grosset & Dunlap, 1947); Sigmund Freud, A New Appraisal, Maryse Choisy (New York: Philosophic Library, 1963); An Autobiographic Study, Sigmund Freud (New York: W. W. Norton & Company, Inc., 1952); The Interpretation of Dreams, Sigmund Freud (New York: Random House, A Modern Library Book, 1950); and A General Introduction to Psychoanalysis, Sigmund Freud (New York: Liveright Publishing Company, 1920, 1935).

† Philip Rieff, Freud: The Mind of the Moralist (New York: Viking Press, 1959).

long hours each day, and usually up until 1 o'clock the next morning. Only a man with such tremendous drive could have published as many articles and books as he put out.

He came of an undistinguished ancestry, his father being a rather unsuccessful wool merchant. His mother was able and bright.

Somehow or other, with almost no money, Sigmund managed to get through medical school, and then he began to do much good scientific research. For years he kept putting out scientific papers and encyclopedic articles. He became one of the world's experts on the microscopic anatomy of part of the brain, and he became an expert neurologist. He wrote an excellent book on the inability to talk that often follows a bad stroke—and he did outstanding work on the nature of the several paralytic diseases of children.

Then he got scholarships which enabled him to go twice to Paris, there to study under the great French neurologists. Freud's early articles show his splendid knowledge of neurologic diseases, and if it had not been for many jealousies, some anti-semitism, and much jockeying of people for the few university titles available, Freud should soon have been given at least an assistant professorship. After a while he did get the coveted University title of Privat Dozent, and years later he was listed as a professor.

In the late 1890's, if Freud had wished to become a consultant in neurology, he probably could have done this, but evidently he did not care to continue in this type of work. While studying in Paris, he became much interested in hysteria and in the effects of hypnotism on the disease, and with this, his fascination with neuroses began. Later, in Vienna, he became a close friend of an older physician named Breuer, who was also much interested in hysteria. Breuer kept "lending" Freud money; he sent him much-needed patients, and he gave Freud many ideas concerning what later became psychoanalysis.

Then, in Freud's peculiar way, and for reasons that are not entirely clear, he turned bitterly on his old benefactor and thereafter hated him. Later, he did the same thing with a certain crackpot numerologist nose-and-throat man named Fliess. For six years Freud, very strangely, made a confidant and close chum of Fliess, and he accepted a number of the man's crazy ideas. It is hard to understand how anyone with Freud's good scientific training could have chosen as his dearest confidant, mentor, and guide such a strange and eccentric person. Finally, the day came when even Fliess could not approve of some weird idea of Freud's, and with this "disloyalty," the close friendship ended.

And here we must examine the most remarkable thing about Freud and his career. Part of his voluminous correspondence with Fliess shows that around 1897 Freud lost all interest in his old microscopic and neurologic researches. Worse yet he abandoned his old scientific methods, and became a gullible person—a mystic, a dreamer, a maker of fantasies, and a man who found it easy to convince himself that a *fantasy* that had come into his mind was a "world-shaking" *fact.*

As one reads his book on the interpretation of dreams, one notes that he keeps saying, as the Pope might do about some article of faith, "This is the interpretation of that dream." So far as I can see, there is little to show how Freud learned to make the interpretations supplied, and there is little to show that with further research he proved that his interpretations were right.

To me, the hardest thing to understand about Freud is how a man who started out in life as a careful scientist—who understood the tremendous need for first gathering many facts of observation, and then having other competent scientists confirm these facts—could have changed so completely, and could have become a literary man, a dreamer, and a sort of philosopher, who no longer cared to use scientific methods. Instead of being impressed by what competent psychiatrists would think of some fantasy of his, he would love the men who agreed with him, and he would have no more to do with those many men who disagreed with him.

As Dr. Jones says, after his great mental change, Freud was a man who could be little influenced by the thoughts of the men about him. He evidently forgot what he once knew well, which is that when a scientist suggests a *theory*, it is only a formula which appears to explain a number of the facts which he has gathered. Then he must gather more facts to see if they fit well into the theory. If they don't, the theory must be modified or scrapped. This is why most scientists hate to dignify Freud's ideas with even the word theory. They prefer to call them "fantasies." Oftentimes they are only analogies, puns or plays on words.

For a long time I wondered what sort of tremendous "brain storm" could have come to change a good scientist into a credulous non-scientist. As Jones said, after the change he became a genius at being willing to believe "in the improbable and the unexpected." His "daemon of creative speculation" took over. He became willing to say things which he knew would cause scientists to hoot at him, and look down on him.

I can easily understand how Freud could have given up his researches in neurology and pediatrics to go into the study of neuroses. I did that sort of thing when I left gastroenterology to go to work in the borderlines of psychiatry. But along the way I kept all of my old scientific ways of observing and thinking and studying.

Freud did not do this. All scientific students of his work whose books and articles I have read agree that with his painful mental revolution in 1897, he gave up his scientific ways of thinking and working. Instead of writing up a study of 50 or 100 cases, he could write a small book on a very silly interpretation *of one case.* As one of my brilliant professional friends used to say to his students, "Beware of the doctor who is always talking about *one case.*"

That Ernest Jones noted the big change in Freud is shown by his statement (I, p. 404) that his Chief had "a creative imagination that, *once it was released from the strict discipline of his scholastic upbringing,* took him to the very confines of thought" (italics mine). How remarkable it is that Jones, who was so devoted to Freud, could see that in order to write all of his fantastic articles and books, The Master *had to get himself released from the restrictions and disciplines of science.*

On page 325, in Vol. I, Jones tells us that on June 12, 1897, Freud, in describing his mental turmoil, wrote, "There followed a period of apathy, and an intellectual paralysis such as I have never imagined." Freud was "passing through a neurotic phase—a curious state of mind which one's consciousness cannot apprehend: twilight thoughts, a veil over one's mind, scarcely a ray of light here and there." Curiously, also, Freud wrote, "I believe I am in a cocoon, and God knows what kind of beast will creep out of it." Jones says that, for a while then, "Every line Freud wrote was a torment." What with Freud's change from his exact and scientific physiology to his new and vague and fantastic psychology (as Jones said), "the mental struggle *must have been titanic*" (italics mine).

I can get some idea of how titanic this struggle must have been for Freud by thinking what would have happened to me, mentally and spiritually, if in 1930, when I had to give up my physiologic researches in a laboratory, I had gone into theosophy or some form of mystical Swedenborgian philosophy. A big stroke or something would have had to have hit me—to destroy the better part of my brain. What I wonder is if the violent mental convulsion which so distressed Freud, and which changed his whole way of thinking and working, had some connection with his early tendency to depressions and severe psychoneuroses.

Perhaps it is important to note that when this tremendous mental upheaval took place, Freud was under the great emotional strain that was "tearing him to pieces" as "he analyzed himself," and along the way became convinced that he had hated his sweet, kindly father, and had loved his mother too much. He wrote Fliess that once on a train, when he was two and a half years old, he saw his mother naked, and then experienced sexual feelings for her! Imagine that! Jones says that Freud's memory had failed him a bit, because the train journey took place when he was four. But even at the age of four what does a child know of sex? Freud apparently felt sure that infants know all about sex.

One thing seems certain and this is that the tremendous mental upheaval in 1897 was not due to any arteriosclerotic injury to his brain, because he was left with all his old kindliness, his ability, and his enormous capacity for work.

As one reads on page after page of Freud's writings, his great concern with sex, and particularly incest, one wonders why he was so obsessed with this subject. Why should he have been so sure that all neuroses are due to some crazy sexual idea? One answer would be that Freud was a sex-ridden man, but Jones tells us that this was not so; he appears to have remained always true to his Martha, and in some ways he was puritanical. There are good reasons for believing that he lost his libido and potentia early—perhaps when he was in his middle forties; and this failure could conceivably have colored his thoughts.

One wonders if his preoccupation with sex could have had something to do with his conviction that no woman could ever have a good psychoanalysis without a "transference," in which she, to some extent, would fall in love with her analyst. This would make her more pliant and less "resistant"—less likely to refuse to accept the analyst's strange interpretations of her dreams, and his perhaps disconcerting accusations in regard to her hostilities and feelings of aggression.

Around 1890, Freud became dissatisfied with the treatment of patients with "continued suggestion," which he was then using, and between 1892 and 1896 he quit using hypnosis. For a while he tried the technique of pressing his hand on his patient's forehead to make him think! By 1894 he was sure that the psychoneuroses are due to the patient's intolerance of memories of hurtful sexual experiences in early childhood—when the child must have had an understanding of sexual intercourse (Jones, I, p. 284). I am glad to read that even Freud found it very hard to explain why a sexual trauma in infancy did no harm *then*—when it was experienced—but worked havoc many years later when it had been practically forgotten. Also, how explain those cases in which a girl is raped or almost raped, and later fails to get any neurosis?

To give an example of Freud's new and often weird type of thinking, such as he adopted when he quit his scientific work, I will give here the substance of an astounding letter which Jones says Freud once wrote to Thomas Mann. In it, Freud reminded Mann that Napoleon had an older brother named Joseph. According to analytic theory, the Emperor must, "of course," have hated him "with a burning hate." But history says that actually Napoleon loved his brother dearly. Hence it is obvious that Napoleon must have "over-compensated," and his early "feelings of aggression" toward his brother must have been "transferred"; and this would explain why Napoleon killed hundreds of thousands of men—they paid the penalty for his having spared his first enemy! Then Napoleon married a widow because her name was *Joseph*ine, and later he invaded Egypt because he wanted to identify himself with Joseph and his brethren of the Bible story. Later, when Napoleon put away Josephine, his downfall started. His disaster in Russia was due to his having been influenced by Joseph's dream that the sun, moon, and stars would bow down before him!

There we have a type of psychonalaytic thinking at its best— just a mess of playing on words. The sad feature of this is that if Freud wasn't spoofing—and I know of no reason to believe that he wasn't serious—he was making a spectacle of himself. No wonder that for years the physicians in Europe laughed and jeered at him.

One of the worst articles by Freud that I have ever read is his 132-page "History of an Infantile Neurosis" (in Vol. 3 of *Collected Papers*, 1925). I can only say that if I had written it my family and friends would have insisted on my being treated by a psychiatrist. The article is full of the account of a dream about a lot of wolves in a tree. A psychotic adult described this dream to Freud as having been experienced by him when he was one and a half years old!

First, Freud swallowed the man's story of the dream, and then went ahead to interpret it at great length. Amusing is Freud's reaction to the man's remembrance that one day in his early childhood his governess' hat blew off. Freud said immediately that this "pointed to the castration fear"; apparently it helped to explain the man's life-time psychosis!

One wonders why it did not occur to Freud that the man's psychosis might better have been explained by the fact that his father was a manic-depressive, his father's brother was a marked eccentric, the patient's sister—apparently a schizophrenic—committed suicide, and many others in the family suffered from "minor nervous troubles." In all fairness to Freud, I should say that once he did admit the neuroses tend to run through some families, but not through others. Unfortunately, his disciples have never used this thought in their writings.

As Dr. Ernest Jones tells us, his hero was honest and upright, and willing at times even to admit that he had been lied to by women who wanted to please him—by telling him the sort of story that they saw he wanted to hear. For instance, a number of hysterical women once lied when they told him what he had felt must be the truth—that their fathers had molested them sexually when they were little.

In his later years he confessed honestly that a number of his theories had not worked out well, and he was not sure that they were correct. He was not sure what he believed, or what he should want his students to believe. It takes a big man to admit such mistakes and doubts. He was big, also, when he admitted that during an analysis one must feed into the mind of the patient some of the ideas one hopes to get back from him. As he said, some patients require more of this "forcing" and some require less. But "without such help nobody comes out of a psychoanalysis" (quoted from Salter). No scientist could have made such an admission and have retained any shred of reputation.

If Freud had worked as a scientist, he would have had to behave as Charles Darwin did: he would have had to write down quickly every serious objection advanced against one of his theories so that he would not conveniently forget it. Even some of Freud's old friends admitted that he had a strong tendency to ignore objections to his theories, and even to get angry with the objector. Dr. Percival Bailey said that Freud considered efforts at any scientific testing of his ideas as not only unnecessary but undesirable! Even Dr. Ernest Jones admitted that Freud had no patience with the scientific method. Freud once wrote that from his college days onward, he had no gift for science.

To show how Freud would have acted if, after his tremendous mental upheaval, he had retained any of his early tendency to use scientific methods, I need only say that when the manic-depressive lad, Otto Rank, came to him with his statement, unfounded on any facts, that neuroses are due to the fright infants get as they go slowly down their mother's birth-canal, Freud would have said, "Before you publish that, find two groups of 100 persons each, one group who were born after a long hard labor, and the other who were born easily and quickly with a cesarian section. If the first group of persons have much more neurosis than is to be found in the second group, you'll have something to talk about."

But Freud just swallowed Rank's idea whole, and later told Ernest Jones that it represented one of the biggest advances in psychoanalysis! For years Freud treated Rank like a son, and only when Rank's psychosis got out of hand and he became a nuisance, did Freud let him go.

Actually, many analytic fantasies are of the type that can

never even be tested—theories such as Nandor Fodor's idea that an infant in the womb, with its as yet undeveloped brain, can be frightened and mentally damaged when its parents are having intercourse.

Very unscientific was Freud's method (followed by many modern analysts) of starting treatment of a patient without first examining him to make sure that he hadn't a brain tumor, brain syphilis, epilepsy, severe cerebral arterio-sclerosis, or some other organic disease that could not possibly be cured with psychotherapy. A friend of mine who makes electroencephalograms tells me the remarkable fact that as yet no analyst has ever sent him a patient. Someone once said that Freud was like a physician who, when a patient came to consult him, examined only his or her external genitalia!

Naturally, I have for long wondered how it came about that a man who was so unscientific, and who all his life preached such a disgusting and unbelievable doctrine of perverted sex *for everyone,* could have come to dominate the thought of the civilized world. As might have been expected, most physicians in Europe promptly rejected Freud's ideas, and would have none of him. But Freud—like a good publicist—went over the heads of the medical profession to the public, who will always listen to any man with weird ideas who startles them, or amuses them, or who promises them an unorthodox cure for their diseases.

It was only after years, when everyone, even the man in the street, was talking in psychoanalytic slang, that we physicians climbed on the bandwagon and began to give honors and professorships to the analysts. As usually happens, very few physicians or laymen ever read enough of psychoanalytic literature to know what it is like, or how silly much of it sounds. If they had, the story might have been different.

Actually, as many men have said, psychoanalysis is far more like a religion than a science. It has its prophet, and its rite of initiation, its insistence on faith and orthodoxy, its insistence on abject confession, its hatred of heresy, and its habit of excommunicating unbelievers. As a Catholic prelate once said to me, "Because we see so clearly that Freudianism is a religion, we dislike it."

Today, I read here and there that some of the more thoughtful and able analysts have become so disillusioned or so disgusted with some of Freud's ideas—such as that of the Oedipus complex, fear of castration, and penis envy—that they are trying to "brush them under the rug." Some of these analysts even joke about Freud's ideas, many are a bit ashamed and on the defensive, and some have, *to some extent*, pulled out of the movement. Others have pulled out entirely, and a few tell me they would like to pull out, but at their mature age they hate to start life over again in a new field. What is good is that some of the ablest analysts are now willing to criticize certain phases of analytic behavior: they are trying to shorten the process of analysis, and some are willing quickly to help a woman with her *immediate* problems, much as any fine old psychiatrist will do.

As Salter said so well in his fine book, many people, on reading the facts he presents, will say, "Oh, no. I cannot believe Freud ever said something so silly. *You must have misquoted him.*" Actually, as Salter says, many things Freud said are so foolish there is no need for misquoting him. When I first read quotations from the story of an "Infantile Neurosis" I said, "No, even Freud could not have said anything so awful," so I read the paper, and found that he *had* said it.

One of Freud's strongest convictions was that the first aim of the analytic treatment consists in attaching the patient emotionally to the person of the physician. As we all know, many weak people greatly want to be dependent on someone—someone to whom they can run often for advice in regard to even small decisions. Today many a wife of a man who for long has been in analysis is greatly depressed or enraged or thinking of divorce. She says her husband is married much more closely to his analyst than he is to her. He is constantly running to the man for help and comfort and strength, and the poor wife is "out in the cold." *

Readers may ask me, "But how did the analysts come to dominate the thinking of the world?" Largely by constantly saying in public such startling or crazy things that newspapers always gave their pronouncements space—sometimes on the front page. For many years in San Francisco, a certain Albert Abrams who called himself a doctor, but in some of his books did not dare put an M.D. after his name, practiced a weird form of medicine. He made one or two million dollars by supposedly diagnosing and treating patients with a very silly contraption which was said to be the last word in electronics. Actually, Abrams showed in one of his books that he did not know enough about electricity to hook up a doorbell!

How did he get patients to come to him from all over the world? By flim-flamming the newspapers. Every so often he would call up a reporter and tell him something like this—that when given a drop of blood from someone he could tell in a minute if the fellow was a Presbyterian, a Catholic, or a Methodist. This startling statement would then shoot all over the world.

Once, when the head of a newspaper chain telephoned to ask me if Abrams could do what he said he could, I laughed and said of course he couldn't. I told how we doctors were often having fun with Abrams, sending him blood supposedly from a sick man but actually from a guinea pig or a rabbit, and getting back a report that the "man" had gonorrhea and syphilis! But "Why, then," asked the Editor, "does he say such things?" "Because you editors are suckers enough each year to give him thousands of dollars' worth of free advertising." "I guess you're right," said the Editor, grouchily, and hung up.

Many analysts have learned this same trick. As I was writing this chapter, and looking for an example, I opened my newspaper and there, in a prominent place, was the statement of an

* See the remarkable story of Mrs. Ferman in *Freudian Psychoantics*, by Maurice Natenberg (Chicago: Regent House, 1953, p. 87).

analyst to the effect that when Johnny fusses at going to the dentist it is not because he is afraid of being hurt. Oh, no. That is too simple. John is afraid that the dentist with his drill (a phallic symbol) will make a sexual assault on the hole in his tooth—a female symbol!

On the second page of the paper I found the report of another bit of "research." An analyst said he had found that when a child gets a pain, soon he is loving it and enjoying it so greatly that he won't give it up! Actually this was nothing new—Freud "discovered" that many years ago. Another analyst said he had discovered that epilepsy is "mental masturbation" (evidently the poor fellow had never heard of the electroencephalograms which commonly show that the epileptic was born with a definitely damaged brain).

Another analyst announced with great excitement that homosexuality results when a child sees his mother naked! This stupid statement—which disregards the abundant evidence of geneticists to show that the sexually confused person is usually born that way—shot around the world as no sensible statement would ever have done; and as a result, from this and other such stupidities, the analyst received high honors from University groups!

For years we were told by Freud that the greatest discovery ever made in psychiatry was that girls envy their brother's penis and boys are constantly afraid of being castrated. Strange, isn't it, that during my half-century of taking long and careful histories from mentally troubled patients, I never heard a single one speak of penis envy or castration fear. I know that analysts will say, "But you didn't know how to make a patient tell you that." However, I doubt if this is the answer because some of our old and very able psychiatrists—good friends of mine—have told me that they too have never been able to obtain this story except occasionally from someone who was once well indoctrinated and brainwashed during years of analysis.

According to Dr. Bailey, Freud said that a patient must

accept the interpretations of his thoughts and dreams by his analyst, otherwise he will be scolded for showing *resistance*. Many a time when a nice patient, being analyzed, is told that his dreams show that his greatest desire in life has been to kill his father and to have sexual intercourse with his mother, he will be horrified, and will say, "Why, no, I never had such an awful idea in my life." But according to many analysts, this only indicates that the patient is showing resistance, and this must be broken down—the man must be convinced that his dreams definitely show that he always wanted to have a child by his mother!

To me, one of the most damning things one could say of leading analysts is that sometimes they write almost unintelligible gobbledegook. Recently I felt shocked when I read Jones' statement that Freud had written an appreciative letter *to one of America's leading analysts* when this man sent him, as a present, a book he had written. Here's a sample of that analyst's prose, which I take at random from a page in one of his books. "It is a methodological error to attempt to interpret psychologically an organic symptom which is the end-result of an intermediate chain of organic processes, instead of trying to understand those vegetative nervous impulses in their relation to psychologic factors which introduce a chain of organic events resulting in an organic disturbance."...."In all of our female cases the diarrhea both means restitution for castrative wishes, and also represents masculine activity in contrast to female receptivity. In one case the wish for restitution by diarrhea seems on a deep level to be the equivalent of giving birth to a child.... The most constant, outstanding feature which determines the specific character of these cases is the wish for restitution as a reaction to guilt for receptive and aggressive-taking tendencies (castration wish)." Imagine a man who could write like that being one of the greatest leaders of the analytic movement!

What often distresses me now is that writers of such material are being honored by universities. A while ago a distinguished analyst was brought over from Europe to give a special lecture. Following is a random sample taken from the report of what the great man said: "The transference phenomena shows us the distortion of our perceptual processes relating to persons in the present by drawing without awareness upon experiences of the past. Transference, like resistance and repression, affects the refraction of our mental organ of apperception. It is the emotional appreciation that a transference has occurred, that a reproduction of a consciously lost emotional relationship to persons of the past has intruded, which it is so essential for the future analytic therapist to experience."

Anyone who has read much analytic patter can doubtless guess what the poor fellow was stumbling about trying to say. To me, the main message that this famous teacher succeeds in giving us is that in the last 50 years practically nothing new has come out of psychoanalysis—nothing but the same old bilge about the "extreme importance of the transference phenomenon." This is a mine which Freud worked out and left empty a half-century ago. How sterile analysis appears to have been, and how sad that the analysts have muffed a great opportunity! If only they had reported exactly what their patients kept telling them every day—without trying to make them say what Freud said they must say—the analysts might have built a big and splendid addition to our knowledge of psychiatry.

Here is a gem of psychoanalytic "research." A while ago that able psychologist, Professor H. J. Eysenck, of London, told us about the report he found *in an official British document,* to the effect that an analyst had learned that the unrest of the miners in the British "pits" was due to the complexes set up in their minds by their having to hack away (with their pick-axe, a phallic symbol) at Mother Earth (a female symbol)! Imagine a man so stupid or shameless as to write "bilge" like that! Because an analyst friend of mine protested to me that no one could have been that silly, I wrote Professor Eysenck, and he answered, "Yes," that that is exactly what he had read.

That Freud himself could at times write something that resembled nonsense can be seen from the following tremendous sentences (quoted from Salter): "This factor exercises a decisive influence upon the outcome of the conflict when a boy finds himself in the situation of the Oedipus complex, and the threat aimed against his narcissism by castration, reinforced from primeval sources, takes possession of him. Driven by the combined power of these two influences, of the immediate real danger and of the remembered phylogenetic one, the child embarks upon his attempts at defense (repressions), which are effective for the moment, but nevertheless turn out to be inadequate when the later reanimation of sexual life brings a reinforcement to the repudiated instinctual demands." After reading this, will the reader wonder why I cannot imagine how the psychoanalysis of children can do any good?

As I copied this I happened to see where that great artist Salvador Dali said that his favorite writer was Kant. Dali said, "I understand almost nothing of what I read, and this in itself fills me with pride and satisfaction!" This, I fear, explains why for years psychiatric journals have gladly accepted papers full of the often silly Freudian jargon.

That very wise man, F. L. Lucas, in his book *Style*, wrote that "The obscurity of pomp is indeed next neighbor to the obscurity of charlatanism, which has so long thrived, *and no doubt will long continue to thrive, on the human passion for being mystified.*"

Fortunately, the public is beginning to laugh at the antics of some analysts. And if I were an analyst, I would be much disturbed over this, because ridicule can be the most destructive of forces. A while ago, the *New Yorker* had fun quoting a paragraph from a recent textbook on psychoanalysis in which the author told his readers how an analyst can get out of the ticklish situation in which he finds himself when the patient turns around and finds him asleep! He can tell the patient that he slept only when the fellow's confessions were of no value—but woke the moment something of value came across!

What often distresses me greatly is the tendency of many social workers and psychiatric nurses to say after only a few moments contact with a mentally disturbed patient, "Your trouble is due to a castration fear, or you hate your father." They are sure they "know it all."

A beautiful case to show the folly and futility of this habit of instantly making a diagnosis, based on one of the usual analytic theories, was that of a young Cuban who came to me complaining of such a markedly premature ejaculation that he had never dared to marry. My able assistant, who in college had a year of psychoanalytic indoctrination, immediately said, "The cause of this is obvious; the man so hates women that he wants to break contact with them as quickly as possible." So far as my young medical friend was concerned, "the case was closed."

But I said, "I, unfortunately, don't *know* these things as you do. I have to ask." So I asked the man if he hated women in general or his usual sexual partner in particular, and wanted to shorten contact with her, and he said, "Oh, no," he liked women and he much loved his usual partner. Then I asked him if his contact *was* short, and he said, "Oh, no," it was *unusually long* because he always made three successive attempts over the course of an hour or more! Usually, by the third time, his tissues had so lost their extreme irritability that he could have a fairly normal "act" with which to satisfy his partner as he much wished to do.

Then I asked my assistant to note how irritable and "jumpy" our patient was and how tremendous his knee jerks were when I hit the tendon with my little hammer. Remarking then that one often sees such tremendous knee-jerks in epileptics, I asked the man if there was any epilepsy in his family, and he said, "Yes," his brother had a severe form of the disease. Then I sent our patient for electroencephalograms, and back came the report, "a typical epileptic record."

Another example out of a hundred I could give to show how stupid, unnecessary and fruitless many an analysis can be was that of a keen, attractive and pleasant woman of 35 whose main trouble was that when her much-loved beau dropped her, she married "on the rebound" a man whom she did not much care for. In the years that followed, she had two sons, and the need for raising and educating them made it impossible for her to get her much-desired divorce. There was just one difficulty in the way, and this was that her husband, on his small law practice, did not make enough money to maintain two separate households—one for him, and one for her and the boys.

Someone then talked her into going to an analyst. A year later, when she dropped in to see me, I asked her, "What does the man advise?" And she said, "He refuses to say anything; he never says a word; he says that *after four more years of analysis I'll know what to do*" (which is standard procedure with some analysts). Fortunately, she then left him, got a good position as a confidential secretary, and, with an income assured, she got her separation. After this she was immediately cured of most of her nervousness!

Freud's idea of sex knowledge in infants is most improbable, for several reasons, one of which is the fact that before the age of four a child hasn't much of an electroencephalogram. Obviously, the brain is not then fully developed. The EEG begins to look like that of an adult at the age of four, and is not typically adult until around the age of eleven!

As I said, one of Freud's favorite ideas was that *every* boy wants to kill his father and have intercourse with his mother; and *every* girl wants to have intercourse with her father. As he said, the Oedipus complex "is at the heart of infantile sexuality, and decisively influences adult sexuality."

In one place in his writings, Freud summed up his teachings, saying that "The impulse desires which are born anew with everybody are those of incest—cannibalism—and lust of murder!" How awful! Why have our people come to so love this sort of thing? Freud also had an idea that if a boy is unable to copulate with his mother he becomes homosexual, or he develops an inferiority complex! Bed-wetting "represents a threat of castration." Loss of teeth, or blindness are symbols of castration.

Naturally, many people just cannot accept this sort of thing —unless, as Lincoln once said, this is the sort of thing they like! According to one eminent analyst, even "Esthetics has its roots in repressed anal-eroticism!" Incidentally, analysts have a whole division of their fantastic world taken up with ideas of oral and anal people. According to one writer, "The 'oral-anal' view of personality and culture, as it may be called, holds that the infant's early experiences in feeding and toilet training determine his adult character, and that this character, in turn, determines the nature of his culture." It is remarkable how the world has taken to its heart this bit of stupidity. I read that people who smoke much, or who like pop or candy, or who bite their nails are showing signs of an oral personality. So far as I can see, the analysts would do well soon to throw these silly fantasies overboard.

As most of us know, the Freudians love to be constantly interpreting according to their theories some harmless little thing that a person has done—such as a slip of the tongue. Everything is grist to their mill. Once, when a girl who was lying on Freud's couch, opened her purse, put in her finger, and then closed the purse again, The Master said that obviously she wished to masturbate. I read that Freud once had a patient who had a lot of trouble squeezing out his blackheads. "Obviously," the pressing-out of the blackheads was a substitute for masturbation, and the tiny cavity which remained was the female genital tract!

To me, one of the least sensible parts of psychoanalysis is the theory of the interpretation of dreams. Nowhere in the course of his treatment of a patient does the analyst seem to express such positive ideas—which, so far as many people can see—are based on little besides analogy or fantasy or the making of puns. I am told that many analysts feel that the interpretation of dreams is the best way in which to learn what is going on in the person's unconscious mind. To give just a few of the interpretations that I have found: for a woman to dream of violets means that she wants to be violated; and to dream of falling means that she wants to be a "fallen woman." For a man to dream of a gate is to be thinking of a woman's vulva—probably his mother's. To dream of flowers on a table means a thought of female genitalia.

According to Freud, dreams deal with the fulfillment of a frustrated wish—usually some sexual desire. Because the idea is in the unconscious, it is not recognized by the patient—for what it means. Freud felt that "the interpretation of dreams is the royal road to a knowledge of the unconscious." I cannot see how Freud could have had any certainty that what he said about a dream was true. How did he know? I wonder if two or three analysts, presented with the story of one dream, would give the same interpretation of it.

As most of us know today, Freud taught that anything that is like a rod, or a stick, an umbrella, a pole, or tree, a dagger, a lance, or a gun, is a phallic symbol. Many written articles have been filled with these fantasies. Similarly, anything that is hollow, or is an entrance, as for instance, a door, or a gate, is an emblem of the female genitalia. Woods and thickets are, of course, pubic hair. Playing the piano means playing with one's self, i.e., masturbation. Any rhythmic activity, such as riding a horse, means sexual congress.

Occasionally one will meet a man who has been terribly distressed by an analyst's accusation that he has been spending his nights dreaming of having intercourse with his mother. I remember one such man who, after starting analysis, went right out and committed suicide. I always suspected it was over his horror of having been accused of incestuous desires, and I felt the surer of this when I read of nice persons who, when accused of shameful sexual desires, "had their nervous system shattered."

Naturally, when scientists study psychoanalysis, one of their first questions is, "Does it work? Does it cure people? Or does it work better than do other types of psychotherapy?"

First, it should be noted that it does not work with people suffering from psychoses or insanity. It is not used in mental hospitals. Freud himself soon concluded that it was of no value in treating people suffering from a depression, schizophrenia, severe anxiety states, a phobia, obsessions, or paranoia. It is used for the treatment of neuroses. But many psychiatrists have objected—saying that if psychoanalytic theory had any truth in it, it ought to help the psychotic patient as well as the neurotic one.

My study of what actually happened to the peculiar people in 673 neurotic families * strongly suggested that psychic troubles of all kinds are related to one another. Why? Because they so often come out of one and the same poor nervous inheritance. Grandfather may have been in a mental hospital; his son may have been an alcoholic; his daughter may have suffered from hysteria; a grandson may have had epilepsy, a nephew may have been an eccentric ne'er-do-well; and several cousins may have been afflicted with "functional" abdominal pains, nervous indigestion, or a love of operations.

During my years of practice I must have talked to a few hundred people who had spent some time in analysis, and I can remember very few who thought it had done them any good. I can remember fewer yet whose relatives or friends would say that after it, the patient was easier to live with!

As we all know, analysts have always insisted on the importance of dredging up from the days of infancy memories of sexual injuries. My analytic friends have no patience with my "superficial" efforts to help many a nervous person with his daily problems. But they forget that even Freud was stumped when people asked him, why didn't the injury show up when the child was hurt? Why did it wait perhaps 40 years to show

* *Practical Leads to Puzzling Diagnoses: Neuroses That Run Through Families* (Philadelphia: J. B. Lippincott, 1958).

up? Why, also, when after the childhood injury has been brought out into the light, do most neuroses go on unchanged? This isn't according to theory; and Jones tells us that the fact was very disappointing to Freud. Many a recently analyzed patient has said to me, "Now that I know why I am a bunch of nerves why don't I get any better?"

To give an example from my own experience: During my first 40 years of life a common nightmare would start with my going perfectly happily through a dark basement. Then someone would brush up against me, someone who had been standing there quietly in the dark, and this would frighten me terribly. I think it is almost certain that when I was less than three years old, someone played this trick on me; but the recognition of this probability has never made it the least bit easier for me to go down into a dark basement. To this day, I dread it. Also, it should be noted that this great fear never gave me a neurosis, or interfered with my happy adjustment to life.

Professor William Ellery Leonard had the same experience. When analysts assured him that his paralyzing phobia which kept him from going any distance from his house was due to his early fright at seeing a locomotive,* that was fine: the only trouble was that it did not enable him to walk any farther away from his house!

It is hard to get from the literature a good answer as to the value of an analysis. Several able psychiatrists have pointed out that, with time—and no treatment at all—most neurotic persons will have periods in which they will be comfortable; hence when, *after 5 years of analysis,* a person says he thinks he is better, it is hard to know how much credit should go to the analyst.

Among those who have tried to appraise the value and significance of psychoanalysis was the late Professor Carney Landis, of Columbia University. To see what the practice was like, he underwent 221 hours of analysis, paid for by the Rockefeller Foundation. Dr. Landis wound up with no enthu-

* *The Locomotive God* (Century, 1927).

siasm for the process; he noted that his analyst rarely said a word to him.

Another eminent professor of psychology who tried out an analysis on himself was Dr. Edwin G. Boring of Harvard. After 168 sessions, Boring gave up, with the feeling that he had wasted his time. A tendency to depression from which he had suffered was left unchanged.

Abraham Myerson, one of America's ablest psychiatrists, after writing to 307 neurologists, psychiatrists, and psychologists to question them about their impressions in regard to analysis, concluded that most of them were not satisfied with it.

Salter tells us that in 1941, the Rockefeller and Carnegie Foundations engaged Professor Robert T. Sears of Harvard to make a study to see if psychoanalysis has value. He studied 166 articles, dealing with efforts to verify scientifically the Freudian fantasies and concluded that few investigators could accept Freud's statements.

Some of the best statistics available are those of Dr. Knight, an eminent psychiatrist, who, in 1941, studied the results claimed for 736 persons labelled as psychoneurotics, or persons with sexual or character disorders, etc. In most cases the results of the treatment (in four clinics) were assayed by the analysts who, naturally, would be inclined to look as favorably as possible on their work. In 27.8 per cent of the cases the treatment was broken off within six months—perhaps because the patient wasn't getting anywhere or he ran out of funds.

Out of the 531 patients who went on with the treatment, there were 158 who saw perhaps a slight improvement, and 54 more who saw no change, or a worsening. Hence Knight concluded that 56.7 per cent of the patients were not helped. There were 157 cases in which the neurosis seemed to be cured, and there were 162 in which it was thought to be much improved, which means that it was helpful in 43.3 per cent.

Dr. Wertham, a very able and sensible psychiatrist, once said that his impression was that 60 per cent of psychoanalyses are "more harmful than helpful." Worse yet, he feared that four out of five were "not indicated"!

In England, E. B. Strauss said he thought that psychoanalysis might cure only from 22 to 25 per cent of well-selected persons.

According to Salter, Dr. A. A. Brill, who did most to "sell the world" on analysis, said that in the eleven years during which he saw 600 stutterers, he analyzed 69 and cured only 4. He said his enthusiasm for treating these persons declined with the length of his experience.

As Dr. Percival Bailey says, if the American Psychoanalytic Association, which once studied the results of treatment by its members, had received a favorable report, it would probably have been published, but so far as he knew, it was not published. I remember that in one such report I read years ago a considerable percentage of the analysts questioned admitted, honestly and bravely, that they were not enthusiastic about the results they were obtaining.

I hear nowadays that there are a number of able analysts in this country—men with a respected name—who are now trying to help people quickly, with their present-day problems. They are practicing ordinary "eclectic" psychiatry. (Eclectic, of course, means that they will use any measure that will help a patient.)

Dr. Bailey can see no evidence that the psychoanalysis of children does any good. I have read that even "Anna Freud and Melanie Klein finally agreed that analysis has little to offer in the way of prevention" of psychotic troubles in children.

Very unfortunate is the isolation of psychoanalysis from all of medicine and from the other forms of psychiatry. The analysts tend to read only those articles and books written by analysts. They tend to ignore a book written by an old-line psychiatrist—no matter how brilliant it may be. Most analysts have little if any contact with those psychiatrists who treat the psychotic and the insane.

Deans of medical schools tell me that typical of the unfortunate isolation of the analysts is the way in which, during luncheon in the school diningroom, all the disciples of Freud are likely to be found gathered closely about one table! Some Deans have told me that the analysts on their staff rarely speak to their colleagues in the other specialties. Obviously, this is unfortunate.

The question is: What is now going to happen to psycho-analysis as a cult? Will it go the way of all previously established cults, and slowly disappear? Some think it will. Always in the past, cults have faded out, their place being taken by other groups. When I was an intern in San Francisco, the Eclectics, the Homeopaths, and a group called, locally, the P. and S., were almost as prominent and influential as were the regular physicians. Now, as I remember, all of the colleges of these people have long since folded up. They are gone and forgotten.

Perhaps the best bet is that in time the Analysts will do as I hear the Osteopaths are now doing in California, where they plan to quit teaching Osteopathy and to get "into the fold" of the "regular" profession as fast as they can.

L'Envoi

THE BOOK IS written and ready to go! I hope it gives an adequate picture of a physician—his life, his ideals, and the work he has loved to do. I hope it will serve as a stimulus to thousands of laymen, doctors, and idealistic medical students to live a life dedicated, not just to making money, but to help in the improvement of medicine and public health.

I hope it makes for better public relations between laymen and physicians. Hundreds of lay readers of my newspaper columns write to say that they feel most sympathy for us physicians when we admit that we have serious problems, and that we have not always solved them perfectly.

I can only hope that through my text there shines forth my lifelong love of medicine and devotion to it, and my lifelong love of people.